The Case for Angels

The Case for Angels

Peter S. Williams

PATERNOSTER PRESS

First published in 2002 by Paternoster Press

08 07 06 05 04 03 02   7 6 5 4 3 2 1

Paternoster Press is an imprint of Authentic Media,
P.O. Box 300, Carlisle, Cumbria, CA3 0QS, UK
and
P.O. Box 1047, Waynesboro, GA 30830-2047, USA
Website: www.paternoster-publishing.com

British Library Cataloguing in Publication Data
A catalogue record for this book is available from the British Library

ISBN 1-84227-185-7

Cover Design by FourNineZero
Typeset by WestKey Ltd, Falmouth, Cornwall
Printed in Great Britain by Bell & Bain Ltd, Glasgow

Contents

'Man has lost his place in the cosmos,
the place *between* angel and beast.'
– Peter Kreeft, *Christianity for Modern Pagans*

'We believe in One God, Son and Holy Spirit,
Creator of things visible ... and of things invisible,
such as the pure spirits which are called angels.'
– Pope Paul VI

'I believe in angels, and I believe that some of these, by the abuse of
their free will, have become enemies of God and, as a corollary, to us.
These we may call devils. They do not differ in nature from good
angels, but their nature is depraved ... [This belief] seems to me to
explain a good many facts. It agrees with the plain sense of Scripture,
the tradition of Christendom, and the beliefs of most men at
most times. And it conflicts with nothing that any of the
sciences has shown to be true.'
– C.S. Lewis, *The Screwtape Letters*

Acknowledgements

My thanks go to:

Steven Carr, for debating the existence of angels with me in the summer of 2001.

Holy Trinity Church, Leicester, for their constant prayers and giving me time to write.

William A. Dembski, for honouring me with a foreword.

Debbie, for proof reading the second draft and making encouraging noises: 'They're not angles, they're angels!'

Gregory A. Boyd, for his commendation.

Ian and Mahesh, for checking my grasp and application of Bayes' probability theorem.

Peter Kreeft, for his enthusiastic commendation.

Paul 'Fluffy' Morgan, for random help.

All at Paternoster Press, especially Lucy Atherton (for dealing with the design and commendation side of things), Jill Morris (for her scrupulous and patient editing), Tony Graham (for overseeing the production of this book) and Robin Parry (for his constructive structural criticism and marginal notes on the first draft, and for providing a free Italian lunch!).

Susan Radford, for tracking down a book I wanted.

David West, for faithful partnership in prayer.

Dallas Willard, for replying to my invitation to comment on his views about angels.

Last, but not least, my parents for their constant support and encouragement.

Foreword

William A. Dembski

Writing on the eve of America's entry into World War II, Bishop Fulton Sheen remarked: 'The masses are capable of far better judgments about world affairs than the intelligentsia. If I wanted a good moral judgment about the war, I should a thousand times prefer to get it from a garage man, a filling-station attendant, a WPA worker, or a delivery boy than from twenty-three PhD professors I know about in just one American university. The reason is not difficult to find. The educated know how to rationalize evil; the masses do not. Evil to them is still evil; they have never learned to sugar-coat it with sophism.' Sheen was perhaps a bit too optimistic about the capacity of the masses to avoid self-deception. Even so, he points insightfully to a rift between high culture and mass culture that is still with us.

Peter Williams' *The Case for Angels* is about one such rift, namely the theological rift between a Christian intelligentsia that increasingly regards angels only as figurative or literary devices, and the great mass of Christians who thankfully still regard them as real (a fact confirmed by popular polls, as Williams notes in this book). This rift was brought home to me at a conference I helped organize at Baylor University some years back. The conference was entitled 'The Nature of Nature' and focused on whether nature is self-contained or points beyond itself. The activity of angels in the world would clearly constitute one way nature points beyond itself.

At that conference, Nancey Murphy, a well-known American theologian, spoke at a session devoted to the mind–body problem. Murphy advocates a physicalism in which humans coincide with their physical make-up. As a consequence, she denies that humans have a soul or spirit (i.e., some irreducible aspect of the human person that ontologically transcends the body). According to her, such a dualism is but a benighted holdover from the early days of Christianity when Greek thought perniciously invaded Christian theology. Once we get beyond these Greek influences and situate Christian theology within its proper Jewish Old Testament context, we'll see that humans are purely physical beings whose immortality consists not in being more than matter but in having their matter reconstituted when God resurrects humanity in the eschaton.

Murphy's exegesis of the Old Testament is itself questionable, and in light of the New Testament her physicalist view of the human person is unsustainable. Even so, her refusal to countenance an immaterial dimension to the human person immediately raises a question about angels, who in Christian theology are immaterial persons. What, then, does Murphy do with angels (and there are plenty of them throughout the Old and New Testaments)? When asked this question at 'The Nature of Nature' conference, she remarked that they are merely figurative or literary devices. But there is a tension in Murphy's position. In the name of a more exact exegesis of the Bible, she rejects the traditional mind–body dualism of Christian theology. Yet that same exegesis is not exact at all when it comes to angels – it simply dismisses them outright. Why is that?

A careful reading of Murphy's work shows that her theology is informed not so much by a desire to exegete Scripture as to bring Christian theology into harmony with advances in science, notably, in her case, with neuroscience. According to her, neuroscience provides decisive confirmation that human consciousness is purely an out-working of a physical system – the brain. But, in fact, neuroscience is still in such a primitive state of development that it provides no such confirmation, at least not by itself. Rather, to provide such confirmation, neuroscience must be combined with a philosophical view that Murphy calls physicalism. According to physicalism, the world and everything in it (including humanity) operates according to purely physical principles. Murphy's rejection of angels and mind–body dualism thus ultimately rests on a philosophical presupposition – physicalism, or naturalism, as it may also be called.

Murphy's rejection of angels and mind–body dualism exemplifies the Christian intelligentsia's increasing rejection of fundamental Christian doctrines. Behind this rejection is invariably some philosophical or ideological precommitment that finds aspects of traditional Christian orthodoxy repugnant. In Murphy's case, it is naturalism or physicalism that conditions her theology. Here at least there is a well-articulated philosophical position that is at odds with Christian orthodoxy. In other instances, there are only vague sentiments. Despite all the violence on our news and entertainment media, ours is a squeamish age. For instance, we no longer care for a God who in wrath punishes sin. Consequently, we invent a permissive God who does not so much save us from sin as coddle us in our sin. In short, we make God a soft, coddled Westerner, like us. This sort of universalism is quite the rage in theological circles these days.

Bishop Sheen's slam against the intelligentsia in favor of the masses, though appropriate to our age, is not appropriate to all ages. Historically, high and mass culture have preferred not to lunge at each other's throats. Often high culture seeks to give expression to what is best in mass culture. To be sure, high culture tends to charge mass culture with vulgarization, and mass culture tends to charge high culture with being out of touch with reality. Yet, since the time of the Enlightenment, high and mass culture in the West have been sharply antithetical. The problem is that high culture has been thoroughly secularized, seeking wherever it can to subvert its Christian roots. At the same time, mass culture has tried as much as possible to hold on to those Christian roots. The result has been a culture war.

Peter Williams' *The Case for Angels* is a refreshing contribution to that culture war and is emblematic of how the terms of that war are changing. In the past, the intelligentsia seemed to hold all the cards. They were in the positions of influence and authority in the culture. They seemed to have the winning arguments. And resistance was confined to intellectual subcultures (ghettos) that had little chance of reclaiming the culture. That is now changing, and Williams' book epitomizes the change. Increasingly, Christian orthodoxy is finding the clarity of mind and firmness of resolve with which effectively to challenge secular ideologies that undermine Christian faith. Williams and this book provide a case in point.

Although this book is ostensibly about angels, less than half of it is directly concerned with angels. Instead, much of the book is concerned with clearing away conceptual stumbling blocks that prevent people from taking angels seriously. Sheen's intelligentsia have been marvellously successful at placing stumbling blocks in the way of Christian orthodoxy. For many intellectuals, these stumbling blocks are decisive and remove any possibility of Christianity being true, and in the case of angels, their being real. Williams identifies the key stumbling blocks that render angels implausible to our intellectual élite and successfully refutes them. Not surprisingly, the biggest of these stumbling blocks is naturalism, and Williams deals effectively with it.

Why is it important to know about angels? Why is it important to know about rocks and plants and animals? It's important because all of these are aspects of reality that impinge on us. The problem with the secular intelligentsia is that they deny those aspects of reality that are inconvenient to their world-picture. And since the intelligentsia are by definition intelligent (though rarely wise), they are able to rationalize away what they find inconvenient. This is what Bishop Sheen was getting at with the previous quote when he referred to the intelligentsia rationalizing evil, and this is what Williams is so successful at unmasking in the intelligentsia's rejection of angels.

There exists an invisible world that is more real and weighty than our secular imaginations can fathom. I commend this book as a way of retraining our imaginations about that reality.

Prologue: Angelology and Christian Integration

Returning the supernatural to philosophy is a project that calls for intellectual and spiritual boldness. Regardless of the state of philosophy, there can be no compromise with the present age ... Only a supernatural, evangelical consciousness wedded to philosophy, belonging to the philosopher living in faith, will be unafraid of challenging the false intellectual currency of the day and will begin the true renewal of the mind ...

– Deal W. Hudson[1]

Angels are worthy of our attention for many reasons. As theologian James Montgomery Boice writes: 'The grandeur and complexity of the angelic world are enough to pique us to study it. But in addition, such study enhances our sense of God's glory. Calvin observes, "If we desire to recognise God from his works, we ought by no means to overlook such an illustrious and noble example" as his angels.'[2] In the New Testament Paul encourages us: 'Whatever is true, whatever is noble, whatever is right, whatever is pure, whatever is lovely, whatever is admirable – if anything is excellent or praiseworthy – think about such things' (Phil. 4:8). Angels (with a capital 'A', good angels) are worth studying because they are true (real), noble, right, pure, lovely, admirable, excellent *and* praiseworthy. Fallen angels (demons) are worth studying because they are real and because it behoves every army, including the army of Christ, to know its enemy (cf. Eph. 6:10–18).

The term 'angel' refers to *an immaterial, purely spiritual creature directly created by God* (cf. Col. 1:16). As such, an angel is a *kind* of

---

[1] Deal W. Hudson, 'The Philosopher and the Supernatural' in Harold Fickett (ed.), *Things In Heaven And Earth* (Brewster, Massachusetts: Paraclete Press, 1998).

[2] James Montgomery Boice, *Foundations Of The Christian Faith* (Downers Grove, Illinois: IVP, 1986), p. 169.

person, for as J.P. Moreland and Scott B. Rae remind us: 'there is no
such thing as a … person plain and simply. There are only … *kinds* of
persons (e.g. divine, human, angelic).'[3] The difference between an
Angel and a demon is not a matter of kind in the above sense, but more
like the difference between a repentant sinner and an unrepentant
sinner.

Angels and demons are inextricably woven into the fabric of scripture and Christian belief. The plausibility of belief in angels is therefore
part and parcel of the plausibility of Christianity, and angels are a matter
for Christian apologetics (the art of giving a reasoned defence of
Christian belief). If angels (good or evil) don't exist, and if Christianity
teaches that they do exist, then this is obviously a point against
Christianity! On the other hand, if angels *do* exist, then this is a point in
favour of Christianity and against any worldview that excludes these
beings. Most notably, if angels exist, then the worldview of secular
atheists, metaphysical naturalism, is false. However, the existence of
angels is not a subject commonly tackled by Christian apologists or
philosophers (theologians of the past few decades have shown slightly
more interest in the subject).[4] Indeed, it is a subject remarkable in its
absence from the writings of modern 'defenders of the faith'. Perhaps the
most notable twentieth-century treatise on angels is the late Mortimer
J. Adler's *The Angels And Us*,[5] composed before his conversion to
Christianity! While it's easy enough to find contemporary philosophers
and apologists who believe in angels, it's rare to find them making more
than a casual remark on the subject. What serious attention angels do
receive comes mainly from writers within the Catholic tradition, such as
philosopher Peter Kreeft.[6] The top philosophers of religion today, Alvin
Plantinga and Richard Swinburne, both discuss demons, but only in

---

[3] J.P. Moreland and Scott B. Rae, *Body & Soul: Human Nature & The Crisis In Ethics* (Downers Grove, Illinois: IVP, 2000).

[4] e.g. Boice, *Foundations Of The Christian Faith*; Gregory A. Boyd, *God At War: The Bible And Spiritual Conflict* (Downers Grove, Illinois: IVP, 1997); Michael Green, *I Believe In Satan's Downfall* (London: Hodder and Stoughton, 1981); Paul Hefner, *Mystery Of Creation* (Leominster, Herefordshire: Gracewing, 1995); R.T. Kendall, *Understanding Theology*, vol. I (Fearn, Ross-shire: Christian Focus, 2000); and B.J. Oropeza, *99 Answers To Questions About Angels, Demons & Spiritual Warfare* (Eastbourne, East Sussex: Kingsway, 1998).

[5] Mortimer J. Adler, *The Angels And Us* (New York: Collier, 1982).

[6] cf. Peter Kreeft, *Angels (And Demons)* (San Francisco: Ignatius, 1995); Peter Kreeft and Ronald Tacelli, *Handbook Of Christian Apologetics* (Downers Grove, Illinois: IVP 1994).

relation to the problem of evil.[7] Prolific evangelical philosopher Norman
L. Geisler touches on the subject (in his massive *Baker Encyclopedia of
Christian Apologetics*), but focuses on the existence of Satan.[8]
Hence, while a host of present-day philosophers believe in angels and
demons (one could additionally mention the likes of William Lane
Craig, William A. Dembski, Gary R. Habermas, Terry L. Miethe, J.P.
Moreland and Dallas Willard), they simply don't pay much attention to
them, at least in their publications. Failure to give angels the sort of
detailed attention given by Thomas Aquinas[9] is not a failure in a
Christian philosopher; but you'd think angels would receive more
attention than they do. While angelology is clearly not so important an
enterprise as natural theology (arguments for God) or Christian
evidences – enterprises to which the above thinkers have made a massive
contribution – I do find this angelic neglect curious. Perhaps there is a
temptation to think that angelology is either too simple to get one's
philosophical teeth into, or so well-trodden a path that nothing new can
or need be added to what has already been said. Neither motivation
bears close examination, as the following pages will show.

I would have thought that the average non-believer would find
the numerous biblical references to angels and demons a considerable
stumbling block to the credibility of Christianity. As theologian Walter
Wink says, 'if you want to bring all talk to a halt in shocked embarrass-
ment, every eye riveted on you … try mentioning angels, or demons,
or the devil. You will be quickly appraised for signs of pathological
violence and then quietly shunned.'[10] The same is true of miracles.
Naturalistic assumptions need to be challenged if accounts of miracles
are not to be dismissed out of hand as impossible. The existence of
angels is surely a parallel case. However, while the topic of miracles has
received excellent and extensive coverage,[11] angels have been brushed
under the carpet. Nor is serious engagement with the issue of angels a
service only to non-Christians, for Christians are not immune from
being influenced by the unbelieving spirit of the age.

---

[7] cf. Alvin Plantinga, *God, Freedom And Evil* (Grand Rapids, Michigan:
Eerdmans, 1974); Richard Swinburne, *Providence And The Problem Of Evil*
(Oxford: Oxford University Press, 1998), pp. 107–8.

[8] Norman L. Geisler, *Baker Encyclopedia Of Christian Apologetics* (Grand
Rapids, Michigan: Baker, 1999).

[9] cf. Thomas Aquinas, *Summa Theologica* @ < http://www.ccel.org/a/aquinas/
summa/FP.html#TOC03 >

[10] Walter Wink, *Unmasking The Powers* (Minneapolis, Minnesota: Augsburg
Fortress, 1986).

[11] cf. Bibliography.

Both the possibility and actuality of angels has important consequences for such subjects as the existence of God and the question of
whether the mind just *is* the brain, or if there's more to it than that. If
finite immaterial beings (angels) exist, why not an infinite immaterial
being (God)? If finite immaterial beings exist, why can't the human mind
be immaterial? Conversely, if human minds are immaterial, or if God
exists, why couldn't (or wouldn't) angels exist? In fact, *there would
appear to be no reason to doubt the possibility of angels existing that
would not equally count against the existence of God*. Therefore, *if
God's existence is possible, the existence of angels is possible*. Whether
or not angels are real is another question, but it is one to which reasonable answers can and will be given.

The Importance of Reason:
Philosophy, Apologetics and Spiritual Warfare

> thinking is honoring God with your mind. Thinking is worshipping.
>
> – James W. Sire[12]

When I tell people that I studied philosophy at university, they often pull
a face that suggests they think I am both clever and useless. (This look is
sometimes followed by the question: 'So, do we exist then?' My usual
response is: 'Who's asking?') Cleverness helps, but I think most people
can grasp some philosophy, if only because most people philosophize on
occasion. Most people wonder about such questions as why they exist,
if there's a God and whether there is life after death; but to really practise
philosophy, one must not only ask such profound questions, but
seek true answers to them through logical argumentation. An argument
is 'a finite set of words arranged in sentences, consisting of one or
more premises and a conclusion, and whose premises are designed to
prove, entail, or provide intellectual support for the conclusion'.[13] Philosophical arguments work by linking premises to a conclusion in such a
way that one has to choose between acknowledging the conclusion or
rejecting either the logical validity of the argument or the truth of at least
one of the premises. An argument places its conclusion in one balance
pan, and some other aspect of reality in the other pan, and tries to

---

[12] James W. Sire, *Habits Of The Mind: Intellectual Life As A Christian Calling*
(Leicester: IVP, 2000³), p. 142.
[13] Stephen T. Davis, *God, Reason And Theistic Proofs* (Edinburgh: Edinburgh
University Press, 1997), p. 1.

establish a link between them such that the weight of the evidence raises the case for belief. It may be useful, as we begin to seek answers to the question of angels, to provide what Peter Kreeft and Ronald Tacelli call a mini-lesson in logic.

> The inherent structure of human reason manifests itself in three acts of the mind: 1) understanding, 2) judging and 3) reasoning. These three acts of the mind are expressed in 1) terms, 2) propositions and 3) arguments. Terms are either clear or unclear. Propositions are either true or untrue. Arguments are either logically valid or invalid. A term is clear if it is intelligible and unambiguous. A proposition is true if it corresponds to reality, if it says what is. An argument is valid if the conclusion follows necessarily from the premise. If all the terms in an argument are clear, and if all the premises are true, and if the argument is free from logical fallacy, then the conclusion must be true.[14]

These are not rules of a game we invented and can therefore change at will. They are the inherent and unbreakable rules of reality itself. Hence, 'To disagree with the conclusion of any argument, it must be shown that either an ambiguous term or false premise or logical fallacy exists in the argument.'[15] To reject the conclusion of a valid argument (one containing no logical fallacy and no terminological ambiguity) one must reject the truth of at least one premise of that argument. A valid argument will convince anyone who finds it harder to reject any of its premises than it is to accept its conclusion. For example, the moral argument for God tries to establish a connection between objective moral value and God's existence (for a brief account of this argument, see Chapter Two). If one acknowledges that the argument is logically valid but nevertheless wish to deny its conclusion (that God exists), one must deny the existence of objective moral value.[16] As Alvin Plantinga notes: 'a person might, when confronted with an argument he sees to be valid for a conclusion he deeply disbelieves from premises he knows to be true, give up (some of) those premises.'[17] It is thus possible to reduce someone from a state of knowledge (e.g. belief that murder is objectively wrong) to a state of delusion (e.g. that murder is not objectively wrong) simply by showing them an argument

---

[14] Kreeft and Tacelli, *Handbook Of Christian Apologetics*.

[15] Ibid.

[16] cf. Peter S. Williams, *The Case For God* (Crowborough, East Sussex: Monarch, 1999).

[17] Alvin Plantinga, 'Two Dozen (or so) Theistic Arguments' @ < http://www. homestead.com/philofreligion/files/Theisticarguments.html >

for God! As George Macdonald (a formative influence on C.S. Lewis) once said, to give truth to him who does not love the truth is only to give more reasons for misinterpretation. However, the more plausible the data one must deny in order to avoid a conclusion, the less plausible one's denial becomes. Of course, arguments differ in the weight of support they attempt to give to their conclusion, in that both the certainty of the premises and the strength of the link between the premises and the conclusion are variable. Nevertheless, arguments always ask you to pay a price for rejecting their conclusions. You can always reject the conclusion *if you are willing to pay the price*. In general then, whether or not a valid argument (for God, angels, or whatever) will convince someone will depend upon *how strongly they desire to avoid the conclusion*. This dynamic is clearly seen at work in the thought of Thomas Nagel, who (writing with admirable candour of a 'fear of religion') admits: 'I want atheism to be true and am made uneasy by the fact that some of the most intelligent and well-informed people I know are religious believers. It isn't just that I don't believe in God and naturally, hope there is no God! I don't want there to be a God; I don't want the universe to be like that.'[18]

The crucial philosophical issue, from the Christian point of view, is pride versus humility: the central problem in knowing is not the world (or race, class, gender, or generation, as postmodernists believe), but the self. The autonomous self bows to no-one and seeks to be the sole arbiter of life and truth. Postmodernism is built upon a foundation of pride, wherein the mythical figure of the autonomous individual arrogates to his or herself the right to determine reality: 'Pride is not first of all thinking too highly of yourself, because it isn't *thinking* first of all but *willing*, just as humility isn't thinking about yourself in a low way but not thinking of yourself at all. Humility is thinking less *about* yourself, not thinking less *of* yourself. Pride is wilful arrogance, arrogating to yourself what is really God's.'[19] Hence, as Peter Kreeft's fictional demon Snakebite warns: 'It's a perilous task to use little shards of light, reason and argument, to confuse [a human]. It may work in the short run, but the very fact that the mortal is using and trusting reason has the tendency to develop in him an unpleasant urge toward humility, of bowing down to truth instead of to his own desires, or peer pressure, or fashion ...'[20] If our aim is to discover the truth, we have to give up our need for control

[18] Thomas Nagel, *The Last Word* (Oxford: Oxford University Press, 1997), p. 130.

[19] Peter Kreeft, *Back To Virtue* (San Francisco: Ignatius, 1992), p. 100.

[20] Peter Kreeft, *The Snakebite Letters* (San Francisco: Ignatius, 1993), p. 17.

so that we can face up to reality rather than trying to fit reality into our schemes. This requires repentance, a turning away from our old way of thinking, not rationalization. The long-term outcome of such repentance is freedom, because we are engaging with reality as it is. A refusal to repent, humbly conforming minds and hearts to the truth, lies at the core of postmodernism: 'To the typically modern mind (and nothing more centrally defines the modern mind than this), objective reality no longer includes the moral dimension of good and evil ... There is no longer anything outside ourselves and the products of our minds to bow down to, conform to, or respect.'[21] For some this is an acknowledged tragedy. For others, it is falsely perceived as a source of emancipation. Faced with the self-contradictory claims of postmodernism (which claims there is truly no truth, absolutely denies absolutes and uses texts to teach that texts have no inherent meaning)[22] I join William P. Alston in diagnosing the root of opposition to truth as intolerance of vulnerability:

> whether what we say is true is determined not by anything we do or think, but by the way things are – the things we are talking about. This vulner-ability to the outside world, this 'subjection' to stubborn, unyielding facts ... seems powerfully repugnant, even intolerable to many. As a Christian, I see in this reaction a special case of *the* original sin, insisting on human autonomy and control and refusing to be subservient to ... God.[23]

So, people can have suspect *motives* for not believing in God, or angels; but they can also have genuine reasons. Not all objections are 'red herrings' or rationalizations. Either way, apologetics is an important and useful part of spiritual warfare, because apologetics should appeal to the whole person, not to some abstract concept of a purely rational decision-making machine. As Pascal wrote, 'every man is almost always led to believe not through proof; but through that which is attractive.'[24] Angels and demons are clearly a topic of fascination that attracts the interest of many in contemporary society, and this is a fact that

[21] Peter Kreeft, *C.S. Lewis For The Third Millennium* (San Francisco: Ignatius, 1994), p. 135.

[22] cf. Douglas Groothuis, *Truth Decay: Defending Christianity Against The Challenges Of Postmodernism* (Leicester: IVP, 2000); Ronald H. Nash, *Life's Ultimate Questions* (Grand Rapids, Michigan: Zondervan, 1999).

[23] William P. Alston, *A Realist Conception Of Truth* (Ithaca, New York: Cornell University Press, 1997).

[24] Blaise Pascal, 'The Art of Persuasion', *Pensées And Other Writings*, Honor Levi (trans) (Oxford: Oxford University Press, 1995).

the church should capitalize upon, just so long as the angelic bait leads to the divine hook.

As for the practical importance of philosophy, one could define it as 'the art of handling ideas', and ideas are the most powerful things around next to God and love. Ideas are mind-altering substances more powerful than any drug. You see, people do things because of ideas. People murdered six million Jews in the holocaust on the basis of certain false ideas; whole cultures rise and fall because of ideas; people commit suicide or endure incredible hardship because of philosophical ideas. Christians should recognize the vital importance to the individual, and to society as a whole, of developing a Christian mind (a mind that operates on the basis of a Christian worldview). As J. Gresham Machen wrote in 1913:

> False ideas are the greatest obstacles to the reception of the gospel. We may preach with all the fervour of a reformer and yet succeed only in winning a straggler here and there, if we permit the whole collective thought of the nation or of the world to be controlled by ideas which, by the resistless force of logic, prevent Christianity from being regarded as anything more than a harmless delusion.[25]

The situation feared by Machen now exists in Western Europe. When a culture reaches the point where basic Christian claims are outside of its plausibility structure, few people will seriously entertain the thought that those claims might be true. Even Christian believers will have a hard time living out, or even believing their Christian worldview, because they will lack the depth of conviction and the integrated intellectual framework necessary for spiritual progress.[26] This is why Christian philosophy is crucial to the practical, spiritual well-being of both church and society, because only Christian philosophy 'can create a plausibility structure in a person's mind, favourable conditions as Machen put it, so Christian ideas can be entertained by that person'.[27]

William J. Wainwright is surely right to note that 'Disbelief is less often the result of intellectual objections than of the clash between religious beliefs and attitudes and sensibilities that have been shaped by

---

[25] J. Gresham Machen, 'Christianity and Culture', *Princeton Theological Review* 11 (1913), p. 7.

[26] cf. Dallas Willard, *The Divine Conspiracy: Rediscovering Our Hidden Life In God* (London: Fount, 1998).

[27] J.P. Moreland @ < http://leaderu.com/aip/docs/moreland2b.html >, p. 2.

an environment that leaves little room for God or the sacred.'[28] Those 'attitudes and sensibilities' are often the result of philosophical objections to faith. These objections are, on the whole, uncritically accepted as part of a media-generated 'climate of opinion' that outlasts the demolition of its intellectual roots. Humanly speaking, the situation in Western Europe looks grim; but we would do well to remember G.K. Chesterton's remark that if people returned to paganism they might rediscover why all the pagans became Christians!

Chesterton also reminds us that when people stop believing in God they don't believe in nothing, but start believing in anything; and that includes New Age belief in 'angels' and 'guiding spirits'. Checking out my local secular bookstore reveals an entire shelf devoted to angels, all New Age works encouraging readers to 'get in touch with their angels' through the use of such occult means as 'spirit writing'. These books are speaking to a need that most philosophers have studiously ignored, 'at the cost of encouraging bad mental habits where religion, belief, and the supernatural are concerned'.[29] Faced with a naturalistic rejection of all things spiritual and a postmodern paganism all too willing to accept every spirit and spirituality going (unless it is Christian), Christians need lovingly and reasonably to invite people on to the middle, narrow path. This calling inevitably involves philosophy.

Some Christians sadly view philosophy with suspicion. They even manage to see support for their attitude in scripture. Colossians warns us to beware 'that no-one takes you captive through hollow and deceptive philosophy, which depends on human tradition and the basic principles of this world rather than on Christ' (Col. 2:8). However, when this passage is read in context, we find that it is a warning against *Gnostic* philosophy.[30] To read this as a condemnation of philosophy in general is to misread it. This misreading is ironic given the meaning of 'philosopher' as one who loves (*philo*) wisdom (*sophia*). Proverbs 8 recommends God's wisdom and John's Gospel explains how the rational 'word' or *logos* of God became incarnate (Jn. 1). All Christians are philosophers, because we all love the incarnate wisdom of God! Colossians warns against being taken captive *to falsehood* through 'hollow and deceptive' philosophy;

---

[28] William J. Wainwright, 'Skepticism, Romanticism and Faith' in Thomas V. Morris (ed.), *God And The Philosophers* (New York: Oxford University Press, 1994), p. 85.

[29] Deal W. Hudson, 'The Philosopher and the Supernatural', in Harold Ficket (ed.), *Things in Heaven and Earth*, p. 115.

[30] Gnostics stressed *gnosis* or knowledge, especially of origins. Gnostics also thought of the material world as evil.

and the 'hollow and deceptive' philosophy that might take the unwary captive is the philosophy 'which depends on human tradition and the basic principles of this world' rather 'than on Christ'. This says nothing against philosophy that is not 'hollow and deceptive', that does not take us captive to 'falsehood', or that depends upon the *logos* of God! An anti-philosophical reading of Colossians has detrimental consequences. Norman L. Geisler and Paul D. Feinberg comment:

> Some Christians are suspicious of philosophy because they have heard stories of others who have lost their faith through the study of philosophy. They have been advised to avoid philosophy like the plague. Upon serious reflection it is clear that this is not wise advice. Christianity *can* stand up to the intellectual challenge mounted against it. The result of such a challenge should not be the loss of faith, but the priceless possession of a well-reasoned and mature faith. Furthermore, there are serious consequences of a failure to be aware of contemporary thought patterns. Rather than being exempt from their influence, one becomes their *unwitting* prey.[31]

At least some members of the body of Christ need to suffer the intellectual onslaught of 'the world' upon the church, for such 'suffering produces perseverance; perseverance, character; and character, hope' (Rom. 5:3–4). As C.S. Lewis said: 'Good philosophy must exist, if for no other reason, because bad philosophy needs to be answered.'[32] According to Titus 1:9 an elder in the church should 'hold firmly to the trustworthy message as it has been taught, so that he can encourage others by sound doctrine and refute those who oppose it'. The apostle Peter wrote that Christians should 'Always be prepared to give an answer to everyone who asks you to give the reason for the hope that you have ... with gentleness and respect' (1 Pet. 3:15). The Greek word translated here as 'give a reason' is *apologia*, and it means 'to give a reasoned defence', as a lawyer would give in a court of law. The apostle Paul considered it his ministry to offer a defence (*apologia*) and confirmation (*bebaiosis*) of the gospel (Phil. 1:7). The Greek *bebaiosis* means 'verification' or 'proof'. Hence Christian apologetics is the art of giving a reasoned defence for Christianity, refuting those who oppose it and offering verification of its truth.[33]

---

[31] Norman L. Geisler and Paul D. Feinberg, *Introduction To Philosophy: A Christian Perspective* (Grand Rapids, Michigan: Baker, 1997), pp. 21–2.

[32] C.S. Lewis, 'The Weight of Glory', *Screwtape Proposes A Toast* (London: Fount, 1998).

[33] cf. Steven B. Cowan (ed.), *Five Views On Apologetics* (Grand Rapids: Michigan: Zondervan, 2000); Michael Green and Alister McGrath, *How*

Apologetics is a neglected aspect of spiritual warfare. 2 Corinthians 10:5 says: 'We demolish *arguments* and every pretension that sets itself up against the *knowledge* of God, and *we take captive every thought to make it obedient to Christ*' (my italics). To answer objections to Christianity, and to advance reasons for Christianity, is to demolish the pretensions of 'the world' and to take captives; and this includes making our own minds obedient to the truth. 'The world', in Paul's parlance, refers to the ideological and political powers opposed to the kingdom of God; and like all spiritual warfare, the battle to worship God with the mind begins at home. A truly Christian commitment to God necessitates a humble commitment to truth and rationality that should never fail to seek honest answers to honest questions. It takes wisdom and discernment to speak the truth in love, as well as doing our homework; but only so will we 'in all things grow up into him who is the Head, that is, Christ' (Eph. 4:15). Faith and reason are not rivals (not even friendly rivals), but soulmates who go everywhere together: 'The faith that the Bible speaks of ... is not just a will to believe, everything to the contrary notwithstanding. It is not a predisposition to force every piece of information to fit the mold of one's desires. Faith in the biblical sense is substantive, based on the knowledge that the One in whom faith is placed has proven that He is worthy of that trust.'[34]

Only the love of truth can motivate someone to accept the conclusion of a sound argument or line of evidence. Logic proves, but only love convinces. As we have seen, even if an argument proves its conclusion beyond reasonable doubt, it is still open to the sceptic to be unreasonable! In a sense then the oft-repeated claim 'You can't argue anyone into the kingdom of God' is true. Likewise, 'You can lead a horse to water, but you can't make it drink.' Still, patient and gentle leading to water is not an unimportant venture (especially when the water of life is involved). Although some Christians have doubts about the usefulness of apologetics (getting your enemy to lower their defences is a clever trick if you can pull it off), the Bible is full of apologetics! Jesus himself said: 'at least *believe on the evidence* of the miracles themselves' (Jn. 14:11, my italics). Either God engages in 'unpractical' apologetics, or apologetics is not unpractical!

---

[33] (continued) *Shall We Reach Them? Defending And Communicating The Christian Faith To Nonbelievers* (Milton Keynes: Word, 1995); Alister McGrath, *Bridge-Building: Communicating Christianity Effectively* (Leicester: IVP, 1994).

[34] Ravi Zacharias, *Jesus Among Other Gods* (Nashville, Tennessee: Word, 2000), p. 58.

Sociologist Peter Berger coined the phrase 'the homeless mind' to describe the effect of modernity on human consciousness. As members of the church, says Stuart McAllister, 'we do not have a homeless mind, but rather a *centred* mind – the mind of *Christ*.'[35] As Douglas Groothuis describes it: 'The renewed mind – a mind alive to the principles of Scripture by inspiration of the Holy Spirit – is the avowed enemy of jargon, superficial opinion, and irrationality. It searches for and utilizes truth; it exposes and corrects error. It develops its God-given rational powers in service of its creator.'[36]

Angelology as an Integrative Enterprise

Alvin Plantinga, perhaps the foremost Christian philosopher of our times, has encouraged Christian philosophers to cast the net of their interests far and wide: 'The Christian philosophical community need not devote all its efforts to attempting to refute opposing claims or to arguing for its own claims ... it ought to do this, indeed, but it ought to do more. For if it does only this, it will neglect a pressing philosophical task: systematizing, deepening, clarifying Christian thought ...'[37] In other words, Christian philosophers can and should get on with the task of doing self-consciously *Christian* philosophy. Angelology, the study of angels, is a prime but neglected candidate for such effort. Angelology requires not only that the Christian philosopher 'refute opposing claims' and argue for Christian claims, but also that they *systematize* – seek to deepen and clarify Christian thought about angels by constant reference not only to theology, but also to relevant philosophical issues. As J.P. Moreland recommends, Christian philosophers 'should continue to apply their craft to the clarification and defence of various Christian doctrines'.[38] This book is my contribution to the task of clarifying and defending the traditional Christian doctrine of angels.

Angelology is a science (at least in the original meaning of that term: *scientia*, or knowledge). Peter Kreeft explains:

---

[35] Stuart McAllister, 'Permanent Things', *Just Thinking*, winter 2001, p. 7.

[36] Douglas Groothuis, *Christianity That Counts* (Grand Rapids, Michigan: Baker, 1994), p. 67.

[37] Alvin Plantinga, 'Christian Philosophy at the End of the 20th Century' @ < http://www.faithquest.com/philosophers/plantinga/20th.html >

[38] J.P. Moreland, 'Philosophical Apologetics, the Church, and Contemporary Culture', *Premise* vol. III, no. 4, 1996, p. 9; @ < http://capo.org/premise/96/april/p960406.html >

Angelology ... uses essentially scientific method: gathering data and formulating theories to explain the data. The theories are controlled by the data. Of course it's not laboratory data. Different sciences have different data ... The data about angels comes from two sources: the Bible and human experience (accounts of people meeting angels) ... Angelology has data, and its theories are justified by its data. For instance, the traditional theory of angels ... says that angels are (1) creatures of God, (2) bodiless spirits, (3) with intelligence (4) and will, (5) who live in God's presence in heaven, (6) obey his will, (7) carry his messages ... (8) assume bodies as we assume costumes, (9) influence our imagination (10) but not our free will, and (11) move material things supernaturally. If any one of the points in this theory were false, the data would be different.[39]

For example, if angels could not assume bodies they could not, being spirits, eat food. However, in scripture angels do occasionally eat food (out of politeness rather than need, cf. Gen. 18:8). Therefore, angels can assume bodies. Angelology thus employs a typically scientific mode of argumentation, namely 'argument to best explanation'. In an argument to the best explanation the conclusion is justified by its being judged the simplest adequate explanation of the available data. Argument to the best explanation is simply a constructive use of Occam's Razor, the rational principle that tells us not to multiply explanatory entities (or their complexity) beyond what is necessary in order to account for the data. The rule with arguments to the best explanation is that the more certain the data, the more certain the conclusion. The nature of the available data means that angelology can sometimes be a rather speculative science; but then, so are many other branches of science. As with any science, one may dispute the data or the interpretation of the data; but to do so is to propose an alternative theory, not to deny the legitimacy of angelology as a broadly scientific subject employing a broadly scientific methodology.

This said, the common distinction between science and philosophy (or theology come to that) is tenuous at best.[40] Angelology is best viewed as an explicitly *integrative* discipline:

Because Christians are interested in truth for its own sake and because they are called to proclaim and defend their views to an unbelieving world and to seek to live consistently with those views, it is important for members of the believing community to think carefully about how to integrate their

---

[39] Kreeft, *Angels (And Demons)*, pp. 28–9.

[40] cf. J.P. Moreland, *Christianity And The Nature Of Science* (Grand Rapids, Michigan: Baker, 1998).

carefully formed theological beliefs with prominent claims in other fields of study ... integration has as its spiritual aim the intellectual goal of structuring the mind so a person can see things as they really are and strengthening the belief structure that ought to inform the individual and corporate life of discipleship unto Jesus.[41]

Let us employ the term 'theology' to stand for any part of the Christian worldview (or exploration thereof) derived primarily from special revelation (that is, God's historical revelation as recorded and contained in scripture). Theological claims about angels must be integrated with relevant claims from other disciplines (e.g. philosophy, psychology) in order to provide the most adequate theoretical account of reality; for neither science nor theology is separable from philosophy, and it is ultimately one's philosophical presuppositions that most affect one's interpretation of scientific theories, whether they be about quantum mechanics, evolution or angelology. One of the spin-off benefits of this integrationist project is 'to maintain or increase both the conceptual relevance of and epistemological justification for Christian theism'.[42] The project of integration is one of a critical but friendly dialogue between disciplines in light of the facts that 'all truth is one' and that 'all truth is God's truth', for 'In conceptual integration, one's theological beliefs, especially those derived from careful biblical exegesis, are blended and unified with propositions judged to be justifiably believed as true from other sources into a coherent, intellectually satisfying worldview.'[43] We might call this project one of 'integrative realism', in that it holds that '[objective] truths about the universe hold independently of the decisions or theorisings of human beings, and these truths form one consistent set. There is no compartmentalisation.'[44] Hence: 'metaphysics is the handmaiden of theology; indeed theology is a branch of metaphysics.'[45] In the course of recommending the integrative project, J.P. Moreland suggests three priorities:

> First, integration should be focused on those areas of study that seem to be intrinsically more central or foundational to the Christian theistic enterprise ... Second, integration should be focused on areas that are currently under heavy attack. A third and, perhaps, less important criterion is this:

---

[41] J.P. Moreland @ < http://leaderu.com/aip/docs/moreland2b.html >, p. 1.
[42] Ibid., p. 5.
[43] Ibid.
[44] Ibid.
[45] Paul Helm, *Faith And Reason* (Edinburgh: Edinburgh University Press, 1997), p. 76.

integration should be focused on those areas of study in which such activity is underrepresented relatively speaking.[46]

Angelology is not particularly central to 'the Christian theistic enter-prise', but it is perhaps more central than is often acknowledged, given the prominence of angels in scripture. Angelology is under heavy attack, at least implicitly speaking. It is suffering from the neglect of Christian thinkers, the anti-supernaturalism of materialists, and from the unbiblical angelology of the New Age movement. Finally, angelology is certainly underrepresented relative to other areas of integration, such as philosophical anthropology or natural theology.

I agree with Douglas Groothuis that a 'Demonic devaluation of reason and argument has ravaged our society'.[47] This devaluation has seeped into the church and it needs to be resisted like the disease it is. Christian philosophy is a God-given antibody by which we obey his command to 'Test everything. Hold on to the good' (1 Thes. 5:21). Philosophy provides the equipment that enables the defence of the faith commanded by scripture. As Augustine put it in his *De Doctrina Christiana* (AD 397): 'If those who are called philosophers … have said anything which is true and consistent with faith, we must not reject it, but claim it for our own use.' Therefore, to apply the resources of philos-ophy to an integrative angelology is a thoroughly biblical undertaking. In what follows I will discuss the possibility, plausibility and actuality of angels as traditionally understood within the Christian worldview.

---

[46] J.P. Moreland @ < http://leaderu.com/aip/docs/moreland2b.html >, p. 2.
[47] Groothuis, *Christianity That Counts*, p. 66.

Chapter One

Plato's Divide

Of course they had no evidence to prove we didn't exist. They just drifted with 'the spirit of the times' and 'the climate of opinion' out of the medieval fire and into the modern fog.

– Peter Kreeft[1]

To some, the very idea that angelology is a serious subject will appear laughable at best. Others will take this proposal in their stride. What accounts for this difference in attitude? It isn't a matter of intelligence. After all, some of the greatest minds have believed, and do believe, in angels. Rather, what generally accounts for this difference is a yet more fundamental difference, a difference in *worldview*. A worldview is a set of assumptions, or presuppositions, that we hold about the basic make-up of reality and that we use to interpret and make sense out of our everyday experience of life, the universe, and everything. A worldview provides answers to fundamental questions, such as:

- *The question of Ultimate Reality*: Is it God, matter, or an impersonal life force?
- *The question of the world around us*: Is it created or uncreated, chaotic or orderly, matter or spirit or both?
- *The question of human nature*: Is it created or uncreated, are we complex machines, sleeping gods, made in God's 'image', free or determined?
- *The question of destiny*: What, if anything, is there beyond death?
- *The question of knowledge*: What is knowledge? How is it possible for us to know?
- *The question of ethics*: What should we do? Is there such a thing as objective right and wrong, good and evil?

---

[1] Kreeft, *The Snakebite Letters*, p. 13.

- *The question of meaning*: What is the meaning or purpose, if any, of human existence?

It has been said that philosophy begins in wonder, and the same is true for worldviews; the journey to a consciously adopted worldview begins with someone saying, 'I wonder' (perhaps, 'I wonder if angels exist?'). This is the first choice, to unreflectively accept whatever worldview assumptions we find ourselves with, or to strike out on our own in search of answers. Either way, we find ourselves presupposing that truth exists and can be known (at least in part), and this implies the acceptance of the common ground rules of reason.[2] From here on in we can divide up the territory over the issue of Ultimate Reality. Is Ultimate Reality material or immaterial, personal or impersonal? If it is immaterial and personal, is it one or many (monotheism or polytheism)? If it is one, is all one (pantheism) or is there a distinction between Ultimate Reality and some less ultimate reality (theism)? Many of these questions lie beyond the purview of this volume, and a thorough treatment of even the most pertinent worldview questions lies beyond my current scope. Nevertheless, this is the conceptual context of angelology, and there are plenty of resources available for those inclined to explore the logical space of worldviews in detail.[3] My current, humbler task is to focus upon one comparatively neglected aspect of the Christian worldview – angels. I will touch on other issues only as they become directly relevant to this end.

Plato's Divide

In his dialogue *The Laws* (Book X) Plato's Athenian (Plato's mouthpiece) notes that: 'all things do become, have become and will become, some by nature, some by art, and some by chance.'[4] According to the Athenian:

---

[2] cf. Norman L. Geisler and Peter Bucchino, *Unshakable Foundations* (Minneapolis, Minnesota: Bethany House, 2001).

[3] A good introduction to world views is James W. Sire, *The Universe Next Door* (Leicester: IVP[3], 1997).

[4] William Dembski's 'explanatory filter' for the detection of intelligent design uses this schema, progressively asking of any product whether it is the result of 'law' (high probability), 'chance' (low probability) or 'design' (detectable by the presence of specified events of sufficiently low probability, or 'complex specified information'). cf. William A. Dembski, *Intelligent Design: The Bridge Between Science & Theology* (Downers Grove, Illinois: IVP, 1999).

[some] people say that the gods exist not by nature, but by art, and by the laws of states, which are different in different places, according to the agreement of those who make them ... and that the principles of justice have no existence at all in nature, but that mankind are always disputing about them and altering them; and that the alterations which are made by art and by law have no basis in nature, but are of authority for the moment and at the time at which they are made ...

This is a fair description of metaphysical naturalism. 'God' exists 'by art', being only an idea in people's minds; hence ultimate reality is amoral and impersonal, having no intentions, and the principles of morality have no objective existence 'out there'. Plato thus delineates two basic worldview options: either the physical cosmos comes before mind; or mind comes before the cosmos. I call this fundamental disjunction 'Plato's divide'. Everything flows from our answer to this most basic of worldview questions. (Alfred North Whitehead said that philosophy is a series of footnotes to Plato. This book is such a footnote.) Christian theism stands on Plato's side of the divide, and asserts that God is the greatest possible being, the Ultimate Reality who freely created an intelligible universe with material and spiritual dimensions, including humans (and angels) made in God's 'image' (having the capacity for love, knowledge and free will) who should worship God and obey him, and who will either exist with God for eternity or not as their choices dictate.[5] These beliefs form the backdrop of the Christian perspective upon existence (one can of course focus more closely upon the details by bringing in beliefs about God's self-revelation in history, particularly in the person of Jesus).[6] The worldview of the secular, God-denying minority, metaphysical naturalism, stands on the opposite side of Plato's divide. As C.S. Lewis explained: 'Some people believe that nothing exists except Nature; I call these people *Naturalists*. Others think that, besides Nature, there exists something else: I call them *Supernaturalists*.'[7]

The most common reason or motivation to doubt the existence of angels is simply the *presupposition* of naturalism, since 'The central claim of metaphysical naturalism is that nothing exists outside the

---

[5] For a more comprehensive analysis of the Christian world view cf. Charles Colson and Nancy Pearcey, *How Now Shall We Live?* (London: Marshall Pickering, 1999); Arthur F. Holmes, *Contours Of A World View* (Grand Rapids, Michigan: Eerdmans, 1983).

[6] cf. the resources on Jesus recommended in the Bibliography.

[7] C.S. Lewis, *Miracles* (London: Fount, 1998[2]), p. 4.

material, mechanical (that is, nonpurposeful), natural order.'[8] A Naturalistic worldview dogmatically excludes the existence of anything immaterial, purposeful or supernatural. A naturalist *must not* believe in angels for angels are supernatural, and as Corliss Lamont says: 'naturalistic metaphysics ... considers all forms of the supernatural as myth [because it] regards Nature as the totality of being and as a ... system of matter and energy which exists independently of any mind or consciousness.'[9] Of course, whether the incompatibility of naturalism and angels is so much the worse for angels, or so much the worse for naturalism, is another kettle of (angel) fish. I happen to think that it's so much the worse for naturalism. Still, the fact remains that: 'Naturalism is antisupernatural, so it will not take seriously Christianity's claim to truths such as the existence of God and the soul, angels and demons.'[10]

Philosopher Barry Stroud, at the University of California at Berkeley, defines *supernaturalism* as 'the invocation of an agent or force which somehow stands outside the familiar natural world and so whose doings cannot be understood as part of it ...'[11] An angel is a clear example of an agent who 'stands outside the familiar natural world', and whose doings cannot be understood as part of a closed system of natural cause and effect. Hence belief in angels means adopting an anti-naturalistic *supernaturalism*; but then, so does belief in God! So too does an acceptance of the traditional conception of the human mind or soul as immaterial. As J.P. Moreland and Scott B. Rae argue: 'a proper understanding of God and angels as spirits and a careful exegesis of Scripture present a biblical anthropology that is inconsistent with physicalism ...'[12] For on the traditional Christian view of things 'The human soul, while not by nature immortal, is capable of entering an intermediate disembodied state upon death ... and of eventually being reunited with a resurrected body.'[13]

Of course, a supernaturalist *might not* believe in angels. A supernaturalist may believe in *one or more* of a whole variety of supernatural

---

[8] Ronald H. Nash, 'Miracles and Conceptual Systems' in R. Douglas Geivett and Gary R. Habermas (eds), *In Defence Of Miracles* (Leicester: Apollos, 1997), p. 119.

[9] Corliss Lamont, *The Philosophy Of Humanism* (New York: Frederick Ungar, 1977), pp. 12–13.

[10] Groothuis, *Christianity That Counts*, p. 89.

[11] Barry Stroud, 'The Charm of Naturalism', *Proceedings And Addresses Of The American Philosophical Society* 70 (1996), p. 44.

[12] Moreland and Rae, *Body & Soul*, p. 10.

[13] Ibid, p. 17.

entities, such as God, gods, angels, the human mind, and ghosts.[14] Supernaturalism as such is not a package deal like naturalism; belief in particular supernatural entities must be approached on a case-by-case basis. Nevertheless, the supernaturalist will at least have to take the question of angels seriously. One can't admit the reality of the super-natural in one instance and then disregard the possibility of the super-natural in another. For the theistic supernaturalist, God is the ultimate reality. Such a belief lays a foundation that is sympathetic to the existence of other supernatural realities, including angels. For the theist, the question of angels is therefore primarily one of evidence. This said, belief in angels is in fact, historically speaking (and I venture, properly speaking), part of the 'package deal' of *Christian* supernaturalism.

Premodernism and Superstition

Christian supernaturalism is, technically speaking, a *premodern* world-view. According to Christian philosopher and theologian William A. Dembski:

> premodernity is identified with superstition ... alchemy, Ptolemaic epicycles, the four humours, the four elements and so on – what C.S. Lewis called 'the discarded image.' Now there is no question that many elements of premodernity needed to be discarded [because they were false]. Nonetheless premodernity had one thing going for it that neither modernity nor postmodernity could match, a worldview rich enough to accommodate divine agency [and, we can add, angels].[15]

Christianity is not premodern in the sense of retaining falsified scientific views, such as belief in the four elements (earth, wind, fire and water). Rather, it is premodern in the sense of retaining certain venerable *meta-physical* beliefs (e.g. the objective reality of God, truth, goodness, beauty, angels and the soul) that were rejected along with belief in alchemy, the four humours, and so on. This double rejection was essen-tially a case of throwing the metaphysical baby out with the scientific bathwater:

---

[14] A *Time* magazine poll found that 69 per cent of Americans believe in the existence of angels, and only 25 per cent believe in ghosts, while 98 per cent of Americans say they believe in God. For the record, I don't believe in gods or ghosts (I am inclined to give ghosts a naturalistic or demonic explanation on a case-by-case basis). cf. Michael White, *The Science Of The X Files* (London: Legend, 1996).

[15] Dembski, *Intelligent Design*, p. 45.

We have been living in an unstable and temporary situation ... suspended between ... the premodern, prescientific world in which we have a cosmic place, meaning and harmony with nature; and the ... scientistic worldview according to which the universe ... is inhuman, alien, unfit for habitation, not a *home* ... We cannot live for long with one foot on the medieval, stable land and one foot in the modern, relativistic boat. We must either find our way back to a home or turn ourselves into machines ... If the old meanings that every premodern civilization saw in nature were really there, then modernity is not demythologized but orphaned ...[16]

The atheistic resort to *scientism*, as throwing the metaphysical baby out with the scientific bathwater is called, is widespread. Returning home doesn't mean giving up on *science*, but on *scientism*.

Scientism and the supernatural

It is salutary to ask oneself, 'Can science really explain everything?' It certainly can't provide every sort of explanation. As Aristotle pointed out, there are several different types of explanation. For example, if we are to give a comprehensive explanation for the existence of a house we must appeal to the existence of the stuff the house is made out of (its material cause), take into account the arrangement of that stuff (its formal cause), explain how that stuff came to be in that form (its efficient cause) and finally we must provide the reason why the house exists, the goal that this arrangement of matter serves (its final cause – to provide shelter). Science explains in terms of contingent material, formal and efficient causes. It cannot explain *why* there is any matter, or *why* the universe ultimately takes the form it does, let alone *why* there is a universe in the first place. Nor can science say the universe hasn't got an efficient cause beyond itself. Theists say that the universe is caused, atheists disagree. Science is incapable of supporting atheists in this disagreement.[17] Science, by its very nature, cannot rule out what Richard Swinburne calls 'personal explanations' (although it can include them as in cryptography). This fact can be recognized in such mundane situations as cooking something in a microwave: Why is the potato getting hot? Answer: because the microwaves are causing the water molecules to vibrate. That's a scientific explanation in terms of natural cause and effect among natural entities. But why is this

---

[16] Peter Kreeft, *Christianity For Modern Pagans* (San Francisco: Ignatius, 1993), pp. 130, 136.

[17] While science cannot rule *out* design, it can rule *in* design (as with SETI, or forensic science). Being thus asymmetric, science not only can't support atheism, but it can (and does) support theism!

happening? Because I want my lunch! This is an explanation in terms of the desires and purposes of an agent. To rule out the existence of spiritual agencies (whether angelic or divine) by reference to science would be just as implausible as refusing to acknowledge that my purpose to have a potato for lunch has anything to do with the potato getting hot.

Failure to appreciate this point has meant that the naturalistic objection to angels has been couched in terms that accuse belief in angels and demons of being *unscientific*. As Rudolf Bultmann notoriously put it: 'it is impossible to use electric light and the wireless and to avail ourselves of modern medical and surgical discoveries, and at the same time to believe in the New Testament world of daemons and spirits.'[18] To formulate this objection into an argument would require an additional premise to the effect that being scientific is the arbiter of rational acceptability. However, is the proposition that 'whether or not a belief is scientific should determine its rational acceptability' a *scientific* proposition? It is not. It is an arbitrary philosophical assertion. The belief that scientific justification is a prerequisite of rationality is self-defeating, because it fails to meet its own standard. This shouldn't be too surprising, since science depends upon several metaphysical presuppositions (such as the uniformity of nature across all time and space) that cannot be scientifically verified. How could it be proven scientifically that only scientifically knowable entities are real? The person who declares that science disproves the existence of God, or any other spirit, is like a person who declares that windows disprove the existence of wind: 'we can see trees through the window, but you can't feel the wind; ergo, trees exist but the wind does not.' Perhaps we need to open the window a bit.[19]

To limit knowledge or existence to that which falls within the narrow competency of the natural sciences is an unjustified and self-defeating leap of faith. There are many things that the natural sciences don't deal with, such as moral and aesthetic values, such as angels and demons, but that doesn't mean these things don't exist! *Scientism* is simply inadequate when it comes to giving an account of reality. Can truth, goodness and beauty be accounted for in purely scientific terms? Can the

---

[18] Rudolf Bultmann, 'The New Testament and Mythology' in H.W. Bartsch (ed.), *Kerygma And Myth* (London: SPCK, 1953).
[19] Robert C. Koons argues that scientific realism is incompatible with naturalism, cf. 'The Incompatibility of Naturalism and Scientific Realism' @ < http://www.leaderu.com/offices/koons/docs/natreal.html >; also in William Lane Craig and J.P. Moreland (eds), *Naturalism: A Critical Analysis* (London: Routledge, 2001).

human mind and personality really be described without remainder by physics, chemistry and biology? Can science explain the existence of an orderly universe open to scientific exploration? I think not. In explaining the universe our rule should not be 'What is the best *scientific* explanation?' but 'What is *the best* explanation?' After all, superstition lurks in more metaphysical categories than the supernatural. As Phillip E. Johnson argues: 'There is no doubt that science has done much to discredit superstition, but sometimes the scientific imagination merely substitutes new materialist superstitions for the old supernatural ones. In place of witchcraft and devil worship, we get psychoanalysis, Marxism, social Darwinism, and space aliens.'[20] Such materialist delusions spring up to fill the spiritual void left by a superficially power-ful but moribund naturalistic philosophy 'that can expel one kind of superstition, but cannot satisfy our spiritual needs'.[21] We need to reject superstition in whatever metaphysical category we find it, rather than relying on an indiscriminate blanket dismissal of all things supernatural that ends up as a form of superstition in its own rite: 'When science is defined as applied materialist philosophy, it automatically excludes the possibility of [angels], regardless of the evidence. Materialist science can be remarkably tolerant of unverified materialist theories, provided that they play a useful role in supporting the claim that a science based on materialism is the only valid way of comprehending reality.'[22] It bears repeating that science *cannot* be the only valid way of comprehending reality, for the very proposal that this is so is *not a scientific proposal*.

We know that 'throughout human history and its varied cultures three great external types of reality commonly have been assumed to exist. These are the external physical world, the world of other minds, and the transcendent spiritual world, for example, of God or the gods [and of angels].'[23] To simply ignore the premodern challenge of non-physical reality, including angels, would be to engage in what C.S. Lewis called 'chronological snobbery': 'the uncritical assumption that whatever has gone out of date is on that account discredited. You must find out why it went out of date. Was it ever refuted (and if so, by whom, where, and how conclusively) or did it merely die away as fashions do? If the latter, this tells us nothing about its truth or

---

[20]   Phillip E. Johnson, 'Darwin and the Supernatural' in Fickett (ed.), *Things In Heaven And Earth*, p. 97.

[21]   Ibid.

[22]   Ibid., p. 98.

[23]   Paul C. Vitz, 'Experiencing the Supernatural' in Fickett (ed.), *Things In Heaven And Earth*, p. 82.

falsehood.'[24] Angelology may be unfashionable, but news of its death is nothing but an unsubstantiated rumour.

The Contemporary State of Naturalism

Naturalism may fairly be dubbed the 'orthodox' metaphysical view of contemporary culture despite the fact that its advocates are a relatively small number of academics with a disproportionate amount of influence. While naturalism remains more academically respectable today than in past centuries, I doubt that it has ever been in such patently poor shape *intellectually speaking*. Terry L. Miethe reports:

> Many philosophers are today talking about the collapse of modern atheism – not necessarily that there are less atheists, but that there is less reason for being one … because of the philosophical, scientific, and ethical evidence for the existence of God. Even the editors of *Philosophy Today* have said: 'No responsible philosopher can escape reflecting upon the unique character and problems of contemporary atheism.'[25]

Naturalism has recently come under an unprecedented barrage of high-calibre intellectual fire on multiple fronts.[26] One can almost feel the tide of naturalism receding. The public seems to have caught on to this mood, if not its rationale: 'In 1900, something like 6% of the world's population were self-confessed atheists. Today that figure has shrunk to just a little over 4% … Every opinion poll for the last two or three decades has shown a steady increase in the level of religious belief.'[27]

---

[24] C.S. Lewis, *Surprised By Joy* (London: Fount, 1977).

[25] Terry L. Miethe in Terry L. Miethe and Anthony Flew, *Does God Exist? A Believer And An Atheist Debate* (San Francisco: HarperCollins, 1991), p. 196.

[26] The most significant figures in the current renaissance of Christian philosophy are Alvin Plantinga and Richard Swinburne (cf. Appendix IV). Also significant is the Intelligent Design Movement (cf. 'What is Intelligent Design?' @ < http://www.reviewevolution.com/whatIsIntelligentDesign.php >; Access Research Network @ < http://www.arn.org >). A good collection of papers critical of naturalism is Craig and Moreland (eds), *Naturalism: A Critical Analysis*. Papers include: Robert C. Koons, 'The Incompatibility of Naturalism and Scientific Realism' @ < http://www.leaderu.com/offices/koons/docs/natreal.html >; and Dallas Willard, 'Knowledge and Naturalism' @< http://www.dwillard.org/Philosophy/Pubs/knowledge_and_naturalism.htm >.

[27] John Drane, *The Bible Phenomenon* (Oxford: Lion, 1999), pp. 10–11.

Anthony O'Hear may dismiss religious belief as 'intellectually unsustainable',[28] and Kai Nielsen may assert that 'for somebody ... with a good philosophical and a good scientific education, who thinks carefully about the matter ... it is irrational to believe in God,'[29] but this is all bark and no bite. If belief in God is so 'irrational', how come there are several Christian scientific and philosophical societies, each with hundreds of members holding good scientific and philosophical qualifications?[30] The fact is that a growing number of scientists and philosophers of science see more evidence now for a personal creator and designer from science than was available in times past.

> In the nineteenth century many scientists thought life could spontaneously arise from sea mud. But that idea was discarded when the complexity of the cell was discovered. In the early 1950s Stanley Miller thought he had a handle on how life may have originated, but now most scientists will frankly admit we have no explanation for the beginning of life. Scientists used to think the universe was eternal, which fit nicely with materialism. Now it has a beginning, with obvious attendant theological overtones. And the anthropic coincidences that Hoyle and others have discovered only add to materialism's woes.[31]

Little wonder the idea of design has undergone a renaissance in the past few decades. If O'Hear and Nielsen are right, why has the number of intellectuals who embrace Christianity increased? In a recent article atheist Quentin Smith highlights the 'influx of talented theists' in philosophy and notes: 'today perhaps one-quarter or one-third of philosophy professors are theists, with most being orthodox Christians.'[32] Indeed, American philosopher Roderick Chisholm believes that while the

---

[28] Anthony O'Hear, *Beyond Evolution* (Oxford: Clarendon Press, 1997).

[29] Kai Nielsen in J.P. Moreland and Kai Nielsen, *Does God Exist? The Debate Between Theists & Atheists* (Amherst, New York: Prometheus, 1993), p. 48.

[30] cf. Society of Christian Philosophers @ < http://www.siu.edu/departments/cola/philos/SCP/ >; Evangelical Philosophical Society @ < http://www.epsociety.org >; The American Scientific Affiliation @ < http://asa.calvin.edu/ASA/index.html >; and Christians in Science @ < http://www.cis.org.uk/ >.

[31] Phillip E. Johnson and Denis O. Lamoureux, *Darwinism Defeated? The Johnson–Lamoureux Debate On Biological Origins* (Vancouver: Regent College, 1999), p. 107.

[32] Quentin Smith, 'The Metaphilosophy of Naturalism', *Philo* vol. IV, no. 2, 05/01/02 @ < http://www.philoonline.org/library/smith_4_2.htm >. Smith notes that in the Oxford University Press 2000–2001 catalogue there were ninety-six recently published books on the philosophy of religion, two presenting 'both sides' and ninety-four advancing theism!

brightest philosophers of a generation ago were atheists, today most of the brightest philosophers believe in God. Smith laments: 'academia has now lost its mainstream secularisation ... If naturalism is the true world-view and a "Dark Age" means an age when the vast majority of philosophers (and scientists) do not know the true world-view, then we have to admit that we are living in a Dark Age.'[33] Of course, what the naturalist considers a Dark Age is for the theist an Age of Enlightenment!

One of the most significant factors in this theistic Enlightenment is the 'nearly unanimous agreement among both theistic and nontheistic philosophers of religion that the logical version of the argument from evil doesn't work'.[34] William Lane Craig explains:

> it is widely recognized ... that the ... coexistence of God and evil is logically possible ... the atheist presupposes that God cannot have morally sufficient reasons for permitting the evil in the world. But this assumption is not necessarily true. So long as it is even *possible* that God has morally sufficient reasons for permitting evil, it follows that God and evil are logically consistent.[35]

A recent incident nicely illustrated this point. One of my friends has a cat called Tia. Listening to Tia mewing for food I mused how she might argue along the following lines: 'I am hungry (a bad state of affairs if ever there was one): if the owner exists (the owner is loving and can procure food to end my hunger) then I would not be hungry; therefore (since I am hungry) the owner doesn't exist.' If Tia argued against the owner in this manner, she would be in the same position as the atheist who argues against God from evil: 'Evil exists: if God exists (God is all-good and all-powerful) then evil would not exist; therefore (since evil exists) God doesn't exist.' I happen to know that Tia's owner exists, that she can procure cat food and that she does love her cat. I also know that Tia's owner had a morally justifiable reason for not preventing Tia's hunger (more food would have been bad for her). Even if we don't know what morally justifiable reason God has for not preventing evil (including

---

[33] Ibid.

[34] Michael Bergmann, *Philosophia Christi* series 2, vol. I, no. 2, 1999, p. 140.

[35] William Lane Craig in debate with Kai Nielsen. Craig has a neuromuscular disease. As Peter Kreeft observes, 'it's significant that most objections to the existence of God from the problem of suffering come from outside observers who are quite comfortable, whereas those who actually suffer are, as often as not, made into stronger believers by their suffering'. Lee Strobel, *The Case For Faith: A Journalist Investigates The Toughest Objections To Christianity* (Grand Rapids, Michigan: Zondervan, 2000), p. 72.

world hunger) an argument against his existence that simply assumes he has none is no more reasonable than Tia's 'anti-owner argument' from 'the problem of hunger'.[36]

The 'free will defence' has played an important role in rebutting the 'problem of evil', for as Alvin Plantinga argues: 'A world containing creatures who are significantly free ... is more valuable, all else being equal, than a world containing no free creatures at all ... To create creatures capable of moral good ... [God] must create creatures capable of moral evil; and he can't give these creatures this freedom to perform evil and at the same time prevent them from doing so.'[37] Adding the admittedly implausible suggestion that all 'natural evil' is caused by demons is none the less sufficient to prove the *logical compatibility* of God and evil. The atheists alleged that it was self-contradictory to believe both in God and evil; the theists have successfully rebutted this accusation.[38]

This is all very well in so far as it goes, but one might wonder just how far that is. Doesn't evil (or the *amount* of evil that exists) at least *count against* the existence of God? Supposing it does, one would still have to take into account all the evidence for the existence of God before deciding if evil counted *decisively* against God's existence. However, evil doesn't even 'count against' God, let alone decisively.[39] Theists can argue that the existence of evil actually counts decisively *for* the existence of God, that it is actually the atheist who engages in a self-contradiction if they believe in evil, and that the more horrifying the evil the more obvious and inescapable this fact is. Consider, for a moment, what it means to claim that something is *morally* 'good' or 'evil'. A moral claim does not describe how the majority of people actually behave. It does not tell us what anyone's subjective preference is. Instead, it is a claim about what people *ought* to do, whether or not they actually do it and is regardless of their actual preferences.[40] If humans

---

[36] Thanks to Jenny for suggesting that I put this illustration in my book.

[37] Alvin Plantinga, 'The Free Will Defence' in Basil Mitchell (ed.), *The Philosophy Of Religion* (Oxford: Oxford University Press, 1971).

[38] cf. Kelly James Clark, *Return To Reason* (Grand Rapids, Michigan: Eerdmans, 1990); John Perry, *Dialogue On Good, Evil, And The Existence Of God* (Indianapolis, Indiana: Hackett, 1999).

[39] For an in-depth discussion of the suggestion that evil counts against God, cf. Daniel Howard-Snyder (ed.), *The Evidential Argument From Evil* (Bloomington, Indiana: Indiana University Press, 1996).

[40] On the nature of moral values cf. Francis J. Beckwith and Gregory Koukl, *Relativism: Feet Firmly Planted In Mid-Air* (Grand Rapids, Michigan: Baker, 2001); Williams, *The Case For God*.

are, as naturalists believe, nothing but tiny anomalies thrown up by blind natural processes for a transient existence in an otherwise hostile cosmos, then it is surely impossible to justify such moral claims. Since the claim that some things are evil is more certain than the claim that humans are 'nothing but' an unintended and temporary cosmic anomaly, and since the two claims are incompatible, we must repudiate at least one of them.[41] This is the heart of the atheist's dilemma; not that they cannot recognize evil when they see it, but that they cannot do so *without embracing a contradiction between their conscience and their worldview*. In this way the problem of evil backfires on the atheist, for as Norman L. Geisler writes: 'to disprove God via evil one must assume the equivalent of God by way of an ultimate standard of justice beyond this world ...'[42]

Steve Kumar reminds us that 'The reality of evil confronts every philosophy of life, and the burden of explaining its origin and existence lies equally upon all.'[43] For example, naturalism implies determinism; but how can I be morally culpable for doing something that I was determined to do by natural forces? Blaming someone for murder would be equivalent to blaming a volcano for the fact that its eruption caused loss of life! Naturalism erases the line between natural and moral evil, reducing the latter to the former. Thus naturalism denies free will and objective ethics, and objective ethics proves free will and disproves naturalism.

The naturalist's problem, as Winfried Corduan sees it, is committing the fallacy of trying to get an ought from an is: 'He or she is trying to justify *prescriptive* moral laws on the basis of *descriptive* data. The atheist is after an obligatory moral code without anything that makes it obligatory. To have commandments, they must be commanded in some way, but the atheist's system does not allow for such a possibility.'[44] Only a theistic worldview allows for such a possibility. The recognition of a moral law thus leads to the recognition of a good moral law-giver, while denying the moral law leads not only to the collapse of the atheist's flagship argument against God, but to the soul-destroying embrace of

---

[41] This argument says nothing against evolution as such, only a purely naturalistic, unintended evolution.

[42] Norman L. Geisler, *Christian Apologetics* (Grand Rapids, Michigan: Baker, 1976), p. 233.

[43] Steve Kumar, *Christianity For Sceptics* (New Alresford, Hampshire: John Hunt, 2000), p. 41.

[44] Winfried Corduan, *No Doubt About It* (Nashville, Tennessee: Broadman & Holman, 1997), p. 87.

nihilism, the view that nothing has any objective value. As R.C. Sproul says: 'To deny [God] is to set one's sails for the island of nihilism ... the darkest continent of the darkened mind ...'[45] The dark continent of naturalistic nihilism is correctly described by atheist Will Provine: 'No God. No life after death. No free will. No ultimate meaning in life and no ultimate foundation for ethics.'[46] Hence, not only is the reality of evil at odds with a naturalistic worldview, but naturalism has nothing positive to say in the face of evil. The Christian, on the other hand, can never forget that God is a God who suffers with us and for us, and who gives eternal life to those who love him.[47]

Alban McCoy, Catholic chaplain at Cambridge University, reminds us that however we view the philosophical problem of evil, 'none of us can escape the second form of the problem: that is the experience of evil.'[48] This is the practical question of *how we are to cope with the experience of suffering*. McCoy suggests that 'Only the conviction that evil can never be the final word ... can ease the sense of futility that so easily arises in the face of evil. Without this, life would surely be, as Macbeth says, no more than "a tale told by an idiot, full of sound and fury, signifying nothing" (*Macbeth* V. v. 16). Even if we cannot make sense of the experience of evil, we need some ground for hope.'[49] With McCoy, I believe that *only God can provide an adequate ground for hope in the face of evil and suffering*. Knowing God's personal involvement in solving the practical problem of evil (especially in my own heart) encourages my confidence in the face of the philosophical problem of evil. As McCoy says:

> The Cross is at once the greatest evil and the greatest good and it is here that we are given grounds for believing that the mystery of sin and evil is within the providence of God, however little we may understand how this might be so ... it is in the Cross that the problem of evil is most clearly manifest, for here, contrary to the view that God must be indifferent to our suffering, he

---

[45] R.C. Sproul, *The Consequences Of Ideas* (Wheaton, Illinois: Crossway, 2000), p. 171.

[46] Will Provine in Russell Stannard, *Science And Wonders* (London: Faber and Faber, 1996).

[47] On the Christian understanding of the afterlife, cf. Kreeft and Tacelli, *Handbook Of Christian Apologetics*; Peter Kreeft, *Everything You Ever Wanted To Know About Heaven But Never Dreamed Of Asking* (San Francisco: Ignatius, 1990).

[48] Alban McCoy, *An Intelligent Person's Guide To Catholicism* (London: Continuum, 2001), p. 17.

[49] Ibid., p. 18.

becomes the victim of evil in order to overcome, on our behalf, the evil we have inflicted on him.[50]

Norman L. Geisler seems to me to be correct when he writes of atheism: 'First, its arguments are invalid and often self-defeating. Second, many atheistic arguments are really reversible into reasons for believing in God. Finally, atheism provides no solution to basic metaphysical questions regarding the existence of the universe or the origin of personality ...'[51] Hence the attractions of theism are not merely predicated on the failures of naturalism, and it is small wonder that 'Even opponents of religious faith are coming to respect its rational integrity.'[52]

Conclusion

It should be obvious by now that in angelology we cannot escape the interrelatedness of all things.

> All knowledge forms one whole, because its subject-matter is one, for the universe in its length and breadth is so intimately knit together, that we cannot separate off abstraction; and then again, as to its Creator, though He of course in His own being is infinitely separate from it ... yet He has so implicated Himself with it, and taken it into His very bosom, by His presence in it, His providence over it, His impressions upon it, and His influences through it, that we cannot truly or fully contemplate it without contemplating Him.[53]

The plausibility of belief in angels, like the plausibility of the Christian worldview as a whole, is intimately linked to the plausibility of the belief that Mind comes before cosmos. The primary issue for angelology is thus the ultimate metaphysical question posed by Plato's divide. The naturalistic response to Plato's divide is impressive in its cultural influence, but shows an increasing lack of rational credibility. Scientism is self-defeating, and naturalism (unlike theism) is unable to account for, or deal with, the reality of evil. Scepticism about angels cannot be justified by the mere assumption of naturalism.

---

[50] Ibid., pp. 16–17, 27.

[51] Geisler, *Christian Apologetics*, pp. 234–5.

[52] Michael Peterson, William Hasker, Bruce Reichenbach and David Basinger (eds), Introduction, *Philosophy Of Religion: Selected Readings* (New York: Oxford University Press, 1996).

[53] John Henry Newman, *The Idea Of A University* (Notre Dame, Indiana: University of Notre Dame Press, 1982), p. 60.

Chapter Two

Angelic Possibility

The materialist assumption that nothing really exists except ... corporal substances does not render the phrase 'incorporeal substance' or the phrase 'spiritual being' self-contradictory or meaningless. It does not, therefore, lead to the conclusion that angels are impossible ... And if the fundamental tenet of materialism ... turns out to be false ... belief in the reality of angels may be true.

– Mortimer J. Adler[1]

In the current cultural climate of metaphysical naturalism it would be easy to feel that belief in angels must be the intellectually suspect product of a will-to-believe in the face of evidence. However, as we saw in the previous chapter, *one ought not to simply beg the question against angels by the mere affirmation of a naturalistic worldview*. With this in mind I will argue for the possibility of angels by defending them against various objections, and by giving some reasons to believe that the human mind and God both exist. The net result will be to show that *for all we know, angels could be real*.

Introducing his now classic book, *Miracles*, C.S. Lewis argued that 'the question whether miracles occur can never be answered simply by experience',[2] for the simple fact that 'What we learn from experience depends on the kind of philosophy we bring to experience.'[3] It is therefore useless, argued Lewis, 'to appeal to experience before we have settled, as well as we can, the philosophical question'.[4] Experience alone is unlikely to convince a committed atheist that a miracle has occurred, for the simple reason that an atheist believes that God doesn't exist and that acts of God are therefore impossible. What goes for miracles goes

---

[1] Adler, *The Angels And Us*, p. 107.
[2] Lewis, *Miracles*, p. 1.
[3] Ibid.
[4] Ibid.

for belief in angels. The question of whether angels exist is unlikely to be settled simply by experience, and it is therefore useless to appeal to experience before we have settled, as well as we can, the philosophical question of whether angels *could* exist to be experienced in the first place. This chapter therefore seeks to deal with the philosophical issues surrounding the *possibility* of angels.

Experience versus Dogma

Weak or fallacious arguments against angels can prove attractive to someone who views the supernatural as superstitious nonsense because of their faith in naturalism. A recent article in *The Philosophers' Magazine* exemplified this fact, illustrating Lewis's dictum that our philosophy affects what we learn from our experience. Resident *Philosophers' Magazine* sceptic Wendy Grossman reflected upon her participation in a talk show dedicated to what she called, with chrono-logical snobbery, 'the medieval belief' that angels exist.[5] Grossman reported: 'One woman told how her parent's angels appeared to her the night before her mother died ... Her mother wasn't even sick, she said, but the next day was taken to the hospital with a suspected chest infection that quickly killed her.' Grossman sought to cast doubt on angels by pointing out that a common factor in angelic encounters is 'that the person in question began to believe in angels at a time of extreme stress in their lives'. She also noted: 'the mother's death described above [is an] obvious [example]'. However, it is hardly a reason for doubt that people tend to encounter angels in times of trouble, since it is a traditional theo-logical assumption that giving comfort is a function of the heavenly host. Wendy's scepticism about angels is, I believe, really faith in naturalism. She dismisses the cautionary aphorism 'God moves in mysterious ways': 'Now, if we could only test that ...' One suspects that 'test' means 'empirically test'. If so, this reveals an implicit commitment to the self-defeating proposition that science sets the boundaries of intellectual acceptability. Besides, Wendy's psychological explanation *doesn't* apply to the above case. The woman encountered angels *before* she knew her mother was sick.

Grossman asks rhetorically why angels don't intervene more than they apparently do: 'haven't they got better things to do, like creating world peace, or ending hunger?' However, casting doubt on angels because they haven't ended world hunger is surely no more effective

---

[5] All quotes from The Skeptic, *The Philosophers' Magazine*, issue 14.

than casting doubt on God for the same reason. The free-will defence is surely effective in either case (cf. Chapter One). Arguing that we know of occasions when angels would intervene in some particular way if they existed, but clearly don't and therefore aren't real, is problematical, in that we obviously don't know this at all. For all we know, Angels could be working their metaphorical socks off to prevent pain and suffering; and we aren't in a position to run a control experiment of a universe without angels to see what the place would be like without them! Naturalism excludes belief in angels, not arguments like those given by Wendy Grossman.

Conceiving Angels

Perhaps many people find it hard to take angels seriously because they find it hard to imagine them seriously (anyone for halos, harps, feathers and nightgowns?). However, physicists don't find it hard to take atoms seriously, even though it has proved very hard to imagine them seriously (anyone for plum pudding,[6] a tiny solar-system or a particle that's also a wave?). Whether the entity in question is an atom or an angel, imagination is not barrier to intellectual seriousness, because we can conceive what we can't imagine. We conceive what can apparently be coherently supposed. We can coherently suppose that both atoms and angels exist. Conceiving is a rational intuition: 'an *intuition* is the way something seems to you upon careful reflection and attention.'[7] We can distinguish between something being *weakly conceivable* for a person when they reflect upon it and see no reason to believe it is impossible, and something being *strongly conceivable* for a person who 'judges that it is possible on the basis of a more positive grasp of the properties involved and of the compatibility of what she is conceiving with what she already knows'.[8] We use intuitions of conceivability throughout our lives. For example, we have a strong rational intuition that a square circle is impossible; and I hazard that you share the intuition that, although extraterrestrial life may not be *actual*, it is at least *possible*: 'judgements that a state of affairs is possible or impossible grounded in conceivability are not infallible ... Still, they provide strong evidence for genuine

---

[6] I think it was John Dalton (1766–1844), father of modern atomic theory, who conceived of atoms as being like plum pudding with smaller, stationary particles evenly scattered throughout the atom – a model now long since superceded.

[7] Moreland and Rae, *Body & Soul*.

[8] Ibid.

possibility or impossibility.'[9] Just as extraterrestrials are conceivable, so angels are conceivable (although neither is easy to convincingly *imagine* – 'little green men' anyone?). We can therefore argue like this: Premise 1) If I can conceive of some state of affairs *s* such that *s* possibly obtains, then I have prima facie grounds for believing that *s* is possible. Premise 2) I can conceive of angels. Conclusion) Therefore I have prima facie grounds for believing that angels are possible.

Angels are *weakly conceivable* in that (as this chapter will show) one can reflect upon the notion of an angel and see no reason to think it impossible. Moreover, angels are *strongly conceivable* in that one can also reflect deeply upon the concept of an angel and see no reason to think them impossible, finding no incompatibility between this concept and anything else one believes to be conceivable (this proposition will be born out by the next chapter). Obviously, not everyone shares this intuition; but people do not always share the same intuitions. While contradictory intuitions cannot all be true, this does not necessarily make it irrational to hold to one's intuitions in the face of some disagreement. The majority of people, including the majority of philosophers and other thinkers throughout history, have shared the intuition that angels are conceivable. Those who don't share this intuition seem to be in this position because they assume that naturalism is true. The burden of proof is therefore on the sceptic. Moreover, it is not enough to believe naturalism to be contingently true in order to justify the intuition that angels are impossible instead of merely nonexistent. Rather, one would have to possess the intuition that naturalism is *necessarily true*. However, 'this view is not defended by any prominent naturalist'.[10] There is therefore a prima facie case for regarding angels to be at least *conceivable* beings, a case that can be bolstered by the rebuttal of the conceptual objections that might be levelled against angels.

Rebuttal of conceptual objections

Some philosophers suggest that the very idea of an immaterial person is incoherent, like the concept of a square circle. The problem with the concept of a square circle is not that none happen to exist, but that none could exist. Unlike the concept of the Loch Ness Monster, which (as far as anyone knows) isn't 'instantiated' (i.e. such that there is an instance of Nessie in the real world) but which *could* be 'instantiated', a square circle couldn't exist because it is a contradiction in terms. Likewise, the

---

[9]   Ibid.
[10]   Paul K. Moser and David Yandell, 'Farewell to Philosophical Naturalism' in Craig and Moreland (eds), *Naturalism: A Critical Analysis*, p. 14.

person who objects that the concept of a bodiless person is incoherent is suggesting that there *couldn't* be any angels or demons (or God). For example, Antony Flew asserts: 'It should certainly be seen as at least very far from obvious that talk of 'a person without a body (i.e., a spirit) is coherent and intelligible.'[11] But what specific reasons are given for thinking this? None. Terry L. Miethe makes the obvious repost: 'is it really any more obvious to talk as if a person is reducible ... to a psychochemical machine, as if this were obviously coherent and intelligible. I think not!'[12] Once again, the weight of human intuition is against the sceptic.

P.F. Strawson argues in his book *Individuals* that for any concept of a thing to be coherent we must be able to uniquely identify or refer to that thing; 'we must be able to pick it out among all other existing or even possible things so that there is no confusion about which thing we are referring too.'[13] This is easy enough with material things (even non-existent ones), says Strawson, since reference can be made to physical properties; e.g. for Nessie: 'A large dinosaur-like creature with a long neck and flippers inhabiting Loch Ness'. When it comes to immaterial things, such material reference is unavailable. Hence, it is alleged, the concept of angels and demons (indeed, the idea of anything immaterial, such as God) is in trouble. One problem with this argument is that *if ideas are themselves immaterial, this objection ends up objecting to itself*. The very attempt to state this objection to immaterial things is self-refuting given any immaterial aspect to the thought or ideas it relies upon. Then again, the number six is not a material object and yet can be quite happily and coherently talked about – so why not angels? The number six, says Davis:

> is surely an immaterial object – the number six does not weigh anything or reside anywhere or take up space. But whether you think the number six is a separately existing thing or just an idea in our minds, the concept of it is obviously a coherent concept and can be uniquely referred to. Take the words 'the only composite number between four and eight.' Won't that description refer uniquely to the number six?[14]

---

[11] Antony Flew in Miethe and Flew, *Does God Exist?*, p. 5.

[12] Ibid., p. 55.

[13] Ibid., pp. 166–7.

[14] Stephen T. Davis, 'God's Actions' in Geivett and Habermas (eds), *In Defence Of Miracles*. For more on this with reference to the existence of God, see Moreland and Nielson, *Does God Exist? The Debate Between Theists & Atheists*.

There are plenty of ways to uniquely refer to angels: by definition ('angels are finite, bodiless persons created by God'), or by their actions (e.g. 'The Angel Gabriel is the Angel who told Mary of God's plan to undertake the incarnation of Jesus'). Why think that *material* reference is a requirement of identification? Such a rule is simply an arbitrary piece of anti-metaphysical bluster.

The concept of an immaterial thing is coherent, but what about the concept of an immaterial *agent*? Some have argued that the notion of immaterial agents is incoherent because what we can dub 'agent words' (such as 'loving', 'cruel', 'aggressive', 'forgiving' and so on) lose their meaning in the absence of a body: 'To be a person, to act justly – he has to behave in certain ways ... But how is it possible to perform these acts, to behave in the required ways without a body?'[15] However, there is no reason why agent words must lose their meaning in the absence of a body, no reason why an immaterial person cannot behave lovingly or cruelly. With Stephen T. Davis:

> I suspect that most atheists understand the sentence 'God spoke to Moses,' even though they think it is false. Using one's vocal cords is of course the normal way that one [human] person speaks to another, but those who insist that what can legitimately be called speaking cannot happen in any other way and that sentences like 'God spoke to Moses' are meaningless are caught in an overly rigid view of language.[16]

If God exists then he can surely work miracles; in which case it is certainly possible for immaterial agents to act and to do so justly.

What if the critic proposes that the problem is not with the concept of an immaterial thing, or with the concept of an immaterial *agent* as such, but with the concept of an immaterial agent *who produces effects in the material world*? Once again, given that God exists and can produce physical effects (e.g. creating the physical universe), one can see that it is indeed possible for an immaterial agent to cause physical effects. If God can survive this criticism, so can angels and demons. As will be seen later, we have evidence that finite immaterial agents *do* produce effects in the physical world; hence, it must be possible! Indeed, one can argue (as I will) that since the human mind cannot be reduced to 'nothing but' the human brain, the mind is clearly capable of causing physical effects (such as my typing these words and your turning these pages). We may

---

[15] Paul Edwards, quoted by Davis, 'God's Actions' in Geivett and Habermas (eds), *In Defence Of Miracles*, p. 169.

[16] Ibid., p. 170.

not know *how* this is possible, but it seems intuitively obvious that it *is* possible. If the human mind is an immaterial cause of material changes in the world, then there is nothing incoherent about the concept of immaterial angelic minds similarly acting on matter.

The description of an angel as a purely spiritual being, an incorporeal personal substance created by God, certainly seems to refer to a unique class of *possible* beings (nothing here is obviously contradictory). As Mortimer J. Adler says, 'An incorporeal substance is a possible mode of being ... The self-evident truth of the foregoing statement lies in the absence of self-contradiction in the conjunction of *substance* with *incorporeal*.'[17] The term 'substance' does *not* mean a *material* thing, but simply a thing that is not a property but can gain and lose properties over time while remaining the same thing. For example, you are a substance because although you have gained various properties as you have grown up (e.g. weight) you are still the same person that was born to your mother. (Even though we might say of someone who has undergone a radical change of character that 'they're a different person', we don't mean it literally because no one is tempted to ask 'a different person than who?') An angel is a substance in the same sense that you are a substance. The fact that you have a body and an angel does not is immaterial.

A more general response to the objection that angels are impossible is simply to point to the arguments in favour of angels! To the extent that these arguments are found to be convincing, so the sceptic should doubt their own scepticism about the cogency of the concept of immaterial things. For now, let us pursue arguments for God and for the immateriality of the human mind, since if either of these entities exist, it would seem likely that angels could exist. I begin with the mind, because this investigation also provides several avenues to approach the question of God's existence.

The mind (and its creator)
There are many views held about the human mind, both within and without Christian circles. Some Christians argue that since we look to the resurrection of the 'spiritual body' Christians can easily embrace a materialistic account of personhood. Quite besides any philosophical problems facing materialistic views of the self, other Christians point to theological issues, like the worry that such an account seems to be at odds with biblical ideas about an 'intermediate state' between death and

---

[17]   Adler, *The Angels And Us*.

resurrection.[18] Naturalists, on the other hand, hold a variety of theories about the mind that, differences aside, are unified in their rejection of supernatural explanations. This rejection is grounded in a central tenet of materialism, namely *the causal closure of the physical domain*. As Jaegwon Kim explains:

> This is the assumption that if we trace the causal ancestry of a physical event, we need never go outside the physical domain. To deny this assumption is to accept ... that some physical events need nonphysical causes, and if this is true then there can in principle be no complete and self-sufficient physical theory of the physical domain ... our physics would need to refer in an essential way to nonphysical casual agents ...[19]

The rejection of the *assumption* of causal closure, and the adoption of a science prepared to make reference to non-physical causal agents *given appropriate empirical evidence*, is precisely the research project advocated by the Intelligent Design Movement. Intelligent Design advocates oppose the dogmatic assumption of causal closure in science and argue in favour of a limited inference to 'intelligent design' from scientific data.

> there exist well-defined methods that, on the basis of observational features of the world, are capable of reliably distinguishing intelligent causes from undirected natural causes. Many special sciences have already developed such methods for drawing this distinction – notably forensic science ... cryptography ... and the search for Extraterrestrial Intelligence ... For intelligent design the first question is ... whether organisms demonstrate clear, empirically detectable marks of being intelligently caused. In principle an evolutionary process can exhibit such marks of intelligence as much as any act of special creation.[20]

---

[18] cf. John W. Cooper, *Body, Soul & Life Everlasting* (Leicester: Apollos, 2000).

[19] Jaegwon Kim, 'The Myth of Nonreductive materialism', *Supervenience And Mind: Selected Philosophical Essays* (Cambridge: Cambridge University Press, 1994), p. 280. Intelligent Design advocates would argue that this is a bridge that has already been crossed with respect to the complex specified information present in various biological systems.

[20] William A. Dembski (ed.), Introduction, *Mere Creation* (Downers Grove, Illinois: IVP, 1998). Theistic evolution proposes *at a minimum* that God caused life by creating and sustaining a finely tuned universe in which sentience would evolve, and *at a maximum* that God also exerted some sort of causal influence on the evolutionary process. I.D. theorists tend to recognize only the minimal form of theistic evolution although the maximal form is, at the very least, closer to the I.D. hypothesis (cf. Keith Ward, *God, Chance And Necessity* [Oxford: Oxford University Press, 1996]).

If Intelligent Design continues to fulfil its youthful promise, one imagines that the naturalistic assumption of causal closure will become less widely held and that this will have knock-on effects in fields such as philosophy of mind[21] and upon the intellectual acceptability of angelology.

The belief that humans are identical with their physical bodies, that mental states just are physical brain states, is called physicalism. Physicalism is a natural result of a naturalistic worldview. Naturalism, as Jaegwon Kim says, 'demands "full coverage" ... and exacts a terribly high ontological price'.[22] According to Kim, 'The shared project of the majority of those who have worked on the mind–body problem over the past few decades has been to find a way of accommodating the mental within a principled physical scheme ... without losing what we value, or find special, in our natures as creatures with minds.'[23] Physicalism is a testing-ground for naturalism and thus for the possibility of angels; for if the price of naturalism as applied to the mind is too high, then the price of naturalism is simply too high, even if this means that one must accept the possibility of angels! If naturalism fails to account for the mind, then naturalism fails. In my judgement, the naturalistic project described by Kim is a conspicuous failure, and hence, so is naturalism.

Physicalism is extremely counter-intuitive, for it holds that my mental life of thoughts and emotions is 'nothing but physical events in my brain and nervous system'.[24] It is this reductive 'nothing but' that is the most important feature of physicalism. However, according to naturalist Ned Block: 'We have no conception of our physical or functional nature that allows us to understand how it could explain our subjective experience ... we have nothing – zilch – worthy of being called a research programme, nor are there any substantive proposals about how to go about starting one ... Researchers are *stumped*.'[25] It is thus hardly surprising to find Ronald H. Nash reporting that 'dualism is making a comeback'.[26]

---

[21] J.P. Moreland suggests 'the ID movement should seek to undergird its strategy with some form of substance dualism in philosophy of mind ...' 'Postmodernism and the Intelligent Design Movement', *Philosophia Christi* series 2, vol. I, no. 2, 1999, p. 100.

[22] Jaegwon Kim, 'Mental Causation and Two Conceptions of Mental Properties', paper presented at the American Philosophical Association, Eastern Division meeting, Atlanta, Georgia, December 1993, pp. 22–3.

[23] Jaegwon Kim, *Minds In A Physical World* (Cambridge: MIT Press, 1998), p. 2.

[24] Ibid., p. 43.

[25] Ned Block, 'Consciousness' in Samuel Guttenplan (ed.), *A Companion To Philosophy Of Mind* (Oxford: Blackwell, 1994), p. 211.

[26] Nash, *Life's Ultimate Questions*, p. 374.

Anthony O'Hear admits: 'science has difficulty in accounting for the appearance and nature of ... self-conscious processes ... It will be natural for the religious to interpret this emergence of ... self-consciousness as revelatory of something deep in the universe, something inexplicable by physics, something behind the material face of the world.'[27] It is perhaps this recognition that serves to buttress physicalism for naturalists. In other words, *physicalism is less a theory predicated on the data than a philosophical necessity forced upon it.*

Consciousness is fundamental to our view of ourselves, but rather than *explaining* consciousness, physicalism really ends up *denying* it by telling us that consciousness is 'nothing but' this or that physical state or property. John Searle is surely right when he says that: 'We could discover all kinds of startling things about ourselves ... but we cannot discover that we do not have ... conscious, subjective, intentionalistic mental states; nor could we discover that we do not at least try to engage in voluntary, free, intentional actions.'[28] Yet physicalism seems to rule out all of these realities. It is very strange to discuss whether my belief that I am hungry is to the left or the right of my belief that angel cake will satiate my hunger! Then again, what weight or mass should we attribute to the thought that an angel cake would be nice to eat? How many thoughts about angel cakes would fit on the head of a pin? If thoughts and beliefs were purely physical things one would expect such questions to be meaningful. Instead, they seem to be nonsensical. Being counter-intuitive doesn't necessarily mean being false, but it does give us cause for scepticism in the absence of convincing evidence to the contrary. If physicalism is indeed a naturalistic presupposition imported into the philosophy of mind, such evidence will be hard to come by.

There is obviously a close association between the mind and the brain. To do something to the brain (through injury, surgery or drugs) is to do something to the mind. On the other hand, it seems obvious that my intention to scratch my nose causes my nose to be scratched, and that this process operates *through* my brain: 'We know, for instance, that the stimulation of certain brain cells near the back of the head produces visual experiences. And we know that when you decide to help yourself to another piece of cake, certain other brain cells send out impulses to the muscles in your arm.'[29] Mind and brain certainly go hand in hand,

---

[27] O'Hear, *Beyond Evolution*, p. 27.

[28] John Searle, *Minds, Brains And Science* (Cambridge, Massachusetts: Harvard University Press, 1984).

[29] Thomas Nagel, *What Does It All Mean?* (New York: Oxford University Press, 1987), p. 28.

but this does not prove that they are the same thing (or that if they are the same thing it is mind that is reducible to matter rather than matter that is, as idealists hold, a manifestation of mind). Nor does it prove that mind is unable to exist apart from matter: 'Things that go together are not necessarily the same, any more than ideas expressed by these words are the same as the words themselves.'[30] Damage to the words in a statement damages *the expression of the meaning* that informs the statement, but it doesn't damage the original intended meaning incarnated by the words. Altering a statement might change the meaning *of the statement*, but it doesn't change the author's intended meaning. Indeed, that original meaning can be restored (resurrected in other words); other words can express the same/identical idea/concept![31] To conclude from the fact that meaning and words go together that meaning *just is* the existence of certain physical shapes (or that meaning can't exist in the absence of such shapes) would be hasty to say the least. Similarly, if I have an accident that means I can't move my body, my intentions to move may remain and the efficacy of my intentions might be restored by an operation. Damage to my body damages the *expression* of my character, but that expression may be restored. To conclude that my character is 'nothing but' the characteristic movements of a certain body would be unwarranted. My character is what informs my characteristic movements, and as such my character is something over and above those movements.[32] As with meaning and character, so with mind.

It seems to me that the strongest motivation for physicalism is simply a commitment to a naturalistic worldview. A physicalist might argue *on the assumption of naturalism* that there is no reason to think that the mind should not be identical with the brain. If there is no reason to think that the mind is not identical with the brain then we are justified (by Occam's Razor) in believing that the mind is identical with the brain (however, the fact that we are within our rights to believe

---

[30] Norman L. Geisler, 'Materialism', in *Baker Encyclopedia Of Christian Apologetics*, p. 445. Richard Swinburne likens the brain to a light socket and the mind to a light bulb. The bulb needs a socket to work, but it can exist apart from the socket and work when plugged into another socket or when attached to a power supply in other ways.

[31] By analogy, Christians believe that persons can be resurrected in a new form, the spiritual body.

[32] My body *limits* what movements can be characteristic of me (flying can't be characteristic of me, given the limits of my body), but it doesn't *determine* what movements are characteristic of me. It might likewise be said that the brain limits who a person can be, but does not determine who they are or who they become.

something does not necessarily guarantee that our belief is true). The non-physicalist would question the first premise of this argument by putting forward reasons to doubt that the mind is identical with the brain (I will myself turn to this task momentarily). It also appears to be the case that the strongest motivation for naturalism is not a response to the evidence, but a rejection of the supernatural.[33] If God exists he is non-physical. If non-physical *finite* minds can exist (whether human or angelic), then there is less reason to reject the existence of a non-physical *infinite* Mind. Physicalism is thus part and parcel of the naturalist's rejection of God. Conversely, if one has reason to think that God exists (or that angels exist), then one has less reason to deny that the human mind could be non-physical.

> If God and, perhaps, angels are paradigm-case persons and since they are immaterial spirits, then it is at least consistent that something be both a person and an immaterial spirit. But more than this, if the paradigm-case persons are immaterial spirits, then this provides justification for the claim that anything is a person if and only if it bears a relevant similarity to the paradigm cases. Arguably, the relevant similarity between other (kinds of) persons and the paradigm cases is grounded in something all persons have in common and that constitutes that which makes the paradigm cases to be persons in the first place, namely, personhood. Personhood is constituted by a set of ultimate capacities of thought, belief, sensation, emotion, volition, desire, intentionality and so forth ... none of these ultimate capacities is physical, and therefore neither is personhood itself.[34]

That physicalism is the result of an assumed naturalism is demonstrated by John Heil's *Philosophy of Mind: A Contemporary Introduction*.[35] Although Heil makes a genuine attempt to show the competing theories in their best light, this is self-consciously 'more than a mere survey of going theories', and as such he rightly makes clear where his sympathies lie, criticizing some theories more than others.[36] Heil tends to treat

---

[33] 'If there is a God, materialism is false. So the truth of materialism must depend on whether or not there is a God ... Materialism could only be asserted as a plausible hypothesis after it has been independently discovered that as a matter of fact there is no God.' Keith Ward, *Religion And Human Nature* (Oxford: Oxford University Press, 1998), p. 137.

[34] Moreland and Rae, *Body & Soul*, p. 24.

[35] John Heil, *Philosophy Of Mind: A Contemporary Introduction* (London: Routledge, 1998).

[36] Heil is surprisingly positive towards idealism (the view that matter is nothing but an idea in an immaterial mind), for 'It banishes problems associated with

the philosophy of mind as a self-contained subject in its own right, although thought about particular philosophical subjects are impossible to divorce from more general philosophical worldview issues. For example, he asserts that: 'modern science is premised on the assumption that the material world is a causally closed system … A natural law is exceptionless.'[37] This statement (the assertion is not argued for) reveals that Heil is a metaphysical naturalist. The view that the cosmos is a closed system of exceptionless natural laws rules out, a priori, the possibility of miracles or the existence of any immaterial, supernatural agents such as God, angels, or the human mind. On the assumption of naturalism there cannot be anything about the human mind independent of its description in physical terms: 'an explanation citing all of the material causes of a material event is a complete causal explanation of the event.'[38] This rules out all teleology (explanation in terms of goals) as traditionally conceived from Aristotle onwards. Heil writes that 'in imagining that [one mental state] could play a role in the production of [a physical state], we seem to be flying in the face of a widely-held belief that the physical order is "causally closed" or autonomous.'[39] (At least here one could take the gesture towards an argument from consent or authority, although this view is not, in fact, all that widely held.) He goes on to say that, 'Whether this is a serious difficulty, or merely a prejudice that we could abandon without jeopardizing the autonomy of physics, is debatable.'[40] Indeed it is. It is just this point that the Intelligent Design Movement has been competently questioning in recent decades. After all, many sciences are built around the recognition of intelligent design (including cryptography, forensic science, archaeology, and the search for extraterrestrial intelligence).

Belief in God makes the expectation of an orderly creation both rational *and* open to exceptions. As C.S. Lewis argued: 'The philosophy which forbids you to make uniformity absolute [theism] is also the

---

[36] (*continued*) causal interaction between minds and the material world [just as simply as materialism], and it does so in a way that bypasses worries associated with parallelism and occasionalism. Rightly understood, idealism is consistent with all the evidence we could possibly have. Moreover, idealism has a kind of elegant simplicity of the sort valued in the sciences' (ibid., p. 34). Nevertheless, Heil seeks a 'less dramatic alternative' (ibid., p. 34). I wonder if a wholly material account of the mind is less dramatic than a wholly spiritual account?

[37] Ibid., p. 23.

[38] Ibid.

[39] Ibid., p. 199.

[40] Ibid.

philosophy which offers you solid grounds for believing it to be general.'[41] Here we meet our first avenue to God. A law of physics never has caused, and never can cause, anything whatsoever: 'The laws are the pattern to which events conform: the source of events must be sought elsewhere ... Science, when it becomes perfect, will have explained the connection between each link in the chain [of events] and the link before it. But the actual existence of the chain will remain wholly unaccountable.'[42] To explain the existence of such an orderly and reliable natural order we must go beyond scientific 'laws'. As Richard L. Purtill writes: 'The theistic scientist has a philosophical reason for expecting laws to be discovered in nature: he thinks that such laws are the product of a mind, namely, the mind of God. The nontheistic scientist, however, can have no such assurance.'[43]

Heil asserts that 'Laws of nature are contingent; they hold in our world, but there is no further reason why they should hold: they just do. Thus, the connection between your physical nature and your conscious experiences, although predictable, is, in the final analysis, imponderable, an inexplicable brute fact.'[44] Here we discover another avenue to God, for several Christian theists, including Robert M. Adams and Richard Swinburne, have defended 'an argument from consciousness for the existence of God based on the existence of mental properties'.[45] In the final analysis, the existent of a reliable God provides an adequate 'personal explanation' not only for the existence of reliable physical laws, but for the correlation between physical laws and mental experience. A tree falls in a wood when there is no one around to hear it. Does it make a sound? The obvious answer to this question requires a distinction between the falling tree causing compression waves in the air and the subjective experience of sound those waves would cause in a person with properly functioning sensory capacities. The falling tree causes compression waves whether or not anyone is around at the time, but it doesn't cause *sound* (in the subjective sense) unless those waves are

---

[41] Lewis, *Miracles*, p. 106.

[42] C.S. Lewis, 'The Laws of Nature', *God in the Dock* (London: Fount, 1979).

[43] Richard L. Purtill, 'Defining Miracles' in Geivett and Habermas (eds), *In Defence Of Miracles*, p. 71.

[44] Heil, *Philosophy Of Mind*, p. 205.

[45] Moreland and Rae, *Body & Soul*, p. 102. cf. Richard Swinburne, 'The Justification of Theism' @ < http://www.leaderu.com/truth/3truth09.html >; Robert M. Adams, 'Colors, Flavors and God' in R. Douglas Geivett and Brendan Sweetman (eds), *Contemporary Perspectives On Religious Epistemology* (New York: Oxford University Press, 1992); Richard Swinburne, *The Existence Of God* (Oxford: Clarendon Press, 1991).

experienced. Material forces act upon our senses which in turn set up electrochemical patterns in our brains, and these patterns *somehow* lead to sensations of colour, sound, smell, etc. Naturalism cannot offer even a partial explanation of that 'somehow'. As Richard Swinburne argues: 'why did not evolution just throw up unfeeling robots? ... Darwinism can only explain why some animals are eliminated in the struggle for survival, not why there are animals and men at all with mental lives of sensation and belief, and in so far as it can explain anything, the question inevitably arises why the laws of evolution are as they are. All this theism can explain.'[46] On the theistic hypothesis, God brings it about that brain events of a certain kind reliably give rise to mental events of a certain kind. The providence of God can here explain what science is in principle incapable of explaining.

Another example of assumed naturalism comes when Heil observes that: 'I have described the world as comprising objects. I take it to be an empirical question – a question for science – what the objects are and what they are like.'[47] Heil clearly begs the question against any non-naturalistic account of the mind. To point out that Heil works with naturalistic assumptions, and that this leads his sympathies in a certain philosophical direction with regards to the philosophy of mind, is not in itself a fait accompli for his arguments or views. Nevertheless, it does suggest that our beliefs about, for example, the existence of God (or the philosophy of science) will have an effect upon our assessment of Heil's arguments. As Heil admits 'Of course it is possible that immaterial minds do intervene in the material world. It is possible that the material world is not in fact causally closed and that natural law is subject to contravention ... *To the extent that we regard the intervention of non-material minds in the material world as implausible*, we should regard ... dualism as implausible.'[48] The Christian does not share the non-intervention intuition because they believe in God. Indeed, as we have briefly seen, theism is able to outshine the explanatory power of naturalism in the very areas that naturalistic assumptions arbitrarily and unfruitfully constrain the philosophy of mind. As Heil says, 'If nothing else, these reflections make it clear that we cannot hope to evaluate claims about minds and the material world without first coming to grips with a host of metaphysical issues.'[49] Thus my own greater sympathies

---

[46] Richard Swinburne, 'The Justification of Theism' @ < http://www.leaderu.com/truth/3truth09.html >

[47] Heil, *Philosophy Of Mind*, p. 177.

[48] Ibid., p. 26, my italics.

[49] Ibid., p. 32.

still lie in the dualistic direction, and this is at least in part because I bring a belief in the existence of at least one supernatural, spiritual personal being to the table – namely God.

It is not only my different worldview that leads me to doubt the merits of a naturalistic approach to the human mind. Despite Heil's sympathetic account of dualism, there are serious arguments for the view that he doesn't cover. Of course, it is unfair to expect an introductory book to cover every argument in the field; and it is noteworthy that Heil can report that 'In recent years, dissatisfaction with materialist assumptions has led to a revival of interest in forms of dualism.'[50] Let us turn, therefore, to some positive arguments for dualism. Remember, while these arguments carry most weight considered cumulatively, it only requires one sound argument to disprove naturalism.[51]

The conceivability of disembodied existence

J.P. Moreland and Scott B. Rae establish a prima facie case for dualism using a modal argument based upon the conceivability of persons existing without bodies.

(1) The law of identity: If m is identical to n, then whatever is true of m is true of n and vice versa.
(2) I can strongly conceive of myself as existing disembodied.
(3) If I can strongly conceive of some state of affairs s such that s possibly obtains, then I have good grounds for believing that s is possible.
(4) Therefore, I have good grounds for believing of myself that it is possible for me to exist and be disembodied.
(5) If some entity m is such that it is possible for m to exist without n, then (a) m is not identical with n and (b) n is not essential to m.
(6) My body is not such that it is possible to exist disembodied; this is, my body is essentially a body.
(7) Therefore, I have good grounds for believing of myself that I am not identical to my body and that my physical body is not essential to me.[52]

---

[50] Ibid., p. 53.

[51] Arguments for dualism employ Leibniz's law of the indiscernability of identicals, which simply states the obvious fact that for any entities x and y, if x and y are identical (they are the same thing), then any truth that applies to x will also apply to y. This law suggests a test for identity; namely that if you find something true of x that is not true of y, or vice versa, then x cannot be identical to y.

[52] Paraphrase of Moreland and Rae, *Body & Soul*, p. 173.

Cartesian certainty

French philosopher René Descartes argued that, since he could be absolutely certain, on pain of self-contradiction, that he was thinking ('I think, therefore I am'), and since he could not be absolutely certain on pain of self-contradiction that he had a body, he could be certain that his thoughts were not identical with his body. In other words, since the physical is something that it is not logically impossible to deny, the physical cannot be identical to the mental, because the existence of the mental *is* logically impossible to deny. If mental entities (such as thoughts) *just are* physical entities, and if it is possible to be absolutely certain that I am performing mental acts ('I think, therefore I am'), then it should be possible to be equally certain that physical entities exist. Yet it is *not* possible to be equally certain that mental and physical entities exist. While it is self-contradictory to think to oneself 'I am not thinking,' it is not self-contradictory to think to oneself 'I have no brain, I am in fact just an immaterial thinking substance.' This argument does not lead us to conclude that we have no brains or that we are nothing but thinking substances; rather, it leads us to conclude that as thinking beings there is more to our minds than our brains.[53]

The distinction between first and third person

Someone other than myself could surely know more about the state of my brain than I do. A scientist can look at my brain with various measuring and imaging devices, whereas I might be totally ignorant about the state of my brain. Indeed, of all people I am in the worst position to know about my own brain. I cannot know anything about it while I am sleeping, whereas a third party can. On the view that my mind just is my brain, it seems to follow that the person who knows most about my brain would know most about my mind. Yet however much a third party knew about my brain they would not know the state of my mind in the special way that I know it. Moreover, I know the contents of my own mental life *incorrigibly*; that is, I am incapable of being mistaken about the content of my self-conscious awareness. For example, it is impossible for me to

---

[53] Descartes went too far in concluding from his argument that he was 'a substance, the whole essence or nature [of which] consists in thinking, and which, in order to exist ... depends upon no material thing; so that this 'I', that is to say, the mind, by which I am what I am, is entirely distinct from the body ... and moreover, that even if the body were not, it would not cease to be all that it is' (Discourse Four, *Discourse On Method And The Meditations* [London: Penguin, 1968], p. 54). This is not to say this conclusion is false, but that it does not follow from Descartes' argument.

mistakenly think that I am in pain. However, it surely is possible for other people, however well informed, to be mistaken about my being in pain. I know my own mind, as it were, from the inside out. Minds are best known from the inside out, but brains are best known from the outside in; thus the mind and the brain cannot be identical.

Qualia

Qualia is the subjective feel or texture of conscious experience. If you picture a pink elephant in your mind you will experience, in your mind's eye, a pink property. There will be no pink elephant in your physical vision, but there will be a pink image in your mind. However, there is no pink elephant-shaped entity in your brain! A brain surgeon couldn't open your brain and see a pink entity while you were having this sense image: 'The sensory event has a property – pink – that no brain event has. Therefore, they cannot be identical.'[54] A variant on this argument is put forward by Moreland and Rae who note that 'Mental states can have the property of familiarity (e.g., when a desk looks familiar to you), but familiarity is not a physical property of something physical.'[55]

The intentionality of beliefs and thoughts

Beliefs have the property of being *about* things. For example, my belief that I am wearing my watch is *about* the whereabouts of my watch. Beliefs and thoughts require *intentionality*: 'intentionality is the mind's ofness or aboutness. Mental states point beyond themselves to other things. Every mental state I have is of or about something – a hope that Smith will come, a sensation of the apple, a thought that the painting is beautiful.'[56] However, it is very difficult to see how matter can have the property of 'aboutness'. As Habermas and Moreland

---

[54] Ibid.

[55] Moreland and Rae, *Body & Soul*, p. 160. John Heil attempts to defuse dualistic arguments from 'qualia' and from privileged access. His rejoinder rests on the distinction between being or having one's own brain-state and observing someone else's brain-state. There may be something in this, but I don't think it touches the nub of the dualist arguments, which could be taken as highlighting the intuitive strangeness of attributing taste, feelings or infallible self-knowledge to one chunk of matter that is inaccessible by other chunks of matter (such as scientists) in a way not true of clearly physical phenomena like mass, spatial position, etc. In other words, qualia and private access go against the grain of the previously established public accessibility of physical phenomena, and this provides an inductive reason to doubt naturalistic accounts of the mind.

[56] Ibid., p. 53.

argue: 'intentionality is not a property or relation of anything physical. Physical objects can stand in various physical relations with other physical objects. One physical thing can be to the left of, larger than, harder than, the same shape as, or the thing causing the motion of another physical object. But one physical object is not of or about another one.'[57] C.S. Lewis hit the nail on the head when he wrote that, 'to talk of one bit of matter as being true about another bit of matter seems to me to be nonsense.'[58] What could possibly distinguish one state of matter from another such that one had the property of being true while the other had the property of being false? Since having a belief is a necessary condition of knowing anything, merely physical objects such as books and computers *and brains* are incapable of knowing. If the mind were just the brain, we would be incapable of knowing this to be so, and thus the physicalist who claims to know that the mind just is the brain thereby contradicts themselves.

While computers undoubtedly possess part of the abilities *of* mind, they do not *have* mind. John Polkinghorne writes that while the human mind is indeed a computer, it is much more than that because we can also 'see', or 'understand', and hence that, 'The exercise of reason is the activity of persons and it cannot be delegated to computers, however cleverly programmed.'[59] As Aristotle argued, 'understanding is not an act of our brain. It is an act of our mind – an immaterial element in our makeup that may be related to, but is distinct from, the brain as a material organ.'[60]

Having intentions
An intention is an inherently teleological 'final cause', whereas scientific explanations are inherently non-teleological; hence: 'Any attempt to reduce intentionality to something nonmental will always fail because it leaves out intentionality.'[61] As William Hasker argues: 'human action has to be understood as fundamentally teleological, but this is impossible if it is to be analysed in terms of the physical interactions of particles which, in themselves, have no capacity to respond to normative or

---

[57] Ibid.
[58] C.S. Lewis, '*De Futilitate*', *Christian Reflections* (London: Fount, 1991), p. 88. cf. Dallas Willard, @ 'Knowledge and Naturalism' @ < http://www.dwillard.org/Philosophy/Pubs/knowledge_and_naturalism.htm >
[59] John Polkinghorne, *Reason And Reality* (London: SPCK, 1992), p. 10.
[60] Mortimer J. Adler, *Aristotle For Everybody* (New York: Simon & Schuster, 1997), pp. 183–4.
[61] John Searle, *The Rediscovery Of The Mind* (Cambridge: MIT Press, 1992), p. 51.

teleological considerations but instead simply follow the mechanistic laws that are natural to them.'[62] If someone attempts to deny that human thought stands in intentional relations we may ask them whether or not they intended to make this denial, or what it was they intended to deny! Since we must take intentionality seriously, physicalism implodes by causing a contradiction between the fact that 'rationality requires a responsiveness to ... teleological considerations'[63] and the fact that 'we cannot reasonably suppose the behaviours of elementary particles to be influenced directly by ... objectives.'[64]

The possible non-existence of the objects of mental activity
Ronald H. Nash points out that physical activity 'requires that any other physical objects related to the event or activity must exist in the physical world'.[65] For example, if the physical activity we're considering is pushing something, there must exist something physical to be pushed: 'However, it is not necessary that the objects of mental activities exist in the [physical] world. Mental activity can take as its object something that does not exist. I can think about things like unicorns, Tinker Bell, and the Wizard of Oz.'[66] Hence mental activity is not identical (and not reducible) to physical activity.

Determinism or moral responsibility
Naturalism implies determinism, because the mind is seen as being identical with the brain, which is a natural, physical system running according to the laws of nature: 'A chunk of matter is inert; it cannot exert its own causal powers and act as a first, unmoved mover or either choose or refrain from choosing to do something. Rather, a material entity does what it has to do given the laws of nature ... and prior causal conditions.'[67] Reasons to doubt the truth of determinism are thereby reasons to doubt the truth of naturalism and physicalism.

One reason to doubt determinism is that it contradicts our concepts of morality. It is not up to the stone whether or not it falls to earth if I throw it into the air. Given certain conditions (being thrown into the air, gravity, etc.) the stone *will* fall back to earth. The stone has no freedom

---

[62] William Hasker, *The Emergent Self* (Ithaca, New York: Cornell University Press, 1999), p. 101.
[63] Ibid., p. 146.
[64] Ibid.
[65] Nash, *Life's Ultimate Questions*.
[66] Ibid.
[67] Ibid., p. 92.

to do anything other than what it is caused to do. If we are thus determined, does it make any sense to retain belief in moral blame or obligation? A moral obligation is something you *ought* to do, something you *should* do; but what use is there for concepts like '*ought*' and '*should*' in a world where every human action is a 'has to'? As William Hasker asks: 'How in reason can a person be held responsible – whether for good or for ill – for doing what she was ineluctably determined to do by forces that were in place long before she was born?'[68] Either we accept determinism and dump moral obligation, or to retain belief in moral obligation and dump determinism. If we dump determinism, then we must also dump naturalism and physicalism, because naturalism and physicalism entail determinism: 'It is safe to say that physicalism requires a radical revision of our common-sense notions of freedom, moral obligation, responsibility, and punishment. On the other hand, if these common-sense notions are true, physicalism is false.'[69]

Moreover, if determinism were true, it would be impossible for anyone to rationally believe anything:

> I am intellectually responsible for drawing certain conclusions, given certain pieces of evidence ... If one is to be rational, one must be free to choose her beliefs in order to be reasonable ... But such deliberations make sense only if I assume that what I am going to do or believe is 'up to me' – that I am free to choose and, thus, I am responsible for irrationality if I choose inappropriately.[70]

Therefore, determinism, which rules out libertarian freedom and with it any obligation to be rational, is necessarily false. If determinism is necessarily false, any theory that requires determinism to be true must also be necessarily false. Naturalism and physicalism both imply determinism. Therefore both naturalism and physicalism are necessarily false: 'It is self-refuting to argue that one *ought to choose* physicalism ... on the *basis* ... that one *should see* that the *evidence is good* for physicalism ...'[71]

If we have been determined to believe what we believe by impersonal physical forces, what reason is there to trust the truth of our beliefs? As H.P. Owen argued: 'if the sum reason for my believing or not believing X

---

[68] Hasker, *The Emergent Self*, p. 85.

[69] Gary R. Habermas and J.P. Moreland, *Beyond Death: Exploring The Evidence For Immortality* (Wheaton, Illinois: Crossway, 1998), p. 60.

[70] Ibid., p. 65.

[71] Ibid. cf. Gregory Koukl, 'Dominoes, Determinism, and Naturalism' @ < http://www.str.org/free/commentaries/evolution/dominosd.htm >

is that I am causally determined to believe it, I have no ground for holding that my judgement is true or false.'[72] This line of thought has proved a rich source of anti-naturalistic arguments. C.S. Lewis argued along similar lines:

> the cause and effect relation between events and the ground and consequent relation between propositions are distinct. Since English uses because for both, let us here use *Because* CE for the cause and effect relation ('This doll always falls on its feet because CE its feet are weighted'), and *Because* GC for the ground and consequent relation ('A equals C because GC they both equal B') ... If an argument is to be verific the conclusion must be related to the premises as consequent to ground, i.e. the conclusion is there *because* GC certain other propositions are true.[73]

If naturalism is true I arrive at the conclusions I do *because* CE they are the natural effects of previous natural causes, but 'a train of reasoning has no value as a means to finding truth unless each step is connected with what went before in the Ground-Consequent relation.'[74] The outcome of a merely physical series of cause and effect *might* be true by luck, but never by judgement. Thus naturalism, and the physicalism to which it leads, cannot profess to give us any *reasons* to accept its truth: 'unless our conclusion is the logical consequent from a ground it ... could be true only by a fluke ... Wishful thinkings, prejudices, and the delusions of madness, are all caused, but they are ungrounded.'[75] Anthony O'Hear agrees with Lewis that 'decisions ... demand a justification logically independent from anything we might discover in scientific accounts.'[76] But once this is admitted, naturalism is out the window: 'Naturalism ... offers what professes to be a full account of our mental behaviour; but this account, on inspection, leaves no room for the acts of knowing ... on which the whole value of our thinking, as a means to truth, depends.'[77] Thus, concludes Lewis:

> acts of reasoning are not interlocked with the total interlocking system of Nature as all other items are interlocked with one another. They are connected with it in a different way; as the understanding of a machine is

---

[72] H.P. Owen, *Christian Theism* (Edinburgh: T & T Clark, 1984), p. 118.
[73] C.S. Lewis, 'Religion without Dogma?', *Compelling Reason*, appendix B (London: Fount, 1999), p. 108.
[74] Lewis, *Miracles*, ch. 3.
[75] Ibid.
[76] O'Hear, *Beyond Evolution*, p. 13.
[77] Lewis, *Miracles*.

certainly connected with the machine but not in the way the parts of the machine are connected with each other. The knowledge of a thing is not one of the thing's parts. In this sense something beyond Nature operates whenever we reason.[78]

The naturalist may want to bring evolution by natural selection into the discussion at this point. Our cognitive abilities might be 'nothing but' an uninterrupted stream of physical causes and effects, they may say, but this stream has been moulded by natural selection. There may be no judgement (in the non-physicalist sense), but everything isn't left to luck. But against this: If it *can* be shown that human cognitive abilities have been moulded purely by evolution (a hypothesis that seems hard to prove), this would point to the existence of 'fine tuning' in the universe that would constitute evidence for the existence of God, and thereby for the falsity of naturalism! The evolution of self-conscious beings with reliable cognitive abilities is surely more likely on a 'Mind first' worldview. On the other hand, if it *can't* be shown that natural selection is up to the task of moulding reliable cognitive equipment, this would give us reason to doubt the naturalistic hypothesis upon which this conclusion is based, because that hypothesis is itself a result of the brain the reliability of which the naturalistic theory calls into doubt. There is no absolute link between the survival value and the truth of beliefs. According to Stephen Stich: 'there are major problems to be overcome by those who think that evolutionary considerations impose interesting limits on irrationality.'[79] Anthony O'Hear likewise admits: 'There is a clear distinction to be drawn between the true and the useful',[80] such that 'success in the evolutionary struggle considered on its own does not guarantee the truth or adequacy of a creature's beliefs.'[81] In either case then, naturalism faces some problems, and this has the effect of undermining physicalism. (For more on this I refer readers to my later discussion of epistemological arguments for God.)

The above considerations combine to convince me that naturalistic accounts of the mind are false and that some form of dualism must be correct. This conclusion supports the possibility of angels, not only by establishing the possibility of immaterial substances existing (if the embodied mind exists, why not a disembodied mind?), but also by disproving naturalism (for if the mind is immaterial, naturalism is false). It

---

[78] Ibid.

[79] Stephen Stich, 'Evolution and Rationality', *The Fragmentation Of Reason* (Cambridge: MIT Press, 1985), p. 56.

[80] O'Hear, *Beyond Evolution*, p. 57.

[81] Ibid., p. 60.

seems odd to suppose that such finite, immaterial minds as ours just happen to exist. The existence of minds is something more at home in a worldview in which an infinite immaterial Mind is foundational. Hence consideration of the human mind leads us to consider the existence of the divine Mind. Indeed, since I have defined angels as beings *created by God* I cannot bracket the question of whether angels are possible from the question of God's existence. If belief in God is supportable, then belief in angels is 'in the clear'. As Keith Ferdinando says: 'if one concedes the existence of at least one supernatural spirit being, God, there is no logical basis for denying the possibility that other spirits, albeit of a different order, may exist.'[82] To justify such a denial would require some argument to the effect that God could not create angels. Given that God is all knowing and all powerful, the chances of producing such an argument would seem to be slim!

Arguments for God

According to Alvin Plantinga: 'theistic belief does not (in general) need argument ... But it doesn't follow, of course, that there aren't any good arguments. Are there some? At least a couple of dozen or so.'[83] I cannot do more here than sketch a few of the arguments that I believe make a compelling cumulative case for God and, as a byproduct, for the possibility of angels. Fuller accounts of most of the following arguments can be found in my book *The Case for God*. I have recommended additional resources for further investigation in the bibliography.

Ontological argument

Anselm argued that the term 'God' must mean 'the greatest possible being'. If we could think of someone greater than God, then *that* being would deserve our worship. But since God *is* 'the being who deserves our worship', he must be 'a being greater than which cannot be conceived'. Anselm's definition of 'God' can be used to argue thus: The greatest possible being must be a being that exists necessarily (that is, one that must exist if it is possible that it exist), because necessary existence is greater than unnecessary, contingent existence. Therefore, if one accepts that God's existence is *possible*, one must also accept that God exists necessarily.

---

[82] Keith Ferdinando, 'Screwtape Revisited' in Anthony N.S. Lane (ed.), *The Unseen World: Christian Reflections On Angels, Demons And The Heavenly Realm* (Carlisle: Paternoster, 1996), pp. 107–8.

[83] Alvin Plantinga, 'Two Dozen (or so) Theistic Arguments' @ < http://www.homestead.com/philofreligion/files/Theisticarguments.html >

Objective value

Francis J. Beckwith writes: 'if moral norms exist, then materialism as a worldview is false, because moral norms are nonmaterial things. If materialism is false, then other nonmaterial things such as God, angels, and souls cannot be ruled out on the grounds that they are not material.'[84] But more than this, objective moral norms (norms whose validity is independent of any and all finite mental states) require an objective standard that can only be found in God, who must therefore exist if objective moral truths exist. There are several ways of showing the link between objective moral norms and God: 1) The existence of a moral law implies the existence of an authoritative moral lawgiver. Only persons can prescribe behaviour as moral values do, and only God could prescribe behaviour with the necessary moral authority. 2) Only persons can obligate behaviour as moral values do, and only God could obligate all people at all times in the same way as moral norms do. 3) Only an ideal mind can contain and exemplify a moral ideal. Impersonal nature is incapable of prescribing, obligating or exemplifying moral behaviour. Neither can imperfect finite minds like our own prescribe, obligate or exemplify absolute moral norms and ideals. By a process of elimination, we are thus led to affirm the existence of an infinite and perfect mind that can and does prescribe, obligate and exemplify the moral ideals which meets us in the realm of ethics.

Aesthetic reality can be divided between our subjective awareness of beauty and the objective beauty of which we are aware.[85] As C.S. Lewis explains: 'Until quite modern times all ... men believed the universe to such that certain emotional reactions on our part could be congruous or incongruous to it – believed, in fact, that objects did not merely receive, but could merit, our approval or disapproval ...'[86] In giving his account of beauty, Lewis draws upon Augustine's definition of virtue as *ordo amoris* or 'appropriate love', defined as: 'the ordinate condition of the affections in which every object is accorded that kind and degree of love which is appropriate to it'.[87] The appropriateness of our emotional reactions depends, at least in part, upon the nature of

---

[84] Francis J. Beckwith, 'Why I am not a Moral Relativist' in Norman L. Geisler and Paul K. Hoffman (eds), *Why I Am A Christian* (Grand Rapids, Michigan: Baker, 2001), p. 16.

[85] cf. Peter S. Williams, 'A Christian View of Beauty' @ < http://www.ht-leicester. org.uk/ >

[86] C.S. Lewis, *The Abolition Of Man* (London: Fount, 1999), p. 14.

[87] Ibid.

the object of our appreciation. As Alvin Plantinga writes: 'To grasp the beauty of a Mozart D Minor piano concerto is to grasp something that is objectively there; *it is to appreciate what is objectively worthy of appreciation.*'[88] Hence our aesthetic reactions can be decent, or can fail to be decent, 'in the old sense [of] *decens*, fitting'.[89] Given this understanding of beauty, it follows that beauty, like goodness, relates to an objective standard that can only be found in God, who is thus 'the most objectively beautiful possible being'. Given that beauty is objective, our judgements about beauty must be measured against some objective standard that the human mind apprehends and employs in aesthetic judgement. This standard of beauty cannot be constituted by any individual finite mental state, or collection of states, or else it would of necessity be a subjective standard. Therefore, there must exist an objective standard of beauty, a standard independent of finite minds. An aesthetic standard or ideal is not the sort of thing that could exist in the physical world. Since the standard of beauty exists neither in finite minds, nor in the physical world, it must exist in an infinite Mind.[90]

Cosmological argument

If anything exists its existence is either dependent upon the existence of one or more things beyond itself, or not. If not, it is an independent thing. Things are either dependent or independent, there is no third option. It is impossible for *everything* to be dependent, for there is nothing outside *everything* to depend upon. Therefore, if something exists, there must exist an independent thing. But something certainly does exist ('I think therefore I am'), so at least one independent thing certainly exists. You and I are clearly dependent things, and every physical thing is apparently dependent. These observations narrow our options with regards to identifying the 'independent thing'. The atheist will want to identify the independent thing with the universe itself, but does this identification make any sense? A wall made up of little bricks may be large, but it's still a *brick* wall. Likewise, a universe made up of dependent things may be large, but it's still a *dependent* thing. The *quantity* of dependent things is irrelevant to the question of ontological *quality*.

---

[88] Alvin Plantinga, 'Two Dozen (or so) Theistic Arguments' @ < http://www. homestead.com/philofreligion/files/Theisticarguments.html >, my italics.

[89] C.S. Lewis, *That Hideous Strength* (London: Pan, 1989), p. 746.

[90] cf. Peter S. Williams, 'Aesthetic Arguments for the Existence of God' @ < http://www.quodlibet.net/williams-aesthetic.shtml >

Design

'What could be more clear or obvious when we look up to the sky and contemplate the heavens, than that there is some divinity of superior intelligence?'[91] So wrote Cicero, and the majority of humanity echoes this insight at one time or another. Even David Hume noted that: 'A purpose, an intention, or design strikes everywhere the most careless, the most stupid thinker; and no man can be so hardened in absurd systems, as at all times to reject it.'[92] The rationality of holding to this conclusion is bolstered by the principle of credulity (we should take things at face value unless we have some reason not to do so), and will be interpreted by the theist as the intended result of properly functioning cognitive faculties aimed at truth and designed (directly or indirectly) by God.

The obvious objection is to say that a naturalistic theory of evolution provides a simpler adequate explanation for the apparent design in nature, which should thus be preferred to theism (by an application of Occam's Razor). However, it is only *naturalistic* evolution that contradicts the intuitive inference to design, and the theist may argue that the *naturalistic* evolutionary explanation, although simpler, is not adequate enough to overturn the *overwhelming intuitive impression* that the universe is an artefact. Besides, there are several aspects of reality that *cannot* be explained by evolution *because they are necessary to the process of evolution itself*, and *these aspects of nature give the impression of design no less than does the whole of which they are such important parts.* The evolutionary challenge therefore fails to contradict the intuitive design argument.[93]

Indeed, the naturalistic origins myth falters at the first fence, for 'the probability of constructing a rather short functional protein at random [is] so small as to be effectively zero (1 chance in 10^{125}).'[94] To put this figure in context, there are only 10^{65} atoms *in our entire galaxy*! Such a staggeringly improbable explanation is the only one available *given naturalistic assumptions*. Moreover, as Neil Broom explains: 'The

[91] Cicero, *De Natura Deorum* vol. XIX, H. Rackham (trans) (Cambridge, Massachusetts: Harvard University Press, 1989).

[92] David Hume, *Dialogues Concerning Natural Religion* (Indianapolis, Indiana: Bobbs-Merrill, 1946), p. 214.

[93] On evolution and the Genesis origins story, cf. Roger Forster and Paul Marston, *Reason, Science And Faith* (Crowborough, East Sussex: Monarch, 1999); < http://www.reason-science-and-faith.com/ >

[94] Steven C. Meyer, 'The Explanatory Power of Design' in Dembski (ed.), *Mere Creation*.

sequence making up a particular DNA strand is not dependent on any preferred bonding between the individual bases. Each base is the molecular equivalent of the dot or dash in the Morse code and can be arranged in any linear combination without breaking the rules of chemical bonding.'[95] In other words, the sequence of amino acids in DNA cannot be explained by reference to the laws of physics or chemistry: 'The chemical laws that bind each base, A, G, C or T, to its neighbour in DNA are lower-level, slave-like laws that must come under the control of a higher principle in a manner exactly analogous to the *intelligent* sequencing of dots and dashes required in Morse Code to create a *meaningful* message.'[96]

William A. Dembski has provided a three-stage 'Explanatory Filter' that reliably identifies intelligent design.[97] Nancy Pearcey explains:

> We detect design ... by applying an 'explanatory filter' that first rules out chance and law. That is, scientists first determine if something is the product of merely random events by whether it is irregular, erratic, and unpredictable. If chance doesn't explain it, they next determine if it is the result of natural forces by whether it is regular, repeatable, and predictable. If neither of these standard explanations works – if something is irregular and unpredictable, yet highly specified – then it bears the marks of design.[98]

For example, the four presidents' faces on Mount Rushmore are irregular (not something generally to be expected from erosion!) and specified (they fit a particular independent pattern): 'Applying the Explanatory Filter, the evidence clearly points to design.'[99] As with Mount Rushmore, so with DNA.

Dembski's filter detects design because intelligent causes can easily achieve something that unintelligent causes (whether they be 'chance'

---

[95] Neil Broom, *How Blind Is The Watchmaker?* (Leicester: IVP, 2001), p. 54.

[96] Ibid.

[97] 'Roughly speaking the filter asks three questions in the following order: (1) Does a law explain it? (2) Does chance explain it? (3) Does design explain it?' – William A. Dembski, 'The Explanatory Filter' @ < http://www.arn.org/docs/dembski/wd_explfilter.htm >. This follows Plato's observation that 'all things do become, have become, and will become, some by nature, some by art, and some by chance' Plato, *The Laws* (book X). cf. William A. Dembski, *The Design Inference* (Cambridge: Cambridge University Press, 1999).

[98] Nancy Pearcey, 'Design and the Discriminating Public' in William A. Dembski and James M. Kushner (eds), *Signs Of Intelligence* (Grand Rapids, Michigan: Baker, 2001), pp. 48–9.

[99] Ibid., p. 49.

and/or 'necessity') find all but impossible; that is, the creation of *specified complexity*. A long string of random letters drawn from a scrabble bag would be complex without being specified. A short sequence of letters (like 'so', or 'the') is specified without being complex. A sonnet by Shakespeare is both complex *and* specified: 'Thus in general, given an event, object, or structure, to convince ourselves that it is designed we need to show that it is improbably (i.e. complex) and suitably patterned (i.e. specified).'[100] The 'Explanatory Filter' is only a *positive* test for design. Suppose an ecologically minded artist carefully distributes leaves in a forest so as to mimic a natural leaf distribution. The filter would be unable to *detect* the activity of intelligent causation in the distribution of these leaves. On the other hand, if the leaves were arranged to spell out the words 'welcome to my forest' the filter *would* detect design, for such an arrangement of leaves is both highly unlikely (complex) *and* specified.

Consider the example of opening a combination lock. Richard Dawkins writes: 'Of all the unique and, with hindsight equally improbable, positions of the combination lock, only one opens the lock ... The uniqueness of the arrangement ... that opens the safe, [has] nothing to do with hindsight. It is *specified in advance*.'[101] Hence the best explanation of an open safe is not that someone got lucky, but that someone knew the specific combination required to open it. Likewise, as biologist Leslie Orgel writes: 'Living organisms are distinguished by their specified complexity. Crystals ... fail to qualify as living because they lack complexity, random mixtures of polymers fail because they lack specificity.'[102] The logical inference is obvious.

Intelligent Design (whether applied to determining cause of death in forensic science or design in nature) can be rigorously cast in terms of information theory:

> the actualisation of a possibility (i.e. information) is specified if independently of the possibility's actualisation, the possibility is identifiable by means of a pattern ... Information that is both complex and specified [CSI] is what all the fuss over information has been about in recent years, not just in biology, but in science generally ... It is CSI that for cosmologists underlies the fine-tuning of the universe ...[103]

---

[100] William A. Dembski, 'Another Way to Detect Design?' @ < http://www.arn.org/docs/dembski/wd_responsetowiscu.htm >

[101] Richard Dawkins, *The Blind Watchmaker* (London: Penguin, 1990).

[102] Leslie Orgel, *The Origins Of Life* (New York: Wiley, 1973), p. 189.

[103] William A. Dembski, 'Another Way to Detect Design?' @ < http://www.arn.org/docs/dembski/wd_anotherwaytodetectdesign.htm >

The fine-tuning of the universe discovered by cosmologists is an example of CSI because it constitutes an unlikely (complex) state of affairs that conforms to a specifiable (non-*ad hoc*) pattern, the pattern of universal constants necessary for a life-permitting universe: 'The fine-tuning of the universe ... is both complex and specified and readily yields design.'[104] The fine-tuning of the universe is identical in nature to the above example of cracking a combination lock. In the case of the cracked combination lock what called out for explanation in terms of an intelligent cause was not merely the fact that an event of small probability had taken place (any long sequence of dialled numbers is equally improbable), but the fact that this small probability was also *specified* (as the sequence necessary for opening the lock). In the case of cosmic fine-tuning, what calls out for explanation in terms of design is not merely the fact that a particular improbable set of physical laws exists, but the fact that this particular set of laws is *specified* (as the set necessary for a life sustaining universe).

> one could think of each instance of fine-tuning as a radio dial: unless all the dials are set exactly right, life would be impossible. Or, one could think of the initial conditions of the universe and the fundamental parameters of physics as a dart board that fills the whole galaxy, and the conditions necessary for life to exist [our specified, non ad hoc pattern] as a small one-foot wide target: unless the dart hits the target, life would be impossible. The fact that the dials are perfectly set, or the dart has hit the target, strongly suggests that someone set the dials or aimed the dart ...[105]

Then again, consider Richard Dawkins' description of DNA:

> at the bottom of my garden is a large willow tree, and it is pumping downy seeds into the air ... Not just any DNA, but DNA whose coded characters spell out specific instructions for building willow trees that will shed a new generation of downy seeds. Those fluffy specks are, literally, spreading instructions for making themselves ... It is raining instructions out there; it's raining programs; it's raining tree-growing, fluff-spreading algorithms. That is not a metaphor, it is the plain truth. It couldn't be plainer if it were raining floppy discs.[106]

---

[104] William A. Dembski, 'The Act of Creation: Bridging Transcendence and Immanence' @ < http://www.arn.org/docs/dembski/wd_actofcreation.htm >, p. 9.

[105] Robert Collins, 'The Fine Tuning Argument' in Kelly James Clark (ed.), *Readings In The Philosophy Of Religion* (Peterborough, Ontario: Broadview Press, 2000), p. 55.

[106] Dawkins, *The Blind Watchmaker*, p. 111.

If it *was* raining floppy discs, and those floppy disks, like DNA, carried a program (for making other floppy disks), wouldn't everyone agree that this information must have originated in some mind or minds? Following Dawkins' usage, both the floppy disk and the willow seed are physical packets carrying complex, specified, encoded information. We know that computer programs come from minds; should we not also conclude that the information encoded by DNA comes from a mind? The search for extraterrestrial intelligence acknowledges that information in radio signals from space would indicate an intelligent source. Astronomers have not found information-bearing signals from space, but molecular biologists have discovered information in the cell. We are not alone.

The most famous design argument is of course that propounded by William Paley, who argued thus: even if we had never seen a watch before, an inspection would lead us to conclude that it was designed and made for a purpose. Observe the world and we see once again an intricate interplay of parts and contingent, complex physical laws arranged together and achieving a collective end (intelligent life forms). The world is analogous to the watch. The watch had a designer, so it is reasonable to think that the world had a designer. Modern knowledge has only increased the strength of this analogy: 'Cells swim using machines, copy themselves with machinery, ingest food with machinery ... highly sophisticated molecular machines control every cellular process.'[107]

Although he didn't employ this precise terminology, Paley pointed out that a watch is *irreducibly complex*. Not only is the purpose carried out by the sum of the watch's parts, but that purpose could not be carried out 'if its different parts had been differently shaped from what they are, or placed after any other manner or in any other order than that in which they are placed ...'[108] Irreducibly complex systems, like a watch, are composed of *a number of mutually interdependent parts, each of which is functionally useless on its own.* This means that such a system *cannot* evolve by natural selection, because until the whole system is functional *there is nothing of advantage in existence to be selected.* (Indeed, manufacturing individual components of irreducibly complex systems would be a drain on resources, therefore constituting an evolutionary disadvantage.) Darwin admitted that the existence of a single irreducibly complex system in nature would falsify his hypothesis: 'If it could be demonstrated that any complex organ existed which could

[107] Michael J. Behe, *Darwin's Black Box* (New York: Free Press, 1996), pp. 4–5.
[108] William Paley, *Natural Theology* (Westmead, Farnborough, Hampshire: Gregg International, 1970).

not possibly have been formed by numerous, successive modifications, my theory would absolutely break down.'[109] Biochemist Michael J. Behe argues that the biomolecular level of life, which was unknown in Darwin's day, is full of 'irreducibly complex' molecular machines that could not have evolved by natural selection:

> A system which meets Darwin's criterion [for falsifying his theory] is one which exhibits irreducible complexity ... An irreducibly complex system cannot be produced gradually by slight, successive modifications of a precursor system, since any precursor to an irreducibly complex system is by definition non-functional ... Now, are any biochemical systems irreducibly complex? Yes, it turns out that many are ... including aspects of protein transport, blood clotting, closed circular DNA, electron transport, the bacterial flagellum, telomeres, photosynthesis, transcription regulation, and much more.[110]

The proposed indicators of design, from Paley's watch analogy to the recent debate over the 'anthropic principle' and 'irreducible complexity', can all be analysed in terms of Complex Specified Information: 'the complexity-specification criterion ... detects design strictly from observational features of the world ... When applied to the fine-tuning of the universe and the complex, information-rich structures of biology, it demonstrates a design external to the universe.'[111]

Epistemological arguments

While epistemological arguments can be employed merely to discredit naturalism and physicalism (see above), they can also be employed as arguments for theism. Atheist Richard Rorty argues: 'The idea that one species of organism is, unlike all the others, oriented not just towards its own increased propensity but toward Truth, is as un-Darwinian as the idea that every human being has a built-in moral compass ...'[112] Alvin Plantinga agrees: 'The fact that my behaviour (or that of my ancestors) has been adaptive ... is at best a third-rate reason for thinking my beliefs

---

[109] Charles Darwin, *Origin Of Species* (New York: New York University Press, 1988), p. 154.

[110] Michael J. Behe, 'Molecular Machines: Experimental Support for the Design Inference' @ < http://www.arn.org/docs/behe/mb_mm92496.htm >

[111] Dembski, 'The Act of Creation: Bridging Transcendence and Immanence', < http://www.arn.org/docs/dembski/wd_actofcreation.htm >, pp. 9–10.

[112] Richard Rorty, 'Untruth and Consequences', *The New Republic*, 31 July 1995, p. 36.

mostly true and my cognitive faculties reliable …'[113] Plantinga dubs this proposition 'Darwin's Doubt': 'With me', wrote Darwin, 'the horrid doubt always arises whether the convictions of man's mind, which has been developed from the mind of the lower animals, are of any value or at all trustworthy.'[114] Plantinga argues that Darwin's Doubt is self-defeating, in that it gives one reason to doubt the naturalistic worldview upon which it is based, and consequently provides some reason to accept a theistic worldview.

Richard Taylor offers an epistemological argument against the naturalism that underlies the naturalistic evolutionary account of origins: Suppose you are travelling by train and, glancing out of the window, you see some stones on a hillside spelling out the words 'Welcome to Wales'. On the basis of this observation you form the belief that you have entered Wales (whether this belief is true or false is immaterial to the following argument). It would be unreasonable of you, says Taylor, to continue in this belief if you came to believe that the stones had not been arranged on purpose to accurately convey information, but had ended up in this formation purely through the operation of natural laws: 'you would, in fact, be presupposing that they were arranged that way by an intelligent and purposeful being or beings for the purpose of conveying a certain message having nothing to do with the stones themselves.'[115] Although it is highly unlikely, the wind *could* have dislodged the stones so that they rolled down the hillside, coming to rest where the ground was pitted by natural erosion in just the right pattern. This would in fact be an instance of CSI that would rightly trigger a design inference (after all, the natural description of an event cannot rule out the presence of design). It is nevertheless *logically possible* that this happen without design – the design filter only offers a *highly probable* inference to design. As Dembski says: 'the complexity-specification criterion … cannot achieve logical demonstration [but] it is capable of achieving statistical justification so compelling as to demand assent.'[116] So, supposing you ignore (or are ignorant of) the design inference these stones would trigger and believe instead that the sign is the result of purely natural

---

[113] Alvin Plantinga, *Warranted Christian Belief* (New York: Oxford University Press, 2000), p. 235.

[114] Letter to William Graham, 3 July 1881.

[115] Richard Taylor, *Metaphysics* (Engelwood Cliffs, New Jersey: Prentice Hall, 1974²).

[116] Dembski, 'The Act of Creation: Bridging Transcendence and Immanence', < http://www.arn.org/docs/dembski/wd_actofcreation.htm >, p. 10.

forces; it would then surely be unreasonable to base your belief that you were entering Wales on this stone formation: 'it would be *irrational* for you to regard the arrangement of the stones as evidence that you were entering Wales, *and at the same time to suppose that they might have come to that arrangement accidentally*, that is, as the result of the ordinary interactions of natural or physical forces.'[117] Taylor now develops his argument by analogy, suggesting that if you came to believe the workings *of your own brain* to be the result of *purely* natural forces it would be similarly unreasonable to base this belief on the reasoning of that very brain.

> It would be irrational for one to say *both* that his sensory and cognitive faculties had a ... nonpurposeful origin and *also* that they reveal some truth with respect to something other than themselves ... If, on the other hand, we do assume that they are guides to some truths having nothing to do with themselves, then it is difficult to see how we can, consistently with that supposition, believe them to have arisen ... by the ordinary workings of purposeless forces, even over ages of time.[118]

If our trust in the stone sign is to be reasonable, we must attribute it to design. Likewise, if our (inescapable) trust in our own cognitive equipment is to be rational, then we must also attribute that to design. As Anthony O'Hear recently admitted: 'in a contest between materialistic atheism and some kind of religious-cum-theistic view, the materialistic conclusion leaves even more mysteries than a view which sees reason and consciousness as part of the essence of the universe.'[119]

Miracles

The argument from miracles does not argue that such-and-such an event is an act of God and that God therefore must exist; that would be to beg the question. To paraphrase Stephen C. Meyer, '[A miracle] can be offered ... as a necessary or best causal explanation ... when naturalistic processes seem incapable [or unlikely] of producing the *explanandum* effect, and when intelligence is known to be capable of producing it and thought to be more likely to have produced it.'[120] G.K. Chesterton mused how: 'an extraordinary idea has arisen that the disbelievers in miracles consider them coldly and fairly, while believers in miracles

---

[117] Richard Taylor, *Metaphysics*, my emphasis.
[118] Ibid.
[119] Anthony O'Hear, *Philosophy* (London: New Century, 2001), p. 125.
[120] Stephen C. Meyer, *The Creation Hypothesis* (Downers Grove, Illinois: IVP, 1994) p. 97.

accept them only in connection with some dogma'.[121] The reverse is closer to the truth: 'The believer in miracles accept them (rightly or wrongly) because they have evidence for them. The disbelievers in miracles deny them (rightly or wrongly) because they have a doctrine against them.'[122]

There are many historical and contemporary reports of miraculous events. In the *British Medical Journal* (December 1983), Dr Rex Gardner describes the full recovery of a young doctor who was so ill that she was expected to die, but for whom several prayer groups were formed: 'Physicians were unable to explain how her chest X-ray film, which had showed extensive left-side pneumonia with collapse of the middle lobe, could, 48 hours later, show a normal clear chest.'[123] Prayer for healing is becoming the subject of serious scientific study.[124] For example:

> Dr [Randolf] Byrd divided 393 heart patients into two groups. One was prayed for by Christians; the other did not receive prayers from study participants. Patients didn't know which group they belonged to. The members of the group that was prayed for experienced fewer complications, fewer cases of pneumonia, fewer cardiac arrests, less congestive heart failure and needed fewer antibiotics.[125]

The Bible contains many examples of predictive prophecy that have been fulfilled hundreds of years later. Many of these prophecies are fulfilled in the person of Jesus. The biblical explanation of this specified, complex information – the existence of a communicative all-knowing God – is proposed as the best explanation of this data.[126]

Desire
That there is a deep need for God within the human heart was recognized by the biblical songwriter who wrote that 'As a deer longs for streams of cool water, so I long for you, O God' (Ps. 42:1 GNB).

---

[121] Ibid., p. 224.
[122] Ibid.
[123] Quoted by John Young, *The Case Against Christ* (London: Hodder & Stoughton, 1994).
[124] Theodore J. Chamberlain and Christopher A. Hall, *Realized Religion* (London: Templeton Foundation Press, 2000).
[125] Phyllis McIntosh, 'Faith is Powerful Medicine', *Reader's Digest*, May 2000.
[126] Prophecy is discussed in more detail in Chapter 4. cf. Prophecy Proves the Bible @ < http://www.geocities.com/Athens/Aegean/8830/prophecy.html >; Geisler and Hoffman (eds), *Why I Am A Christian*.

Christian writers through the ages have echoed this theme of longing. Augustine wrote in his *Confessions* that: 'You made us for yourself, O Lord, and our hearts are restless till they rest in you.' Pascal wrote of how 'There is a god-shaped vacuum in the heart of every man, and only God can fill it.' Chesterton expressed this by saying that 'Christian optimism is based on the fact that we do not fit in to the world.'[127] That this restless desire apart from God predicted by the theistic hypothesis exists, and that people who believe they have discovered relationship with God seem to have discovered the object that satiates this desire, is evidence in favour of the theistic hypothesis. As Pascal argued: 'Man tries unsuccessfully to fill this void with everything that surrounds him, seeking in absent things the help he cannot find in those that are present, but all are incapable of it. This infinite abyss can be filled only with an infinite ... object ... God himself.'[128]

According to C.S. Lewis: 'Creatures are not born with desires unless satisfaction for those desires exists. A baby feels hunger: well, there is such a thing as food ... If I find in myself a desire which no experience in this world can satisfy, the most probable explanation is that I was made for another world.'[129] A man's hunger does not prove that he will get any food; he might die of starvation. But surely hunger proves that a man comes from a race which needs to eat and inhabits a world where edible substances exist: 'In the same way', says C.S. Lewis, 'though I do not believe (I wish I did) that my desire for Paradise proves that I shall enjoy it, I think it a pretty good indication that such a thing exists and that some men will.'[130]

Experience

Religious experience is far more convincing in the first person than in the third person, and quite reasonably so.[131] Nevertheless, religious experience, even considered in the third person, is evidence for God.

The theist may argue that throughout human history a host of individuals have claimed to have known and had a personal relationship with God. This

---

[127] G.K. Chesterton, *Orthodoxy* (London: Hodder & Stoughton, 1996), p. 114.

[128] Pascal, *Pensées And Other Writings*, p. 181.

[129] C.S. Lewis, *Mere Christianity* (London: Fount, 1986).

[130] Ibid.

[131] As William Lane Craig says: 'in the context of an immediate experience of God, its rational to believe in God in a properly basic way ... In the absence of overwhelming arguments for atheism, it seems to me perfectly rational to go on believing in the reality of that experience.' Strobel, *The Case For Faith*, p. 84.

claim has been made across cultural and geographic boundaries as well as over time. For the atheist's claim that there is no God to be true, every single one of these individuals must be wrong about the matter that they themselves would characterize as the most important human concern.[132]

Many, perhaps most, people from different eras and widely different cultures claim to have experience of the divine; and that includes atheists! Jean-Paul Sartre's experience, paradoxically, caused him to abandon belief: 'I had been playing with matches and burned a small rug. I was in the process of covering up my crime when suddenly God saw me. I felt His gaze inside my head and on my hands ... I flew into a rage against so crude an indiscretion, I blasphemed ... He never looked at me again.'[133] Of course, for many, the experience of God is one to be cherished. If it is unlikely that so many people could be wrong about this profound experience then it is likely that God exists. Moreover, the principle of credulity encourages us to take religious experience at face value, unless there is sufficient reason to doubt it: 'It is a basic principle of knowledge ... that we ought to believe that things are as they seem to be, until we have evidence that we are mistaken ... If you say the contrary – never trust appearances until it is proved that they were reliable – you will never have any beliefs at all. For what would show that appearances were reliable, except more appearances?'[134] If you lack religious experience yourself, then it is reasonable to trust the reports of those with such experience. Such testimony carries, by the principle of credulity, a prima facie validity. You may wish to reply that you have reasons against the existence of God that override this prima facie validity, but it seems to me that the denial of God at least requires the existence of some such defeater.

J.P. Moreland delineates 'causal' and 'direct perception' arguments for God from experience. Both arguments focus on what Rudolf Otto called 'numinous experience': 'Numinous experience is one in which the subject (allegedly) has some sort of direct apprehension of a personal Being who is holy, good, awesome, separate from the subject, and One upon whom the subject depends in some way for life and care.'[135] In the causal argument 'a person cites certain experiences of spiritual power

---

[132] Paul D. Feinberg in Cowan (ed.), *Five Views On Apologetics*, p. 161.

[133] Jean-Paul Sartre, *Words* (London: Penguin, 2000), p. 102.

[134] Richard Swinburne, 'Evidence for God' in Gillian Ryeland (ed.), *Beyond Reasonable Doubt* (Norwich: Canterbury Press, 1991).

[135] J.P. Moreland, *Scaling The Secular City* (Grand Rapids, Michigan: Baker, 1987), p. 232.

and transformation, his changed life, his new ability to handle problems in a way not available to him before his conversion (or before some special numinous experience after conversion), and postulates God as the best explanation for his change.'[136] Relevant testimony is not hard to come by. William Lane Craig confesses: 'God has transformed my life, my attitudes, my relationships, my motivations, my marriage, and my priorities through his very real ongoing presence in my life …'[137] Moreland notes that the cogency of this causal argument: 'rests in the ability of the God hypothesis to explain the data more adequately than … other hypotheses [alone]'.[138] He points out that attempts to explain away religious transformation by the power of psychological or sociological factors alone must assume the existence of a common causal factor (or a small number of factors) responsible for the transformation. However, 'such a strategy becomes less plausible as the diversity increases in the nature and scope of religious transformation … since the working of God seems to be the major, perhaps the only, constant factor at work in such experiences.'[139] After all:

> Religious transformation has occurred for thousands of years, in primitive cultures and advanced ones, in young and old people, in those well educated and those without education, in cool, calm people and emotional, hysterical people, in those in a religious culture and those in an atheistic culture. Such differences in time, place, upbringing, temperament, and age are good evidence that the common causal factor in such cases is God.[140]

Moreover, in Christianity such transformation is tied to 'objective events (the resurrection) and an objective interpretive grid (the Bible) which render such transformation probable'.[141] As Moreland explains: 'If Christ is risen from the dead and scripture promises for a new life are true, then one has a basis for predicting that certain patterns of life change will occur. When such cases of change do in fact happen, they serve as positive confirmations of the Christian hypothesis …'[142]

The direct perception argument, 'seeks to show that there is a close analogy between the religious form of perception in numinous experiences and the sensory form of perception in visual experience, and

---

[136] Ibid.
[137] William Lane Craig in Strobel, *The Case for Faith*, p. 86.
[138] Moreland, *Scaling The Secular City*, p. 232.
[139] Ibid.
[140] Ibid., pp. 233–4.
[141] Ibid., p. 234.
[142] Ibid.

since we know the latter to be cognitive and (usually) verdical, there is justification for taking the former to be cognitive and (usually) verdical'.[143] Moreland argues that 'there are several reasons for holding that there is a close analogy between sensory perception and numinous perception. And since we know that the former is (usually) verdical, there is good reason to take the latter as (usually) verdical.'[144] Of course, there are disanalogies between sensory and numinous perception; but to point this out is not in itself an argument against numinous perception, because disanalogy is an essential feature of *all* argument by analogy. Numinous perception is clearly analogous to sensory perception, so the only question is how strongly analogous it is. Thus the question is not whether this is evidence for God, but *how strong* this evidence is.

The most obvious disanalogy between sensory and numinous perception is the fact that numinous perception is non-empirical. While God can often be sensed 'in' or 'through' nature, God is not a part of nature like a tree or a mountain. Rather, as Alvin Plantinga has pointed out, belief in God is like our belief in other minds. No human has ever had empirical sensory perception of another person's experience, although we all know what it is to know what someone else is feeling or thinking. Someone else's experience just isn't the sort of thing that is open to *sensory* perception; neither is God. If the fact that 'other minds' are not perceivable by the empirical senses does not make belief in 'other minds' irrational, then neither does the fact that God is not perceivable by the empirical senses make belief in God irrational (the same point applies to belief in angels). Besides, 'it is a category fallacy to fault ... God [or angels] for not being an empirical entity ... It is not part of the nature of a spirit to be visible empirically as a material object would be. It is a category fallacy to ascribe sensory qualities to God or fault him for not being visible.'[145] I submit that numinous religious experience provides adequate grounds for two valid arguments for God that surely contribute *some* weight to the case for God.

Meaning

'The way we approach and view our mortality depends upon our views of what are the ultimate ends of our actions and desires, what offers us true satisfaction, and what is the source of the positive or negative

---

[143] Ibid., p. 235.
[144] Ibid., p. 240.
[145] Ibid., p. 227.

value that anything may possess.'[146] For the Christian, our ultimate end and true satisfaction is eternal life with God, the source and summit of all value. For the naturalist, our ultimate end is extinction, true satisfaction is a temporary and fragile distraction from that end, and all thought of values is, as Michael Ruse says, 'just an aid to survival and reproduction ... and any other meaning is illusory'. As Terry L. Miethe writes: 'If God does not exist, we are very hard pressed to find any real order or personal meaning, let alone true happiness, in a world that would finally be naturalistic, mechanistic, and deterministic.'[147]

Our choice is thus between theism, or the no meaning, no purpose, no future and no value worldview of nihilism. Nihilism is the inevitable terminus of naturalism, for meaning is impossible to find without God. *Meaningfulness is the coincidence of purpose and value* (after all, what's the point of purpose if it isn't valuable?). Thus, *for life to be objectively meaningful is for life to have an objective purpose that is objectively valuable*. Only God can provide this. If God exists, then we have a purpose, a reason why we exist, a goal and a meaning. On the other hand, if no God exists, then the universe has no creator, no meaning or purpose, and we have no creator, and so no meaning or purpose. Therefore, *if existence is meaningful, God must exist*. As G.K. Chesterton argued, 'this world of ours has some purpose; and if there is a purpose, there is a person.'[148]

To say that it is objectively *good* to accept nihilism, or that it is rationally *bad* to accept theism, would be self-contradictory, because nihilism is the utter denial of such normative concepts. Therefore, *our choice is between God on the one hand and self-contradiction on the other*. To choose self-contradiction is absurd. While the nihilists may shrug their shoulders and demand, 'So what? That's the point of nihilism', those of us who remain on the sunny side of the metaphysical street, can find no rational, moral or existential motive for crossing over. The grass isn't greener on the other side.

The evidence cumulatively points to the actuality of two immaterial realities (the human mind and God), a state of affairs that disproves naturalism and clearly supports the possibility of angels.

---

[146] Ivon Soll in J.E. Malpas and Robert C. Solomon, *Death And Philosophy* (London: Routledge, 1998), p. 23.

[147] Terry L. Miethe, *Why Believe? God Exists!* (Joplin, Missouri: College Press, 1998), p. 28.

[148] G.K.Chesterton, *Orthodoxy*, p. 83.

Angels and Theological Scepticism

I am not surprised that naturalists don't believe in angels, since they don't believe in anything supernatural on principle. I take it that the above arguments for the mind and for God challenge that assumption beyond breaking point. What I do find surprising, or at least disappointing, is that some *theologians* think that angels are not real (of course, theologians are not necessarily Christians).[149] Brian Hebblethwaite (who is a Christian) writes that 'Such belief is certainly not part of the creed and cannot be held to belong to the essence of Christianity.'[150] I agree; but I also think such disbelief both theologically awkward and factually incorrect.

In order to reconcile scepticism about angels with their faith, Christians who doubt angels adopt a demythologized account of them. Thus Brain Hebblethwaite asserts that: 'it is quite possible for Christians, without forsaking the heart of the Christian matter, to think of angels as symbolic personifications of God's own communications with the human world and of devils as projections of the evil tendencies which afflict us human beings individually and collectively ...'[151] I concur that this is *possible*, but I do not think it necessary, plausible or wise. Such disbelief goes against all of the positive arguments for angels that I will examine in Chapter Four. Just how damning a criticism this is, readers will have to judge for themselves. There are, however, some issues relating to such theological scepticism that I will deal with here. The first issue is how we should approach biblical hermeneutics, the art of understanding what the Bible says (in what follows I will assume that the Bible is, in some non-trivial sense, 'the word of God' – however, I will briefly argue for this assumption in Chapter Four).

Angels and hermeneutics

It is the *whole* Bible that is the word of God. Each manuscript was written for its own particular purpose, and few if any of the authors imagined that what they were writing was going to be collected together into one entity. Putting all these pieces together as a unity (and there is great unity as well as diversity within the biblical writings) has a divinely intended effect

---

[149] A university graduate recently told me that only one of her theology teachers had been a Christian. As an exercise in empathy, non-Christians should ponder how they would feel about being taught evolution by a young-earth creationist!

[150] Brian Hebblethwaite, *The Essence Of Christianity* (London: SPCK, 1996), p. 75.

[151] Ibid., pp. 75–6.

upon the meaning of each part, just as a composer's placing of certain notes together in a piece of music alters how we perceive, and are meant to perceive, the individual notes. Each part of the Bible, therefore, is best read *within the context of the whole*. Finding out about the genre and context of a particular biblical book or letter can be very helpful in understanding it, but it would be wrong to concentrate on such matters to the exclusion of the wider picture. Given that scripture is both the word of its human authors *and* the word of God, it should be born in mind that the intended meaning of its human authors may not necessarily be the last word on determining what the Bible actually means *as the word of God*. Interpreting biblical literature by the standards appropriate to its literary forms and genres is simply a good *first step* in this process.

One of the Psalms contains the sentence: 'There is no God.' But if we widen the context we see that it says, 'The fool says in his heart, "There is no God"' (Ps. 14:1). What applies to a single verse of scripture also applies to whole books. Ecclesiastes examines the meaninglessness of life without relationship with God, but in the context of the Bible we are obviously not meant to conclude that life is meaningless, but that life is meaningful because God *can* be known. The book of Job contradicts the assumption, which underlies other parts of the Old Testament, that suffering is always deserved. (Job never discovers *why* he has suffered so much, but he does discover that he can believe in the existence of God despite his undeserved suffering, because God meets him in the midst of his pain. Job is enabled to believe that his suffering is undeserved *and* that God is almighty and good. Although Job doesn't know *how* it can be true that God can co-exist with undeserved suffering, Job knows *that* there is no contradiction in this belief, because he knows both that undeserved suffering exists *and* that God exists. Both suffering and God are facts of Job's experience, and since truth cannot contradict truth, it must be true that the existence of God and suffering (even undeserved suffering) are not incompatible. This knowledge is enough, both for his mind and for his heart.) Likewise, it is clear that the concept of angels undergoes development during the historical course of biblical revelation: 'The character of Satan (the word means "adversary") first appears as the name of a figure in the court of Jahweh, a functionary whom Jahweh allowed to be the agent by which evil happened to good men in order to try them out ... By the time the Book of Job was written, however, "Satan" has become a named character ...'[152] Thus, 'In the Book of Job [Satan] appears as the partner of God, who on behalf of God puts the righteous one to the test.

---

[152] Michael Perry (ed.), 'The Demonic and Exorcism in the Bible', *Deliverance: Psychic Disturbance And Occult Involvement* (London: SPCK, 1996²), p. 138.

Only in post-biblical Judaism does the devil become the adversary of God, the prince of angels, who, created by God and placed at the head of the angelic hosts, entices some of the angels into revolt against God.'[153] As B.J. Oropeza points out: 'Satan's primary role as a courtroom accuser is unique to the Old Testament.'[154] It was under the influence of Zoroastrianism that 'Satan, the adversary, probably evolved into the archdemon'.[155] From here 'Christianity, probably influenced by the angelology of Jewish sects such as the Pharisees and the Essenes as well as of the Hellenistic world, further enhanced and developed theories and beliefs in angels and demons.'[156] Hence, 'By the time of the New Testament, Satan has become a name of God's archetypal enemy. That is his role through out the New Testament ...'[157] Considering this development within the context of the Bible taken as a whole should lead us to adopt a 'demythologized' view of the figure of Satan *as he appears in certain Old Testament stories*. This move is quite compatible with belief in the literal existence of Satan as depicted in the New Testament and in the authority of scripture. The vital question for Christians is not *whether* we should demythologize, but *how far* we should extend such 'demythologization'. In general terms the answer is surely 'no further than necessary', but how far is that?

Those who are sceptical about the existence of angels are apt to take the fact that beliefs about angels have metamorphosed over time as evidence that such belief is *nothing but* the result of the contingent interaction of superstitious and legendary mythmaking, and that we should therefore demythologize all scriptural accounts of angels. However, such a reductive approach is far from necessary (it also ignores the individual nature of the scriptural evidence for angels). We cannot determine or dismiss the truth of a belief simply by describing its historical origin and development; there is nothing incongruous about accepting such development as part of a progressive but none the less authoritative revelation. Rejecting the complete literal factuality of some biblical angelology does not require us to reject biblical angelology *in its entirety*, because we are led to such a partial rejection *by scripture itself!*

---

[153] *Encyclopaedia Britannica*, 'Satan and the origin of evil' @ < http://www.britannica.com/eb/article?eu=67473 >

[154] Oropeza, *99 Answers To Questions About Angels*, p. 96.

[155] *Encyclopaedia Britannica* @ < http://www.britannica.com/eb/article?eu=117210&tocid=33975 >

[156] Ibid.

[157] Perry (ed,), 'The Demonic and Exorcism in the Bible', *Deliverance: Psychic Disturbance And Occult Involvement*.

Christians needn't have their view of Satan fixed by the book of Job at the expense of the New Testament's view of things, and rejecting the former in no way requires a rejection of the latter. Indeed, the evidence does not really call for a *rejection* of any biblical angelology. Rather, it calls for certain incomplete understandings to be subsumed and refined by later, more complete understandings of the same subject matter, somewhat as a scientific theory is sometimes subsumed into a more adequate theory rather than replaced by a completely different hypothesis. Altering the Old Testament understanding of Satan in the light of the New Testament picture of Satan is less like replacing Aristotle's astronomical theories with those of Copernicus than it is like replacing Newton's theory of gravity with Einstein's.

We need a sophisticated understanding of scripture that permits the existence of *some* internal development without detracting from the truth of the Bible when taken in its totality and correctly interpreted. As theologian Keith Ward writes:

> the Bible does not claim to be dictated by God word for word. Very few Christians have taken a 'dictation' view of the inspiration of the Holy Spirit. It is more typical to think of the Spirit as overseeing the writings of many different individuals, to ensure that, *taken together*, they convey insight into spiritual truth, without putting words one by one into their minds ... It seems clear that *the personalities and beliefs of the writers were not simply over-riden by the Spirit*, but rather used to build up a set of documents which would, *as a whole*, give insight into the nature and purpose of God.[158]

If the Bible may contain such developments as those examined above, we need some way of settling disputes between passages and books, a way of reading the Bible *in context*. I would advance criteria such as:

(1) Placing greater weight on the more obvious over the less obvious. Augustine noted, 'Virtually nothing is unearthed from these obscurities which cannot be found quite plainly expressed somewhere else.'[159] Thus, we 'should proceed to explore and analyse the obscure passages, by taking examples from the more obvious parts to illuminate obscure expressions and by using the evidence of indisputable passages to remove the uncertainty of ambiguous ones'.[160]

---

[158] Keith Ward, *Christianity: A Short Introduction* (Oxford: OneWorld, 2000), p. 109, my italics.

[159] Augustine, *On Christian Teaching* (Oxford: Oxford University Press, 1999), p. 33.

[160] Ibid., p. 37.

(2) Allowing for progressive revelation.
(3) Reading the Old Testament in the light, or through the lens, of Jesus and New Testament theology.
(4) Bringing the responsible use of sources of knowledge besides scripture to bear on interpreting scripture in the spirit of the integrationist project of 'faith seeking understanding' described earlier: 'our interpretation of Scripture must be viewed in the context of what the church community has said through the ages (tradition) and what our reason tells us today.'[161] As Augustine warned, 'We must show our Scriptures not to be in conflict with whatever [our critics] can demonstrate about the nature of things from reliable sources.'[162]

A common-sense view of the Bible that takes its methodological cue *from the Bible itself* will allow one to admit the presence of imperfect human understandings contained within scripture *without detracting from the inspiration, truth or reliability of the Bible as God's word* when a) taken as a whole and b) interpreted according to good hermeneutical principles such as those given above. Truth is one, and 'all truth is God's truth', so we cannot compartmentalize scripture from science or philosophy or archaeology, etc. We can be confident that what the Bible really affirms as true really is true in the way affirmed; but as Charles Hodge warned 'Theologians are not infallible in the interpretation of Scripture.'[163] Nor should we deny, therefore, that theology, science, philosophy, and so on, are useful resources that have something to contribute to our interpretation and understanding of God's word. As Howard J. Van Till comments:

> The problematic practice that we must guard against in our reading and interpretation of Scripture is the frequent failure to acknowledge that the Scriptures, although they do indeed provide the foundation stones for our 'training in righteousness,' constitute but one of the sources provided [by God] for our intellectual growth. If a multiplicity of intellectual resources is provided [by God] for the growth of a Christian's knowledge of God and his works, then any practice that so elevates one resource so as to

---

[161] Jean Pond in Richard F. Carlson (ed.), *Science & Christianity: Four Views* (Downers Grove, Illinois: IVP, 2000), p. 54.

[162] Augustine, *De genesi ad litteram* vol. I (Mahwah, New Jersey: Paulist Press, 1982), p. 21.

[163] Charles Hodge, *Systematic Theology* vol. I (Grand Rapids, Michigan: Baker, 1992), p. 59.

effectively exclude or demean all other sources is, in my opinion, counter-productive.[164]

I believe that scripture is inerrant (unfailingly correct) in whatever it really asserts as the word of God, where 'whatever it really asserts as the word of God' is sometimes discernable (if at all) only after extensive and careful consideration of all the relevant data, including information from outside scripture. As Kelly James Clark argues, reason and revelation cannot but go hand in hand.

> although people often oppose revelation to reason and suggest that revelation is superior, there can be, in the end, no real opposition. Here is the problem: Each person must decide (tacitly or explicitly) that a purported revelation *is* revelation. Each person must decide that what is being said in some particular holy writ *is* the voice of God. Each person must decide *what* is being said and then what it *means*. And each person must decide what it *means today* that God said something a long time ago. At every level ... reason is operative ... Every take on Scripture is interpretation – and interpretation is a function (at least partly) of ... reason.[165]

For example, if the scripture seems to say that the sun goes round the earth and science contradicts this assertion *with greater certainty than the certainty attached to our interpretation of scripture*, then science will cause us to correct our interpretation of scripture; for truth is coherent, truth cannot contradict truth, and all truth is God's truth.[166] As Augustine said: 'Anyone with an interpretation of the scriptures that differs from that of the writer is misled, but not because the scriptures are lying.'[167] Augustine made a great deal of sense when he advocated what we might call 'the love rule of hermeneutics'.

---

[164] Howard J. Van Till in J.P. Moreland and John Mark Reynolds (eds), *Three Views On Creation And Evolution* (Grand Rapids, Michigan: Zondervan, 1999), p. 211. This position does not mean we should not place great weight on what we think Scripture says, but sometimes our understanding will be less certain than at others.

[165] Kelly James Clark in Cowan (ed.), *Five Views On Apologetics*, p. 262. 'The phrase "The Bible says ..." begs a lot of questions ... What *does* the Bible say? To whom is it saying it? What is the context, background and literary form of the passage in question? Is it to be taken literally, or figuratively, or allegorically?' David Winter, *But This I Can Believe* (London: Hodder & Stoughton, 1980), p. 112.

[166] The same principle applies to the interpretation of the creation narratives in Genesis in relation to science. cf. Moreland and Reynolds, *Three Views on Creation and Evolution*.

[167] Augustine, *On Christian Teaching*, p. 27.

So anyone who thinks that he has understood the divine scriptures or any part of them, but cannot by his understanding build up this double love of God and neighbour, has not yet succeeded in understanding them. Anyone who derives from them an idea which is useful for supporting this love but false to say what the writer demonstrably meant in the passage has not made a fatal error, and is certainly not a liar.[168]

Christians who demythologize *all* scriptural references to angels probably fall within Augustine's category for the person who is 'misled' but has 'not made a fatal error and is certainly not a liar'. One hopes that they would place me in the same category! The question of angels will not be settled by name-calling. Rather, we need to pay attention to the hermeneutical spiral: 'After the philological and grammatical issues have been examined, and after the biblical and historical contexts have been established, proposed interpretations are subjected to comparisons with our knowledge base and revised accordingly.'[169] I assume that Christians who don't believe in literal angels are drawn to a non-literal interpretation of apparently literal texts when it comes to subjecting interpretation to comparison with our knowledge base. This suggests that these Christians believe our knowledge base includes information that contradicts the literal interpretation of *any* scriptural references to angels *with more certainty than attaches to a literal interpretation of the relevant biblical passages*. If this were so, if some facet of scientific or philosophical knowledge (or theological knowledge come to that) clearly and compellingly contradicted belief in literal angels, then Christians would surely have to agree that all biblical references to angels must, despite appearances, be symbolic. After all, the only remaining alternative would be that the Bible was straightforwardly *wrong*! While this thought might cheer the secularists, Christian trust in the Bible as a

---

[168] Ibid.

[169] Wayne Frair and Gary D. Patterson in Carlson (ed.), *Science & Christianity: Four Views* (Downers Grove, Illinois: IVP, 2000), p. 24. We should, however, bear in mind Douglas Blount's caution: 'we should *not* be surprised that an inerrant book (or collection of books) makes claims which seem to us implausible. After all, since considerations of humility give us reason to expect some of our beliefs about, say, morality to be false, it would *hardly* be surprising if some of the moral claims made by an inerrant book (or collection of books) seemed to us to be false. Indeed, it would be surprising if all its claims seemed to us to be true!' Douglas Blount, 'The Authority of Scripture' in Michael J. Murray (ed.), *Reason For The Hope Within* (Grand Rapids, Michigan: Eerdmans, 1999), pp. 420–21. We have warrant for the wisdom of being prepared to live with a degree of mystery.

whole has warrant (and justification) enough to place a question mark over such a concession.[170] Hence, while recognizing that the implicit argument of the angelic demythologizers is valid, I believe it to be unsound. Since the argument is valid, one need only reverse its premise to construct a valid argument for the opposite conclusion. Doubters may argue: '1) the Bible (as a whole, etc) does not teach falsehoods, 2) angels can't/don't exist, 3) therefore the Bible (as a whole, etc) does not teach that angels exist', but believers can just as validly argue: '1a) the Bible (as a whole, etc) does not teach falsehoods, 2a) the Bible (as a whole, etc) teaches that angels exist, 3a) therefore angels can and do exist.' Indeed, the first argument has an *ad hoc* appearance lacking in the second (it certainly *seems* that the Bible teaches the existence of literal angels). As far as I can see, there is no information in our knowledge base that contradicts the literal interpretation of scriptural references to angels with more certainty than attaches to a literal interpretation of the relevant passages.

Theologians who object to angels – a response
Theological disbelief in angels and its attendant demythologization may simply be a capitulation (perhaps unconsciously) to the sceptical spirit of the age. Richard Harries is correct when he points out that 'if the sincerity and intellectual integrity of liberal theologians can be challenged, so too can that of those who wish to defy the spirit of the age by asserting a firmly supernatural view of the faith. For there is human motivation for defiantly going against the current as well as for swimming with it … the only question that matters is the truth of what is discussed.'[171] It is nevertheless legitimate to point out the role played by assumptions in academic debate. For example, theologian Walter Wink confesses: 'I had never been able to take demons seriously. The idea that fallen angels possessed people seemed superstitious.'[172] This is a psychological report, not a reasoned argument for disbelief. Wink simply *assumes* the falsity of traditional angelology and proceeds *on this basis* to explain away such belief: 'It is merely a habit of thought that makes people think of the Powers as personal beings.'[173]

---

[170] For an exposition and defence of the warranted nature of Christian belief in Scripture see Plantinga, *Warranted Christian Belief*.

[171] Richard Harries, *C.S. Lewis: The Man And His God* (London: Fount, 1987), p. 41.

[172] Walter Wink, *The Powers That Be: Theology For A New Millennium* (New York: Galilee Doubleday, 1998), p. 5.

[173] Ibid., p. 27.

In the same vein, Wink rejects the pre-modern, biblical, theistic worldview and adopts what he calls an 'integral' worldview, because he thinks 'it makes the biblical data more intelligible for people today than any other available worldview, the ancient one included.'[174] For Wink: 'This integral view of reality sees everything as having an outer and an inner aspect ... soul permeates the universe ... This is not pantheism, where everything is God, but pan*en*theism (*pan*, everything; *en*, in; *theos*, God), where everything is in God and God in everything ...'[175] For the panentheist, matter and 'God' are two sides of the same coin, different 'aspects' of one and the same reality. Hence: 'This integral worldview ... is given modern representation by the Moebius strip ...'[176] This proposal seems to promise 'to take us beyond the naturalism that recognizes no reality other than this world, but [fails to] unambiguously acknowledge a reality which is other than ourselves and not just some profound aspect of our own being.'[177] Panentheism leads to an essentially naturalistic attitude towards reality, for like naturalism it denies the existence of an independent, transcendent, supernatural realm or ultimate reality. Clearly, Wink is not simply *demythologizing* angelology within a biblical worldview, but *remythologizing* angelology within an unbiblical worldview. His presumption against angels is a function of his rejection of the Bible's pre-modern worldview. This rejection seems to be based, in turn, on an uncharitable interpretation of that worldview: 'few of us in the West who have been deeply touched by modern science can actually think that God, the angels, and departed spirits are somewhere in the sky, as most ancients literally did.'[178] But of course, one may accept the pre-modern, biblical worldview without accepting the literal truth of such language. To suggest otherwise is to propose a false dilemma. As C.S. Lewis noted:

---

[174] Ibid., p. 20.

[175] Ibid., pp. 19–21. Panentheism comes in a variety of forms, including 'process philosophy'. cf. John B. Cobb Jr and Clark H. Pinnock (eds), *Searching For An Adequate God: A Dialogue Between Process And Free Will Theists* (Grand Rapids, Michigan: Eerdmans, 2000).

[176] Wink, *The Powers That Be*, p. 21.

[177] H.D. Lewis, *Philosophy Of Religion* (London: English Universities Press, 1965), p. 128.

[178] Walter Wink, *The Powers That Be*, p. 20. Of course, science is incapable of falsifying even a literalistic interpretation of such language. Nor is being incapable of scientific falsification a mark of irrationality, since the proposition that this is so cannot itself be scientifically falsified.

what we mean may be true when the mental images that accompany it are entirely false ... When a man says that he grasps an argument he is using a verb (*grasp*) which literally means to take something in the hands, but he is certainly not thinking that his mind has hands or that an argument can be seized like a gun ... If absurd images meant absurd thought, then we should all be thinking nonsense all the time.[179]

The biblical writers may talk about angels inhabiting the heavens as a modern theologian may talk of grasping an argument. Neither assertion need be literally true in order to convey literal truth. It should be obvious that even if early Christians took such biblical imagery literally (a questionable assumption), 'this would not mean that we are justified in relegating their doctrines as a whole to the lumber-room.'[180] Indeed, Wink simply swaps one metaphor for another: 'The integral [panentheistic] worldview reconceives that spatial metaphor not as "up" but "within".'[181]

While there is a relation of appropriateness between different metaphors and the worldviews they represent, one can hardly arbitrate between worldviews by pointing out the absurdity of taking its metaphors, however appropriate, literally! Does it really make any more sense, literally speaking, to say that God is 'within' the universe (panentheism) than it does to say that God is 'without' (yet present to) the universe (theism)? Of course not, and such a criticism is totally beside the point *in either case*. The salient question is that of the ontological relationship between the world around us and ultimate reality. Theists believe that the universe is freely created by God and is therefore ontologically distinct from God. Panentheists believe that God is 'within' the universe and that the universe is not freely created by God. Such a 'withinness' theology excludes the possibility of nature transcending miracles as dogmatically as does naturalism, for on the panentheistic view: 'divine influence in the world is a fully natural part of the normal causal processes of the world, never a supernatural interruption thereof.'[182] Evidence for miracles, such as Jesus' resurrection, is therefore evidence against panentheism.[183] Then again, if God is the 'inner aspect' of the physical cosmos (and its evils), how can one justifiably differentiate between absolute good and evil? If the physical cosmos

---

[179] Lewis, *Miracles*, pp. 73–6.
[180] Ibid., p. 78.
[181] Wink, *The Powers That Be*, p. 20.
[182] David Ray Griffin, 'Process Theology and the Christian Good News' in Cobb and Pinnock (eds), *Searching For An Adequate God*, pp. 5–6.
[183] cf. resources on Jesus' resurrection in the Bibliography.

bears the signature of intelligent design, the inference to a transcendent designer is in no way undermined by saying that 'God' is the 'withinness' of the very thing that points to design!

Walter Wink's approach to theology seems to me to be a typically postmodern case of allowing the tail to wag the dog. Wink accommodates worldview beliefs to what 'people today' find subjectively 'intelligible' (i.e. culturally acceptable and user-friendly), rather than seeking to accommodate people's beliefs to a worldview affirmed on the independent grounds of its objective truth. Besides, isn't the pre-modern, biblical worldview (metaphysically speaking) itself a part of the 'biblical data' that Wink seeks to make more 'intelligible'? If so, isn't his entire project self-contradictory?

Wink wants to take the spiritual realm of angels and demons depicted in the Bible as seriously as he can within the constraints of his non-biblical worldview. To this end he hypothesizes that the 'powers' mentioned in the New Testament are nothing but the inter-subjective character of social institutions: 'The Powers That Be are more than just the people who run things. They are the systems themselves, the institutions and structures that weave society into an intricate fabric of power and relationships.'[184] Wink finds support for this view in the fact that the seven letters to the churches in Revelation are addressed, not to the church congregation, but to the congregation's angel: 'The angel seemed to be the corporate personality of the church, its ethos or spirit or essence.'[185] Hence, according to Wink, 'the demonic arises when an angel deviates from its calling'.[186] Wink even flirts with the hypothesis that such 'angels' have an *emergent* personal nature: 'I prefer to think of the Powers as impersonal entities, though I know of no sure way to settle the question ... For the present I have set aside the question of the actual status of these Powers, and instead have attempted to describe what it was that people in ancient times were *experiencing* when they spoke of "Satan", "demons", "powers", "angels", and the like.'[187]

It may be that *some* biblical references to angels and demons can be interpreted as symbols for 'the spirituality of actual entities in the real world'.[188] For example, such an interpretation seems to be a *possible* reading of the 'authorities' and 'powers of this dark world' mentioned by Paul in Ephesians 6:12. However, a distinction would also seem to

---

[184] Wink, *The Powers That Be*, p. 1.
[185] Ibid., p. 3.
[186] Ibid., p. 6.
[187] Ibid., p. 27.
[188] Wink, *Unmasking The Powers*, p. 172.

flow from that text between the 'powers *of this dark world*' and the 'spiritual forces of evil *in the heavenly realms*' (my italics). Therefore, while Wink's 'withinness' may have a legitimate place in Christian thought about spiritual forces, it should not be adopted as a universal interpretative device. Gregory A. Boyd comments, 'as much as Paul might see demonic activity in structural societal evil, he clearly does not equate the demonic powers with structural societal evil.'[189] One theological problem with accepting Wink's theory across the board is that some biblical references to angels and demons are surely read most naturally as intending the ascription of particular actions to literal personal beings of a non-divine, but spiritual kind. There is certainly a place within Christian theology for recognizing the corporate spirituality of institutions; and if there were good reason to deny the existence of angels in the traditional sense Wink's theory would be an attractive alternative to simply ditching angelology altogether (especially if combined with a psychological demythologization of demon possession, which is hard to interpret institutionally). However, I don't believe that these are our only alternatives.

To accept a wholly demythologized angelology, even within a biblical worldview, would require us to ride roughshod over a large amount of biblical data that is not easily amenable to such interpretations (e.g., the various messages and warnings conveyed by angels to Mary, Joseph and the disciples; or the incident in Acts 12 – examined in Chapter Four – where Peter is sprung out of jail by an angel.) This being so, such a drastic move would require an impressive amount of evidential justification. As we have seen, Wink fails to provide anything approaching such a justification. However, other theologians (of a more orthodox stripe than Wink) *have* proposed various well-meaning justifications for their disbelief in angels.

Brian Hebblethwaite argues that it makes facing the problem of evil easier if we view 'the whole creative process whereby finite persons are fashioned from below in and through a regularly structured physical universe [i.e. evolution] as necessary not simply for the formation of the values of *human* life, but as necessary for the formation of *any* finite creaturely persons.'[190] Questions about evolution aside, Hebblethwaite might, strictly speaking, be right in making this claim. However, might does not necessarily make right. Aside from the motivation provided by the attempt to produce a theodicy, this proposal has no independent warrant (I can think of no intrinsic reason to think that an omnipotent

---

[189] Boyd, *God At War*, p. 276.
[190] Hebblethwaite, *The Essence Of Christianity*, p. 76.

God couldn't create finite creaturely persons without using a physical process), and anyone who agrees that angels are possible will see Hebblethwaite's argument as rather *ad hoc*. Moreover, anyone happy to accept the conclusion that the problem of evil is a philosophical damp squib, will see little if any warrant for accepting Hebblethwaite's theodicy and its attendant angelic objection. One needn't hold that a physical world is a necessary means to the end of creating finite creatures to exonerate God's creation of a physical world. After all, a physical world is a necessary means to the end of *physically embodied* finite creatures, and the total value of such a world and the ends it makes possible would seem sufficient justification for such a creation. As Herbert McCabe argues:

> you cannot make material things that develop in time without allowing for the fact that in perfecting themselves they will damage other material things ... You may be tempted to argue that it would be better not to have lions at all – but *if you think along those lines you have to end up thinking that it would be better not to have any material world at all* ... A world without any defects ... would be a world without any natural order in it. No reasonable person objects to an occasional withdrawal of natural cause, a miracle from time to time; but a world without any natural causes ... would not be a natural material world at all. So the people who would like [God] to have made a material world without suffering ... would have preferred him not to have made a world ... But ... *most people are pleased he made such a world ... The accusation that God made it does not seem very damning.*[191]

Norman L. Geisler notes a problem with the suggestion that God should have made only non-material creatures: 'The problem is that, while no angel can die of food poisoning, neither can they enjoy a prime rib. While no angel ever drowned, neither has any angel ever gone for a swim or went water skiing. No angel has ever been raped, but neither has any angel ever enjoyed sex or the blessing of having children (Mt. 22:30).'[192] Even granting Hebblethwaite's necessary condition theodicy, God still had a choice between creating a physical world and not creating a physical world. Since he has created, we know that what he has created is overall a good thing (although not morally obligatory); but this conclusion follows *whether or not God had other morally good types of creation available to him,* and *irrespective of whether he availed himself of these possibilities.*

---

[191] Herbert McCabe, *God Matters* (London: Mowbray, 1987), pp. 31–3, my italics.

[192] Geisler, *Baker Encyclopedia Of Christian Apologetics*, p. 223.

According to scripture, not all angels are good. Some have turned against God. The possibility of such a fall can be demonstrated: 'If angels are persons (selves) they have intellects and wills. If they have wills, they can choose between good and evil. If they can choose between good and evil, they can choose evil. If they choose evil, they become evil. So if there are good spirits, there can be evil spirits.'[193] Hebblethwaite has some questions: 'what could possibly tempt a pure spirit, unencumbered with the lures of a physical origin, to fall from grace? Why should such fallen spirits be permitted to wreak havoc in nature or the human world? What is the point of keeping them in being, let alone in active interference with the world, if they have rendered themselves wholly unredeemable?'[194] These are good questions. I think there are good answers.

Christians believe that *while human beings are presently sinful, in heaven we will be sinless.* God has created humans so that we can exercise our free will in forming our characters either in openness to God or the self-centredness that leads to rejecting God. Once someone has chosen to accept relationship with God on God's terms (being forgiven by grace) then, in heaven, God will cause that person to be without sin. Christian tradition suggests that *this self-same process applies to angels,* but that unlike humankind, angelkind have already chosen for or against God: 'Angels were created with free will and tested ... Some chose to love and serve God. Others chose to rebel.'[195] As the *Catechism of the Catholic Church* says: 'Angels and men, as intelligent and free creatures, have to journey toward their ultimate destinies by their free choice and preferential love.'[196] Those finite spirits who rejected God are now demons. Those who did not reject God are now Angels: 'If an angel chose a good character, that was fixed for ever. If an angel chose a bad character, that too was fixed for ever.'[197] That is, God did not begin by creating Angels or demons, but by creating angels (finite spirits) with the freedom to accept grace (thereby becoming Angels) or to reject it (thereby becoming demons). Such a theory would seem to be a necessary component of angelology, given the apparent impossibility of any morally perfect being freely choosing to reject God.[198] As Richard

---

[193] Kreeft, *Angels (And Demons),* p. 111.

[194] Hebblethwaite, *The Essence Of Christianity,* p. 76.

[195] Kreeft, *Angels (And Demons),* p. 116.

[196] *Catechism Of The Catholic Church* (London: Geoffrey Chapman, 1994), p. 74.

[197] Swinburne, *Providence And The Problem Of Evil,* p. 36.

[198] cf. Williams, *The Case For God.*

Harries asks: 'If the angels were created perfect and placed in the perfect environment of the presence of God, how could they have fallen?'[199]

Harries alleges that: 'if there are fallen angels, God created them in the first place, and he knew they were going to fall.'[200] On the basis of God's implied responsibility for the existence of fallen angels, and the assumption that such responsibility would count against God's existence, Harries draws the conclusion that demons are nonexistent, saying 'it is necessary to reject the idea not only of one devil but of all devils.'[201] Hebblethwaite agrees with Harries, and for similar reasons: 'The Judeo-Christian tradition has popularly been taken to affirm the existence of … angels – incorporeal spirits, living in God's immediate presence, unencumbered by mortality, not set – and that must mean not needing to be set [as Hebblethwaite's theodicy requires creatures to be] –at a distance from God and built up from below in and through a whole evolving universe.'[202] Both scholars are surely right to prefer belief in God to belief in angels when they perceive a contradiction between these two beliefs; and if there was no alternative account to the popular angelology that Harries and Hebblethwaite attack, I would be inclined to agree with their rejection of angels. However, the traditional angelology of Christendom is in fact just such an alternative theory. Harries and Hebblethwaite have attacked a 'straw man' (or a 'straw angel'!).

Hebblethwaite's 'popular tradition' is only partially correct, and only partially traditional. The problem is with the claim that angels are 'not set – and that must mean not needing to be set – at a distance from God'. One needs to ask of the phrase 'not needing to be set at a distance from God' the question: '*At what stage of their existence?*' The good angels are not now at a 'distance' from God, nor will they ever be; but does this statement necessarily hold true in the past tense as Hebblethwaite assumes? I see no reason to make this assumption, and given the problems it causes for angelology, every reason to abandon it. As Mortimer J. Adler reports: 'According to Aquinas, the angels were not created in a state of bliss, which consists in being confirmed in goodness by the gift of grace; for if that were the case, no angel could have turned away from God. "The fall of some angels," he writes, "shows that the angelic nature was not created in that state".'[203] Only those

---

[199] Harries, *C S. Lewis: The Man And His God*, p. 38.
[200] Ibid.
[201] Ibid.
[202] Hebblethwaite, *The Essence Of Christianity*, p. 75.
[203] Adler, *The Angels And Us*, pp. 86–7.

angels who freely chose to serve God were transformed into the wholly good beings Angels are today. Those who did not choose to serve God thereby became demons. What if, as Harries notes, God could foresee that some angels would rebel?[204] The immediate moral responsibility for rebellion belongs to the fallen angels, not to God. God is of course responsible for creating the *possibility* of a fall resulting in demons, but this possibility was not only an intrinsic component of creating creatures with significant free will (which is a good thing), but the necessary condition of the existence of Angels (who are wholly good things).

> What glory would God receive if angels and all humans were pre-programmed to worship him? What genuine love relationship could God share with his creatures if they were forced to love him? Both angels and humans can choose what is evil instead of what is good, yet having freedom of choice itself is a good thing. There could be no love for God and no godly character development without the real potential to choose against God ... Apparently God thought it a greater good to share a mutual love relationship with some of his creatures than to have all his creatures love and worship him involuntarily.[205]

If the nature of this choice in the context of its antecedent conditions is a mystery, it is no more a mystery in the case of angels than it is in the case of humans. Richard Swinburne affirms and extends the traditional theory.

> Embodied humans are not the only kind of rational agent with free will there could be. God might well create non-embodied free agents; and some of them might indeed choose the bad. We may perhaps regard the initial choice of character by the angels as one extended in time, and, given that, if it is good that God should give us the ultimate choice over the period of our lives on Earth of being allowed to fix our characters beyond further change, it would seem to be similarly good that God should give to angels also the ultimate choice of being allowed to fix their characters. And he might well also, in giving them that initial choice, have promised them temporary and limited power over the world when they fixed their characters. That would have given a deeper significance to their choice than it would otherwise have ... If freedom and responsibility are good things, it is good that there be angels who have it, as well as humans ... angels could only choose the bad if

---

[204] One might wish to question whether God *could* foresee what non-existent creatures with free will *would do were they to be created* and point out that once such creatures are created there is no going back.

[205] Orpeza, *99 Answers To Questions About Angels, Demons & Spiritual Warfare*, p. 88.

they were tempted so to do, being already subject to bad desires, the bad must have pre-existed any bad choice by angels.[206]

Since this bad cannot have come from nature, or from the angels themselves, it must have come from God. Some may find this thought disconcerting, but several points should be born in mind. First, it admits of a necessary condition theodicy (without this state of affairs there would have been no freely chosen angelic love and so no Angels). Secondly, it has its roots firmly in scripture and Christian tradition. According to Paul: 'the creation was subjected to frustration, not by its own choice, but by the will of the one who subjected it [i.e. God], in hope that the creation itself will be liberated from its bondage to decay and brought into the glorious freedom of the children of God' (Rom. 8:20–21). Paul goes on to write that: 'God has bound all men over to disobedience so that he may have mercy on them all' (Rom. 11:32). Classical angelology simply applies Paul's teaching to angels. Thomas Aquinas affirmed: 'the angels did not have from the beginning of their creation that ultimate beatitude which is beyond the power of nature; because such beatitude is no part of their nature, but its end; and consequently they ought not to have it immediately from the beginning.'[207] This is certainly no harder to accept than Hebblethwaite's angel-denying alternative of an evolutionary history as the necessary condition of free will. Is it really *impossible* for almighty God to gift creatures with significant free will unless he uses the tool of nature?!

Hebblethwaite finally objects that: 'blaming things on the devil distracts us from facing up to the evil in the human heart and from our own responsibility, at least for moral evil.'[208] But this simply need not be the case. The devil cannot be blamed for sin, only for temptation (cf. Jas. 1:13–15). Hence human responsibility remains intact. This objection really begs the question, for one might just as well note that blaming everything on the human heart and human responsibility distracts us from facing up to the reality of demonic evil!

Richard Harries complains that: 'it seems morally intolerable to have hordes of fallen spirits hovering about leading us into sin. There is enough to contend with in human life anyway, arising from our existence as a creature that is at once flesh and spirit, without that as well.'[209] The real question is whether we have in fact got too much to contend

---

[206] Swinburne, *Providence And The Problem Of Evil*, p. 108.
[207] Thomas Aquinas, *Summa Theologica*, Question 62, Article 1.
[208] Hebblethwaite, *The Essence Of Christianity*, pp. 75–6.
[209] Harries, *C.S. Lewis: The Man And His God*, p. 38.

with, more to contend with than could possibly be reconciled with the existence of God. As a theist, Harries must think not; but in this case his complaint undermines itself. I doubt it is more morally intolerable that demons should tempt humans to sin than it is that human culture should do so, or that other people should do so. Harries' complaint adds nothing new to the traditional problem of evil, a problem that has been well and truly defused in philosophical terms.

Conclusion

Angels are at least weakly conceivable. The main reason for doubting this is the assumption of naturalism, an assumption challenged (in my judgement, beyond breaking point) by the problem of giving an adequate naturalistic account of the human mind, and by the arguments for God's existence.

A demythologized angelology is a possible (if strained) alternative to the wholesale rejection biblical authority *given sufficient reason to doubt the possibility of literal angels*. However, all of the objections to angels have been found wanting.

I will take it as read from now on that angels are *possible* and that traditional Christian angelology is therefore at least rationally permissible. Still, even if the objections to angels fail, the question remains as to whether (and why) we should believe in angels, and what we should believe about them.

In the course of rebutting arguments against angels I have already begun the task of formulating a more detailed account of the angelic nature. Having such an account makes angels not only weakly conceivable, but strongly conceivable, thereby adding to the *plausibility* of angels. I will therefore take a chapter to discuss the hypothetical *nature* of angels, before arguing that this nature is not merely a possibility, but an instantiated reality.

Chapter Three

An Angelic Assay

Bodies without minds – nothing unusual about that ... equally familiar ... are minds associated with bodies ... But minds without bodies – that is, indeed, an extraordinary prospect. Therein lies the fascination of angels.

– Mortimer J. Adler[1]

This chapter takes up the task of showing that angels are not merely *possible* (weakly conceivable), but that they are *plausible* because they are 'strongly conceivable'. Something is 'strongly conceivable' for anyone who 'judges that it is possible on the basis of a ... positive grasp of the properties involved and of the compatibility of what she is conceiving with what she already knows'.[2] To this end I will present an ontological assay of angelic nature. An assay is 'a list of the various constituents [properties, etc.] that composes some entity's being'.[3] I think that the following assay gives an approximately true picture of what angels are actually like; but in terms of arguing the case for angels this chapter should be taken as an attempt to provide a plausible conception of what angels *might be like if they exist.*

Consider the following description of an encounter with an angel:

The sound was quite astonishingly unlike a voice. It was perfectly articulate; it was even, I suppose, rather beautiful. But it was, if you understand me, inorganic ... Blood and lungs and the warm, moist cavity of the mouth are somehow indicated in every voice. Here they were not. The ... syllables sounded more as if they were played on an instrument than as if they were spoken: and yet they did not sound mechanical either. A machine is something we make out of natural materials; this was as if rock or crystal or light had spoken of itself. And it went through me from chest to groin like the

---

[1] Adler, *The Angels And Us*, p. 3.
[2] Moreland and Rae, *Body & Soul*.
[3] Ibid., p. 194.

thrill that goes through you when you think you have lost your hold while climbing a cliff.

That was what I heard. What I saw was simply a very faint rod or pillar of light. I don't think it made a circle of light either on the floor or the ceiling, but I am not sure of this. It certainly had very little power of illuminating its surroundings. So far, all is plain sailing. But it has two other characteristics which are less easy to grasp. One was its colour. Since I saw the thing I must obviously have seen it either white or coloured; but no efforts of my memory can conjure up the faintest image of what that colour was ... How it is possible to have a visual experience which immediately and ever after becomes impossible to remember, I do not attempt to explain. The other was its angle. It was not at right angles to the floor. But as soon as I have said this, I hasten to add that this way of putting it is a later reconstruction. What one actually felt at the moment was that the column of light was vertical but the floor was not horizontal – the whole room seemed to have heeled over as if it were on board ship. The impression, however produced, was that this creature had reference to some horizontal, to some whole system of directions, based outside the Earth, and that its mere presence imposed that alien system on me and abolished the terrestrial horizontal ... The fact that it was quite obviously not organic – the knowledge that intelligence was somehow located in this homogeneous cylinder of light but not related to it as our consciousness is related to our brains and nerves – was profoundly disturbing. It would not fit into our categories. The response which we ordinarily make to a living creature and that which we make to an inanimate object were here both equally inappropriate ... I felt sure that the creature was what we call 'good', but I wasn't sure whether I liked 'goodness' so much as I had supposed.

I think this is the most successful fictional encounter with an Angel (it's from C.S. Lewis's science fiction/fantasy novel *Perelandra*).[4] Interestingly, the description is largely negative. Indeed, this passage is successful *precisely because of its carefully chosen vagueness*. An angel is neither organic, nor mechanical; it is unearthly, and meeting one is not the pleasant experience some might fondly imagine. As Charles Colson writes: 'In biblical accounts angels aren't cute, pudgy babies with wings. The first thing an angel says is, "Don't be afraid." In other words, real angels are a fearsome sight.'[5] We need to purge our thoughts about Angels of guilt-by-association with personally comfortable images of diminutive cherubs. The same point, as Lewis's Screwtape reveals, goes

---

[4] cf. C.S Lewis, *Out Of The Silent Planet*, *Perelandra* and *That Hideous Strength* (London: Pan, 1989).

[5] Charles Colson, *Answers To Your Kid's Questions* (Wheaton, Illinois: Tyndale House, 2000), p. 32.

for belief in demons: 'If any faint suspicion of your existence begins to arise in his mind, suggest to him a picture of something in red tights, and persuade him that since he cannot believe in that (it is an old textbook method of confusing them) he therefore cannot believe in you.'[6] This popular image of demons is the symbolic creation of medieval art. It is a peculiarly modern mistake (born, perhaps, of too much TV) to confuse reality with symbol and to reject the former on the basis that we cannot take the latter with literal seriousness.

On the other hand, adherents of the New Age movement, as Douglas Groothuis observes, 'are not skeptics about the supernatural. If anything, they tend to be credulous.'[7] Adopting a pick-and-mix approach to their sources of information on angels, New Age followers accept everything that subjectively 'works for them'. This data (from the Bible, apocryphal literature, etc.) is then interpreted, often out of context, in the light of the New Age worldview.[8] Colson notes that the 'angels of New Age thinkers don't sound very much like the ones in Scripture ... New Agers tell of angels that appear on command ... These angels never ever confront or challenge anyone. They make no demands on our behaviour or character. These are the "imaginary guides" of the New Age movement, not real angels.'[9] Here is something that unites New Ageism and naturalism while separating both from the wisdom of pre-modernity. Pre-modernity sees our problem as conforming the mind to reality, and the solution as a humble acknowledgement of truth. For naturalism and the New Ageism alike, the problem is how to conform reality to our desires, and the solution is technique. As C.S. Lewis warned, demons are 'equally pleased by both errors and hail a materialist or a magician with the same delight'.[10] Whether the technique in question is 'the scientific method', or occult practices (e.g. 'contacting your angel/higher self'), the focus is on humanity (or the individual) proud and autonomous at the centre of a consequently hollow universe. Thus modernist scientism and postmodern New Ageism both seek knowledge (of ultimate reality, by means natural or supernatural) for the sake of shaping reality in our image, while pre-modernism seeks knowledge (of ultimate reality, by means natural and supernatural) for the sake of shaping the self in the image of ultimate reality. It is hardly surprising that naturalists and New Agers alike end

---

[6] C.S. Lewis, *The Screwtape Letters* (New York:Collier, 1982), p. 33.
[7] Groothuis, *Christianity That Counts*, p. 148.
[8] cf. Sire, *The Universe Next Door*.
[9] Colson, *Answers To Your Kid's Questions*, p. 33.
[10] Lewis, *The Screwtape Letters*.

up playing God in their different ways (the latter more literally than the former), for only the theist sees ultimate reality as a someone else worth bowing down to.

In so far as the following assay and its premises conflict with New Age angelology, and in so far as those premises and the conclusions built upon them are defensible, it should serve as a philosophical corrective; for as Douglas Groothuis warns: 'New Age "open-mindedness" notwithstanding, biblical teaching stands at odds with the New Age mindset. Not everything billed as spiritual is of the same spirit. The differences are real and important.'[11]

A handful of premises form the basis for constructing the following angelic assay:

(1) 'God' means an infinite spirit, the 'greatest possible being' (this is true by definition).
(2) Humans are more like God than anything else we know (besides angels), having a naturally embodied finite spiritual mind (cf. Chapter Two).
(3) By definition, 'angel' means a naturally unembodied, finite, spiritual person.
(4) If they exist, angels are therefore higher than mankind but lower than God in the hierarchy of types of being.
(5) By definition, Angels are wholly good and demons are evil.

Given these premises it is possible to work out (with a mixture of certainty, probability, plausibility and possibility) a great deal about angelic nature. While I will draw upon scripture to fill in the details, the reliability of scripture as a source of data is irrelevant to the usefulness of the resultant assay in proving the plausibility of angels. In terms of arguing the case for angels, I am not begging any questions. Angelology involves a measure of guesswork, but it can and should be *highly educated* guesswork. Giving a detailed conception of angels might be thought a somewhat audacious task; nevertheless, it is both possible and worthwhile. As Peter Kreeft argues:

> We don't *see* pure spirits, and we can't *imagine* them. That doesn't mean we can't *know* or *understand* them. We can see and imagine the difference between a five-sided figure (a pentagon) and a six-sided figure (a hexagon), and we can also intellectually understand that difference. We cannot, however, sense or imagine the difference between a 105-sided figure and a

---

[11] Groothuis, *Christianity That Counts*, p. 192.

106-sided figure [perhaps an angel can]. Both *look* to us simply like circles. But we can understand the difference and even measure it exactly. So we can understand some things we can't see.[12]

It is worthwhile trying to understand angels because they are intrinsically interesting, and because if we lack any assay of angels we will lack any reason to demur from even the strangest angelic theory or story. Indeed, we will lack criteria by which to judge any angelic theory or story as plausible or implausible in the first place (a fact sceptics and New Agers alike should note).

The Nature of Spirit

The existence of an angel depends upon their being created and sustained in existence by God (cf. Neh. 9:6 and Col. 1:16). There is nothing implausible in this; as atheist J.J.C. Smart admits: 'Surely an omnipotent being could have created ... spirits directly ...'[13] The name 'angel' comes from the Greek *angelos* and denotes a messenger, the function most frequently performed by Angels in the Bible. Thus Augustine noted that *Angels are spirits by nature and messengers by function.*

To define 'spirit' simply as 'an immaterial (noncorporeal) substance' is inadequate, for as Antony Flew warns: 'to characterize something as incorporeal is to make an assertion that is at one and the same time both extremely comprehensive and wholly negative.'[14] Hence J.P. Moreland and Scott B. Rae note that: 'A positive characterization of "spirit" is needed to give content to notions [about] God, angels and disembodied persons.'[15] Moreland and Rae suggest that this can be done by thinking of spirits as 'the kinds of substances that possess the ultimate capacities for thought, feeling, consciousness and active volitional power'.[16] A substance is: 'an essentially characterized particular that sustains absolute sameness through (accidental) change and that possesses a primitive unity of parts, properties and capacities or powers ...'[17] An immaterial

---

12 Kreeft, *Angels (And Demons)*, p. 39.
13 J.J.C. Smart and J.J. Haldane, *Atheism And Theism* (Oxford: Blackwell, 1996), p. 27.
14 Antony Flew in Miethe and Flew, *Does God Exist?*, p. 6.
15 Moreland and Rae, *Body & Soul*, pp. 154–5.
16 Ibid., p. 155.
17 J.P. Moreland, 'The Explanatory Relevance of Libertarian Agency' in Dembski (ed.), *Mere Creation*, p. 266.

substance with the ultimate capacities for thought, feeling, conscious-ness and active volitional power is appropriately called a *spirit*. A particularly relevant Old Testament term, frequently translated as 'spirit', is *ruach*. While *ruach* can refer to an invisible and *unconscious* power (e.g. wind) it can also refer to an invisible *conscious* power distinct from the body. Dallas Willard defines 'spirit' as *non-physical personal power*: 'Thoughts, feelings, willings and their developments are so many dimensions of this spiritual substance, which exercises a power that is outside the physical.'[18] Willard kindly provided the following comments upon his definition of 'spirit':

> The point about spiritual beings (including angels) as non-physical energy – my precise phrasing is 'unbodily personal power' – is very important ... there is no contradiction involved in the idea of non-physical or spiritual energy unless you define 'energy' in such a way that it must be a function of what is physical ... Definitions aside, anything has energy that is capable of doing work, i.e., bringing about change. Of course ideas, emotions, choices and so forth do work all the time, and without them we wouldn't be having this discussion. I know that there is a long discussion about whether or not the mind is the brain ... I have been a part of that discussion for decades ... and I think the weight of the discussion in the last decade among philosophers has definitely gone against identity [of mind with brain] ... What leads some people to think energy is a function of matter is a misreading of the equation $E=MC^2$. The universe of discourse in which this equation was developed was not energy, but matter ... it was never intended, and there was nothing that went into its proof, about energy in general. Rather, it is a statement about all of matter: namely, that the quantity of energy it contains is equal to its mass times the square of the speed of light. So, as is now said, there is enough energy in a raisin to supply New York City with electricity for one day. The equation, then, says nothing about energy in general, and it is a good thing it does not, for then its proof would have to have been different.[19]

An angel, being a spirit, clearly satisfies the classical definition of a person (by Boethius); namely that 'a person is an individual substance of a rational nature'. An angel is just as much a person as you are. A *person* can be more briefly defined as 'a conscious purposive agent'.[20] To be *conscious* means to engage in 'acts of thinking, feeling, desiring, willing, believing and knowing'.[21] To be *purposive* means 'to have desires,

---

[18] Willard, *The Divine Conspiracy*, pp. 93–4.
[19] Dallas Willard, personal correspondence.
[20] Davis, 'God's Actions' in Geivett and Habermas (eds), *In Defence Of Miracles*, p. 164.
[21] Ibid.

intentions or aims, and set out to achieve them'.[22] To be an *agent* means to be something with the ability 'to do or achieve things in the world'.[23]

The consciousness of angels

According to Moreland and Rae, there are at least five different types of conscious mental state: 'sensation, thought, belief, desire and act of will'.[24] A *sensation* is a state of awareness, such as a conscious awareness of a colour, sound, texture, smell or taste. A *thought* is 'a mental content that can be expressed as an entire sentence and that only exists while it is being thought'.[25] Thoughts have the non-physical property of being *about* something, and can have the non-physical properties of being either true or false, good or bad. A *belief* is someone's view of how things are. A *desire* is a felt inclination to do, have, avoid or experience particular things. An *act of will* is a voluntary exercise of active power. I hypothesize, on the premise that angels are persons and as such are analogous to humans, that angels have all five mental states. I will discuss each in turn.

Sensation

As persons, angels must be self-aware. Although angels have no bodies, and so no physically perceived sense data, they still have states of awareness or modes of consciousness. These states apparently include awareness of the physical world, and might including such humanly familiar things as shapes, colours, sounds, textures, smells and tastes. In a famous paper about the possibility of disembodied human existence, H.H. Price pointed out that: 'When we are asleep, sensory stimuli are cut off ... But we still manage to have experiences. It is true that sense perception no longer occurs, but something sufficiently like it does ... we are provided with a multitude of objects of awareness, about which we employ our thoughts and towards which we have desires and emotions.'[26] Something analogous to such dream perception, although corresponding to the real world, could be true of angelic sensation. We should distinguish between *imagining* (the objects of which may or may not be objectively real) and *imaging* (the objects of which are objectively

22 Ibid.
23 Ibid.
24 Moreland and Rae, *Body & Soul*, p. 158.
25 Ibid.
26 H.H. Price, 'Personal Survival and the Idea of Another World' in John Hick (ed.), *Classical And Contemporary Readings In Philosophy Of Religion* (Engelwood Cliffs, New Jersey: Prentice Hall, 1970), p. 373.

real). To have non-physical sense experiences of the physical world an angel needs to exercise a capacity of imaging, not imagination. It is hard enough to imagine what the sense experience of a cat or a dog is like, let alone what the sense experience of an angel is like; but such angelic experiences do not seem to be incoherent.

H.H. Price extended his dream-world analogy to cover meeting other disincarnate persons: 'There is no reason why an image-world should not contain a number of images which are telepathic apparitions; and if it did, one could quite intelligently speak of "meeting other persons" in such a world. All the experiences I have when I meet other persons in this present life could still occur, with only this difference, that percepts would be replaced by images.'[27] I'm not saying that this theory *does* apply to angels, only that it *could* apply. At the very least, it gives us a picture of how angels might have telepathic sense experiences of each other.

Thought

As persons, angels have intelligence: 'The word intelligent derives from two Latin words, the preposition inter, meaning "between", and the verb lego, meaning "to choose or select". Thus according to its etymology, intelligence consists in choosing between.'[28] (Playing with the children's construction toy Lego, involving as it does repeated choosing between many pieces in order to select the most appropriate brick for the task in hand, is a paradigm example of an intelligent activity.) Although not omniscient (Mt. 24:36), Angels exceed humans in intelligence (1 Pet. 1:12, 2 Pet. 2:11).

E. Michael Jones highlights the fact that: 'Far from being two mutually exclusive compartments hermetically sealed off from each other, the intellectual life turns out to be a function of the moral life of the thinker.'[29] As Proverbs puts it, as a man 'thinketh in his heart (or mind) so is he' (Prov. 23:7 AV). We know that Angels are wholly good. Therefore we know that the intellectual life of Angels is unaffected by sin, but positively affected by their moral perfection, a perfection that primarily consists in loving God with all their heart, mind and strength. As Paul writes, 'those who live in accordance with the Spirit have their minds set on what the Spirit desires' (Rom. 8:5). Angels must be good

---

[27] Ibid.

[28] William A. Dembski, 'Redesigning Science' in Dembski (ed.), *Mere Creation*, p. 112.

[29] E. Michael Jones, *Degenerate Moderns* (San Francisco: Ignatius, 1993), p. 258.

thinkers, both in the intellectual and the moral sense. Paul tells us that 'the mind controlled by the Spirit is life and peace' (Rom. 8:6); and this too surely applies to Angels.

If angels are intelligent, do they have language? Paul writes of 'the tongues ... of Angels' (1 Cor. 13:1). We learn from scripture that Angels talk not only to men and women when they are sent as God's messengers (Acts 12:8ff.), but that they talk to each other (Zech. 1:11ff). When Angels talk to a human they must of course use that human's language, either by producing effects in the hearer's mind, or by using an assumed body (a matter to be discussed later) to produce the appropriate sound waves. Among themselves and without bodies angels must communicate telepathically.

Belief

Angels have knowledge, so they must have beliefs, since knowledge requires belief. We have already noted that angels are not omniscient and that they nevertheless know more than humans know. One wonders whether Angels are infallible. In their natural state they certainly cannot be deceived by physical sense data, since they have none. Neither can their beliefs or belief forming processes be adversely affected by sin. While Angels are not necessarily infallible, it would seem that Angels are at least less fallible than humans.

Desire

As spirits, it is clear that angels have no desires for bodily pleasure or the avoidance of bodily pain, since they have no body. Nevertheless, it seems reasonable to think that angels do have inclinations (which may be felt inclinations) to do, have, avoid or experience certain things. For example, one imagines that Angels have an inflexible inclination to do the will of God, and therefore to avoid being outside the will of God. One imagines that demons have an inflexible inclination to avoid doing the will of God if possible, and thereby to ensure that they are outside of his will.[30] Demons often evince a desire to avoid judgement by Jesus, both in the New Testament and in contemporary exorcisms. It would seem to be the case that angels have emotional states.

Mortimer J. Adler infers that 'Angels cannot have acquisitive desires, for there is no way in which they can improve or perfect themselves by acquiring external goods.'[31] However, this leaves open the possibility

---

[30] Demons can never be outside of the *permissive* will of God, although they are allowed by God to exercise their freedom in opposition to his *positive* will, as are we.

[31] Adler, *The Angels And Us*, p. 138.

that angels have desires for *internal goods* such as goodness, beauty and knowledge. Of course, an Angel is already wholly good in terms of *quality*; but this does not mean an Angel cannot add to its goodness in terms of *quantity*. Knowledge is good, and so an angel who gains knowledge gains an internal good. All goodness is beautiful, and so while an Angel's beauty is as pure as its goodness, the *amount* of its internal beauty will increase along with the quantity of its knowledge or other internal good.

Act of will: active volition power

John Damascene affirmed that: 'An Angel is an intellectual substance, endowed with liberty.'[32] Being endowed with liberty means that persons are 'unmoved movers who simply have the power to act as the ultimate originators or their actions'.[33] Persons have libertarian free will, the ability to either exert or refrain from exerting active power. Or, more poetically, as Emily Dickinson wrote:

> A DEED knocks first at thought,
> And then it knocks at will.
> That is the manufacturing spot,
> And will at home and well.
> It then goes out an act,
> Or is entombed so still
> That only to the ear of God
> Its doom is audible.[34]

As we have already seen, according to traditional angelology angels were created with the power to freely choose the good of loving God or the evil of rejecting him. Since wholly good beings would have no power to sin by rejecting God, this theory requires us to posit a certain original and divinely intended imperfection in the primordial angelic nature. This original imperfection contributed to an overall good state of affairs, being the necessary precondition of angelic freedom to love God and to be transformed by grace into a sinless mode of existence. Some angels chose to love God and were confirmed by God's grace in a state of total moral goodness, thus becoming Angels. Other angels rejected God

---

[32] Quoted by Fr. Pascal P. Parente, *The Angels* (Rockford, Illinois: Tan, 1994), p. 35.

[33] Moreland and Rae, *Body & Soul*, pp. 129–30.

[34] Emily Dickinson, 'The Deed', *The Complete Poems Of Emily Dickinson* (Boston: Little, Brown, 1924).

and became demons, falling further down the path of imperfection made possible by their original estate. As C.S. Lewis wrote:

> All angels … are equally 'Supernatural' in relation to *this* spatio-temporal Nature, i.e. they are outside it and have powers and a mode of existence which it could not provide. But the good angels lead a life which is Supernatural in another sense as well. That is to say, they have, of their own free will, offered back to God in love the 'natures' He gave them at their creation. All creatures of course live from God in the sense that He made them and at every moment maintains them in existence. But there is a further and higher kind of 'life from God' which can be given only to a creature who voluntarily surrenders himself to it. This life the good angels have and the bad angels have not: and it is absolutely Supernatural because no creature in any world can have it by the mere fact of being the sort of creature it is.[35]

While original moral imperfection was a necessary precondition of angels freely choosing to love God, imperfection is not a necessary condition of free will per se. God is morally perfect and has free will! God is free to choose between any and all equally good states of affair. God's loving nature was exercised in the fact that he chose to create although he was under no obligation so to do. God could have created spiritual beings with wholly good moral characters, but then they would not have been free to *choose* whether or not to love God. A 'love' that is not freely given is not worthy of the name. Thus God freely created finite spiritual beings who could freely choose an existence that precludes the freedom to sin but which includes the freedom to choose between any and all volitional acts within their power that are good. This is the freedom currently enjoyed by Angels, and there is nothing incoherent about asserting that Angels are both wholly good and endowed with free will (this is presumably the type of freedom to be enjoyed by humans in Heaven).

Acts of active volitional power, whether originated by a human, an angel, or by God, are supernatural occurrences: 'When an agent exercises libertarian agency, the act is supernatural in the sense that it cannot be subsumed under a law of nature plus initial conditions, and in this sense agent acts transcend nature.'[36] Hence C.S. Lewis writes that 'The rational part of every man is supernatural in … the same sense in which *both* angels and devils are supernatural.'[37] Any supernatural act

---

[35] Lewis, *Miracles*, p. 180.
[36] J.P. Moreland, 'The Explanatory Relevance of Libertarian Agency' in Dembski (ed.), *Mere Creation*, p. 287.
[37] Lewis, *Miracles*.

in causal contact with the natural realm is a temporary exception to the natural order of things; that is, to what would have happened if the supernatural cause had not acted. Thus we should see the actions of rational agents 'in terms of libertarian agency and believe that free acts leave *scientifically detectable gaps* in the natural world'.[38] However, as Lewis pointed out, once a supernatural act has been performed, subsequent events proceed according to natural law: 'If events ever come from beyond nature altogether she will [not] be incommoded by them ... The moment it enters her realm it will obey all the natural laws.'[39] Hence my arm, when I cease to make it rise, quite naturally falls to my side; and a tombstone, rolled away by an angel, when released from the angelic power, quite naturally falls to the ground (Jn. 20:1).

Persons can engage in basic and non-basic actions. Non-basic actions, like constructing a set of shelves, are done by doing other actions (hammering, screwing, etc.). Basic actions are actions done without the performance of any intermediary action. When an agent performs a basic action they begin by conceiving an ultimate, teleological end they intend to accomplish, and then they freely and immediately bring about that state of affairs. For example, when I wave hello to someone I simply conceive the goal of waving hello and then freely exercise my ability as an agent to wave hello. When God created the cosmos he conceived the cosmos as an end he would achieve and freely exercised his omnipotence to bring it about that the cosmos began to exist and was sustained in existence. While human basic acts are restricted to the movement of an individual body, the basic actions of angels, like God's basic actions, are not thus limited. On the other hand, when an agent performs a non-basic action they begin by conceiving of an ultimate, teleological end they intend to accomplish, then they conceive of various sub-acts they need to perform as means to their ultimate end, and then they freely perform each sub-act in order to achieve their intended goal. As agents angels are able to perform both basic and non-basic actions.

Can angels act to produce effects in the natural world? It is strongly conceivable that if angels existed, they could interact with matter. Besides, intending to raise your arm brings it about that your arm raises, and sitting on a pin causes you to feel pain, so spirit–matter interaction is perfectly intelligible in that it obviously takes place every day in humans:

---

[39] Lewis, *Miracles*, p. 63.

[38] J.P. Moreland, 'Science, Miracles, Agency Theory and the God-of-the-Gaps' in Geivett and Habermas (eds), *In Defence Of Miracles*, p. 143.

I have no idea (nor even a very firm opinion) whether psycho kinesis actually occurs, but I am quite sure that it is conceivable – that the notion of psycho kinesis is coherent. And if it is conceivable, it seems a short step to hold similarly that an immaterial thing [such as an angel] can conceivably cause physical events to occur – to act as an agent ... It does not seem that anyone is in a position to insist dogmatically that no event in the physical world can be brought about by an immaterial thing. After all, it is a crucial tenet of mind-body dualism that this sort of thing commonly occurs.[40]

How an angel can be the immaterial cause of a material effect is no more mysterious in principle than how the human mind can cause material effects (e.g. my typing this chapter), or how an immaterial God can cause the existence of the entire universe. There may be little else to be said in any of these cases besides that effects are brought about by acts of volition within the range of an agent's power.

Angels and space

The infamous question about how many angels can stand on the head of a pin was never asked by any medieval theologian. Nevertheless, this mocking question has a serious point and a serious answer 'that follows from the consideration of how an angel, lacking a body, occupies a particular place'.[41] Being immaterial, although angels may be in definite places or make things happen in definite places, this is 'not because angels are present there as matter but because they are spiritually present'.[42] What does it mean for someone to be 'spiritually present'? Since spirit is mind and will, 'spiritual presence is attention and willing'.[43] Spiritual presence for angels is analogous to that of humans or God, with these differences, that human spiritual presence (at least on earth) is mediated through the limited perspective provided by embodiment, and God's spiritual presence is unlimited. God is omnipresent, a term that means being spiritually present *to* everywhere and everything. By contrast, angels and humans have a limited capacity for spiritual presence, although the capacity is greater in angels than in humans. The answer to the question 'How many angels can "stand" on the head of a pin?' is therefore 'However many can be spiritually present to the head of a pin at one and the same time.' The relationship between angels and space

---

[40] Davis, 'God's Actions' in Geivett and Habermas (eds), *In Defence Of Miracles*, p. 170.
[41] Adler, *The Angels And Us*, p. 19.
[42] Kreeft, *Angels (And Demons)*, p. 68.
[43] Ibid.

according to traditional angelology as summarized by Fr Pascal P. Parente: 'An Angel ... is said to be present or localized in a particular place ... by virtue of his power being applied to a specific object or a particular place ... he does not fill or occupy space ... His presence in a place is determined, and occasionally made known, by his activity there and not by his substance ...'[44] It would seem to follow that an angel *needn't* have a spatial location even in this analogous sense, for an angel could surely refrain from exercising its power of thought or activity on any object whatsoever and focus its entire attention upon something immaterial, such as an idea in its mind, on itself, on another angel, or on God. Hence it is perfectly possible for angels to exist in the absence of any space–time continuum (just as it is possible for God so to do).

In the process of arguing for the existence of the human soul, Richard Swinburne reasons:

> A person has a body if there is one particular chunk of matter through which he has to operate on and learn about the world. But suppose that ... a man now finds himself no longer able to operate on the world, nor to acquire true beliefs about it; yet still to have a full mental life, some of it subject to his voluntary control. He would be disembodied. Or suppose, alternatively, that he finds himself able to operate on and learn about the world within some small finite region, without having to use one particular chunk of matter for this purpose. He might find himself with knowledge of the position of objects in a room (perhaps by having visual sensations, perhaps not), and able to move such objects just like that, in the ways in which we know about the positions of our limbs and can move them. But the room would not be, as it were, the person's body; for we may suppose that simply by choosing to do so he can ... shift the focus of his knowledge and control, e.g. to the next room. The person would be in no way limited to operating and learning through one particular chunk of matter. Hence he would have no body. The supposition that a person who is currently a man might become disembodied ... seems coherent.[45]

If such a scenario is coherent when applied to an initially embodied human spirit, it is certainly coherent when applied to an originally un-embodied spirit (an angel).

One might well ask what explains the specific extent of an angel's ability to operate on and learn about the world, and I think that the only answer is that God must simply freely choose what powers any

---

[44] Parente, *The Angels*, p. 37.

[45] Richard Swinburne, *The Evolution Of The Soul* (Oxford: Clarendon Press, 1986), p. 152.

particular angelic nature has. We might conjecture that God has reasons for creating angels of various capacities, according to his various purposes for them.

Since the 'location' of an angel is determined 'by virtue of its power being applied to a specific object or a particular place',[46] an angel can pass from one location to another 'with the rapidity of thought'.[47] Hence angelic motion 'is not really locomotion but merely an instantaneous change of place ... His motion consists in transferring his attention and activity from one object to another without having to pass successively through the intermediate places and space. He can, however, follow a continuous motion through space when his activity demands it.'[48] The idea that angels can move instantaneously from one place to another in this sense goes back to Aquinas. Mortimer J. Adler tells of how, when he explained this concept to the quantum physicist Niels Bohr, he was amazed and said, 'That's exactly the point of modern quantum theory. So a thirteenth-century theologian discovered one of the basic principles of modern nuclear physics seven hundred years ago!'[49] As Peter Kreeft says, 'Aquinas deduced from philosophical principles a kind of movement that modern science induced from observation and experiment.'[50]

Angels and time

Angels and demons are 'immortal creatures'.[51] As such, they neither reproduce nor die a natural death (Lk. 20:36) as do humans. This means they have a great deal of experience at performing their angelic or demonic work.[52] Nevertheless, angels are temporal creatures. Would the belief that angels existed before the cosmos (cf. Job 38:4–7) conflict with the unity of time and space in Einsteinian physics? It would not: 'It is coherently conceivable that something has temporal extension, in virtue of extending over time, even though that thing is not extended in physical space. It is not self-contradictory, on other words, to hold that something is temporally extended but not a body.'[53] As William Lane

---

[46] Parente, *The Angels*, p. 38.

[47] Ibid.

[48] Ibid.

[49] Adler, *The Angels And Us.*

[50] Kreeft, *Angels (And Demons)*, p. 70.

[51] *Catechism Of The Catholic Church*, p. 76.

[52] It also means that as the human population increases there are fewer angels and demons per head of population.

[53] Paul K. Moser and David Yandell, 'Farewell to philosophical naturalism' in Craig and Moreland (eds), *Naturalism: A Critical Analysis*, p. 4.

Craig argues: 'An un-embodied consciousness that experienced a succession of mental states, say by counting, would be temporal; that is to say, time would in such a case exist, and that wholly in the absence of any physical process.'[54] Medieval theologians coined the term *aeveternity* for angelic time: 'Unlike eternity, it has a beginning and a before and after; but unlike the time of material creatures, it is not measured by matter or space, and it has no ending.'[55]

Angelic numbers and organization

There is scant evidence to answer the question as to how many angels there are. Jesus says to Peter, 'Do you think I cannot call on my Father, and he will at once put at my disposal more than twelve legions of angels?' (Mt. 26:53). A 'legion' was composed of around six thousand men, so 'more than twelve legions' means over seventy-two thousand Angels. This gives us a lower limit to the number of Angels. The book of Revelation speaks of 'thousands upon thousands, and ten thousands times ten thousand' of Angels worshipping before the throne of God (Rev. 5:11); but since Revelation is highly symbolic it is doubtful that this number (a little over 100 million) is meant literally. The Greek word for 'ten thousand' (*myrios*) that appears in this passage probably indicates simply a number too large to be counted by ordinary means.

As for demons, 'Scripture never gives us the number of demons that exist.'[56] However, there are some clues. Paul says that Gentile idolaters are worshipping demons when they worship their idols (1 Cor. 10:20–21), and even assuming that demons are behind only a fraction of idol worship we are probably left with a large number. When Jesus exorcises the tomb-dwelling man from the region of Gerasene, what was apparently a single evil spirit reveals: 'My name is Legion ... for we are many' (Mk. 5:9). When Jesus allows these demons to enter a nearby herd of pigs, 'The herd, about two thousand in number, rushed down the steep bank into the lake and were drowned' (Mk. 5:13). If we assume that one pig equals one demon, we will conclude that there are at least about two thousand demons. Indeed, since it is unlikely that all the demons in existence would have possessed this one man, we would be led to infer that there are probably many more than two thousand demons. However, it is not certain that one drowned pig equals one demon, since it is surely possible that the drowning of an entire herd could be

---

[54] William Lane Craig, 'Design and the Cosmological Argument' in Dembski (ed.), *Mere Creation*, p. 350.

[55] Kreeft, *Angels (And Demons)*, p. 93.

[56] Ibid., p. 73.

accomplished by only a few demons. We cannot, therefore, confidently affirm anything on the basis of this incident beyond the existence of 'many' demons. Last but not least, Mary Magdalene had seven demons exorcised from her by Jesus. In the final analysis then, we should admit our ignorance and rest with the knowledge that whatever the number of fallen angels, they are no match for God.

Angels are apparently organized into different ranks or groups (Jude 9; Lk. 1:19). Whether these angelic ranks are merely different offices, or whether they correspond to different types of angel, it is hard to say. It may be that some angels are more powerful than others. Just how many ranks or types of angel one thinks there are mainly depends upon how one interprets the various spiritual powers listed by Paul in Ephesians 6. I think that the terms 'angels', 'archangels', 'cherubim' and 'seraphim' all refer to different angelic ranks, and that terms such as 'powers' and 'thrones' refer to the fallen, inter-subjective, corporate spirituality of human institutions.

There is little indication that demons imitate the ranking of Angels, other that they are dominated by Satan. It may well be that some demons concern themselves with corrupting and using the corporate reality of institutions. However, 'indicating clearly distinct classes or ranks of an angelic hierarchy is a difficult and speculative task.'[57]

Angelic appearances

Since angels are bodiless spirits they have no appearance in themselves; they are invisible. It's not that angels have bodies that can't be seen (like the invisible man), but that *they have no body to be seen*. Nevertheless, they can apparently cause themselves to look like anything they want, either by manipulating our imaginations or, as has already been mentioned in passing, by 'assuming' a body. Peter Kreeft calls this 'putting on disguises',[58] but I think a better description would be 'putting on appearances'. Given that angels have this ability, there would seem to be no intrinsic limitation on the appearance they adopt. Rather, they may simply adopt whatever appearance is most suitable for the occasion. Suitability would seem to be dictated, at least in part, by the expectations of those appeared to. Thus it is no surprise that in the Bible angels often appear simply as young men dressed in white, or that in modern reports angels have wildly differing appearances. I suppose that the modern-day equivalent of a young man dressed in white might very well be a young man or woman dressed in jeans and a T-shirt! The

---

[57] Oropeza, *99 Answers To Questions About Angels*, p. 25.
[58] Kreeft, *Angels (and Demons)*, p. 68.

important point is that there is nothing impossible or even implausible about an Angel adopting either a real or an apparent appearance. According to Moreland and Rae:

> your natural kind is 'human person,' and it is essential to you that you belong to that kind. However, it is not essential to being a human person that you are embodied. Rather, it is essential to being a human person that you have the natural capacities for informing and developing a body. When science studies your body, it studies the actualisation of capacities for embodiment within the soul. It is necessary for a human being that it have these capacities, but it is not necessary that these capacities are actualised.[59]

Nevertheless, humans begin their existence as embodied souls, and although the Bible indicates that humans pass through a temporary state of disembodied existence between death and resurrection, we will continue our existence in the new heaven and earth as souls embodied in 'spiritual bodies'. Hence the human mind is primarily intended and designed by God for embodied existence, this being its most natural state:

> What it means for a person to be embodied is for a person to bear some of the following relations to his or her body, relations I characterize in the first person. I am sensorially bound up with my body in that I feel with these fingers and this skin, I see with these eyes, smell with this nose, eat and taste with this mouth, hear with these ears. I can have some sensory apprehension of the inside of my body ... as when I feel my heartbeat or have a stomach ache ... it is by means of my body as a whole that I interact with other persons and material objects. In my acting in the world, my body is transparent to my intentions in the sense that ... I can ... act in a basic, nonmediated fashion ...[60]

Angels, on the other hand, do not begin their existence as embodied beings, and (as far as we know) are not destined for eternal embodiment, not even with a 'spiritual body'. Hence angels are not primarily intended or designed by God for embodied existence. As a matter of course then, angels are persons who do not normally stand in any of the above relations to any particular body whatsoever. As we have seen, this is a perfectly coherent, strongly conceivable state of affairs; even if it is rather difficult to imagine. However, an angel might none the less

---

[59] Moreland and Rae, *Body & Soul*, p. 175.
[60] Charles Taliaferro, *Consciousness And The Mind Of God* (Cambridge: Cambridge University Press, 1994), pp. 116–17.

possess the ultimate capacities necessary for embodiment. This means that it is perfectly coherent to imagine that an angel might become embodied, certainly temporarily. Indeed, it would seem from the biblical data that Angels do indeed become temporarily embodied with human bodies. As Peter Kreeft charmingly puts it: 'Angels sometimes "assume" bodies, as we would put on a costume or hire a tuxedo or a limo.'[61] In fact, it would seem that the best hypothesis given the data is that when angels become embodied they are embodied *in spiritual bodies*, that is, in bodies like that of the resurrected Jesus and like those to be received by humans upon our resurrection. On other occasions however, it is possible that angels influence our imagination by telepathy: 'Then it *looks* as if there is a body there, but there isn't. In this case, a camera would not record anything. It would in the first case, if they "assumed" bodies.'[62] Such assumed bodies 'are not literal, living human bodies. They did not come out of a mother's womb. They don't *have* to eat or breathe. They did not grow; they were manufactured ... They are masks.'[63]

It would seem to be the case that demons cannot assume bodies. B.J. Oropeza observes: 'there is no biblical reference to demons' manifesting themselves physically.'[64] There are two possible explanations for this fact. The first explanation is that the angelic fall somehow impaired a natural angelic potentiality for temporary embodiment, or that this ability was only bestowed upon angels who did not reject God. On this explanation the difference between Angels and demons when it comes to bodies is intrinsic. The second explanation is that God manufactures the bodies assumed by Angels, and that God refuses to manufacture bodies for demons to assume. On this explanation the idioplastic difference between Angels and demons is extrinsic. Occam's Razor enjoins us to accept the latter, extrinsic theory, because it is simpler to assign the power of creating bodies to God alone than it is to attribute it to angels as well. One might speculate that it is due to the non-availability of divinely created bodies to assume that demons seek to inhabit human bodies through possession. As C.S. Lewis mused: 'I don't think evil, in the strict sense, can create, but it can spoil something that Another has created.'

---

61   Kreeft, *Angels (And Demons)*, p. 52.
62   Ibid.
63   Ibid.
64   Oropeza, *99 Answers To Questions About Angels*, p. 74.

Angelic gender

Angels do not marry: 'At the resurrection people will neither marry nor be given in marriage; they will be like the angels in heaven' (Mt. 22:30; cf. Mk. 12:25). The image of God in humanity is divided into masculine and feminine aspects such that marriage offers a fuller picture of God than the individual (Gen. 1:26–7). Since Angels do not marry, and since Angels are made in God's image (they are persons), one might conjecture that Angels are neither masculine nor feminine, but that each Angel encompasses and unifies both masculinity and femininity. It is true that Angels who appear in the Bible are consistently male. However, we cannot apply our habitual association between physical appearance and gender on the basis of how Angels assuming bodies in the midst of a patriarchal society choose to appear.

Transcendental Assay

Another way to approach an understanding of the angels is through the elucidation and application of the traditional transcendental values of truth, goodness and beauty. C.E.M. Joad described these values well.

> In regard to the nature of Value, the traditional view ... seems to me to be correct. The Values, on this view, reduce themselves to three, Goodness, Truth and Beauty ... they are both objective in the sense that they are found by the human mind ... and not projected into things or contributed to them by our own minds, and ultimate, in the sense that whatever we value can be shown to be valued because of the relation of the thing valued to some one or other of the three Values. Thus while other things are valued as means to one or other of these three, *they* are valued as ends in themselves.
>
> Moreover, these Values are not just arbitrary, pieces of cosmic furniture lying about ... but are revelations of a unity that underlies them, are, in fact, the ways in which God reveals Himself to man ...[65]

The Old Testament word for 'truth', *emeth*, indicates reliability and fidelity of character, whether in behaviour (Gen. 24:49), promises (2 Sam. 7:28), or just laws (Neh. 9:13). In the Bible 'Truth is first a matter of inner character and only derivatively a quality of words and deeds.'[66] According to Os Guinness:

---

[65] C.E.M. Joad, *The Recovery Of Belief* (London: Faber and Faber, 1951), p. 177.
[66] Ibid., p. 34.

character was traditionally understood as the inner form that makes anyone or anything what it is – whether a person, a wine, or a historical period ... Character was the deep selfhood, the essential stuff a person is made of, the core reality in which thoughts, words, decisions, behaviour, and relationships are rooted. As such, character determined behaviour just as behaviour demonstrated character.[67]

Character is thus a matter of the heart and mind, a matter of the spirit. Angels clearly have character. The derivative use of *emeth* to refer to the reliable nature of statements that 'tell it how it is', statements of good character, grew out of the use of *emeth* to refer to a character that is oriented towards truth in being honest and reliable.

Thus the biblical concept of truth is inherently ethical: 'It is because truth is conformity to fact that confidence may be placed in it or in the one who asserts it, and it is because a person is faithful that he or she would be careful to make statements that are true.'[68]

In the New Testament the concept of fidelity is carried more by *pistos* (faithful) than by *alethes* (true), although the link between *pistos* and *epist*emology (the theory of truth and knowledge) is apparent. Biblically speaking, epistemology is the study of how our beliefs can be faithful to reality. Christians have thus traditionally accepted the description of truth provided by the Greek philosopher Aristotle: 'If one says of what is that it is, or of what is not that it is not, he speaks the truth; but if one says of what is that it is not, or of what is not that it is, he does not speak the truth.' The Herodians said to Jesus, 'we know that you are a man of integrity [truth – *alethes*], and that you teach the way of God in accordance with the truth' (Mt. 22:16), implying that Jesus' personal fidelity underlay the truth of his assertions about God. After all, it is common sense to be wary of claims made by one who is an habitual liar, and to take with due seriousness the words of people judged likely to be 'in the know'. Angels are good messengers (as their name denotes) because the truth of their message is guaranteed by the moral truthfulness of their character. Of course, when accepting an angelic message one must first check that the message is being given by an Angel and not a demon! One point to note here is that Angels give messages from God, not from themselves. Secondly, if the angel has assumed a body, one knows that it therefore is not a demon (because demons cannot assume

---

[67] Os Guinness, *Time For Truth* (Leicester: IVP, 2000), p. 49.

[68] Roger Nicole, 'The Biblical Concept of Truth' in D.A. Carson and John D. Woodbridge (eds), *Scripture And Truth* (Grand Rapids, Michigan: Zondervan, 1983), p. 290.

bodies). Finally, a genuine Angelic message will never contradict the Bible, as the message of many New Age 'angels' do.[69]

Good and evil exist, and are pertinent both to our search for truth and to our handling of the truth: 'we cannot divorce morality from truth and reason', writes Keith Ward, for 'the disinterested pursuit of truth is itself a normative, moral obligation. It is one of our chief moral obligations to seek truth and to be reasonable.'[70] Truth demands honesty; honesty not only in the sense of telling the truth as one sees it (unless to do so infringes a greater obligation), but honesty in the sense of being prepared to have that true *'under standing'* which is the virtuous desire and ability to *stand under* the authority of the truth as that which *ought* to be believed. Thus, the more one understands about God, the more truth one can and must stand under. As wholly good beings, Angels must stand under all the truth that they understand.

'Virtue epistemology' stresses the importance of moral values in the pursuit of cognitive excellence: 'Thinking about epistemology as encompassing the pursuit of intellectual virtue, while presently unfashionable, was the dominant way of casting epistemological concerns in the writings of Aristotle, Augustine, Thomas Aquinas and other philosophers of the ancient and medieval tradition.'[71] This tradition recognizes that 'If we fail to oversee our intellectual life and cultivate virtue, the likely consequences will be a maimed and stunted mind that thwarts our prospects for living a flourishing life.'[72] As W. Jay Wood explains:

> A vicious moral character can undermine good thinking just as effectively as some physical disability. The two-way causal connection between right thinking and morality, between the intellectual and moral virtues, is a prominent motif that runs through many religious traditions; it is also attested by common sense. Arrogance, dishonesty, pride, pugnacity, laziness and many other vices undermine our ability to think well ... We cannot be fully intellectually virtuous without also being morally virtuous ... When we

---

[69] cf. Patty Tunnicliffe, 'What in Heaven's Name? An Analysis of the Messages and World Views Coming from Aliens and Modern Day Angels' @ < http:// ses.edu/journal/issue2_1/2_1tunnicliffe.htm >

[70] Keith Ward, *The Battle For The Soul* (London: Hodder & Stoughton), p. 70.

[71] W. Jay Wood, *Epistemology* (Leicester: Apollos, 1998), pp. 16–17. Peter Kreeft notes: 'Virtue comes from the Latin word *virtus*, which meant manliness, or virility. Thus, as one wag notes, the word which used to mean a man's ability to impregnate a woman ... came to mean a woman's ability not to be impregnated by a man.' Kreeft, *Back to Virtue*, prelims.

[72] Wood, *Epistemology*, p. 17.

succeed in harmonizing these aspects of our lives, we achieve what ancients and moderns alike call integrity.[73]

A person's virtue (or lack thereof) can have an effect upon the functioning of their cognitive apparatus, just as brain damage would affect their computational abilities: 'proper cognitive functioning (and ultimately intellectual virtue) requires that we function properly on a moral and emotional level as well. In order to function properly in the sense necessary for warrant, we must pay attention to our emotions and other facets of our interior life, such as the disposition of our wills and moral characters.'[74] Thomas Dubay relates how '[John Henry] Newman once observed ... that worldly people commonly make the fatal error of assuming that they have the capacity and right to judge religious truth without a preparation of their hearts by virtuous living. This is like a tone-deaf critic claiming to pass judgement on a Mozart concerto or symphony.'[75] Virtues are:

> the qualities ... and characteristics that make a man or woman true, good, and beautiful as a person ... A virtue is a power to be and to act, to live a gospel goodness such as love, patience, chastity, honesty, affability, magnanimity, justice, humility ... A deep rootedness in these gospel goodnesses brings a progressive freedom from ... egocentrism and ugly addictions. One is liberated to live gloriously and with growing delight ...[76]

Growth in virtue is growth in the fruit of the Holy Spirit. As Paul writes: 'we, who with unveiled faces all reflect the Lord's glory, are being transformed into his likeness with ever-increasing glory, which comes from the Lord, who is the Spirit' (2 Cor. 3:18). The Holy Spirit is the divine gardener, growing in us his fruit (this fruit is one fruit with many aspects, like a blackberry): 'the fruit of the Spirit is love, joy, peace, patience, kindness, goodness, faithfulness, gentleness and self-control' (Gal. 5:22–3). Not that we become perfect overnight; but we should see change in the right direction over time. Angels, being wholly good by the grace of God must be characterized by the fruit of the Spirit, and by its wholeness. Angels are consistently described as holy by scripture

---

[73] Ibid., pp. 17, 19.

[74] Ibid., p. 174.

[75] Thomas Dubay, *The Evidential Power Of Beauty* (San Francisco: Ignatius, 1999), p. 271. Aristotle wrote: 'It is not possible to be good in the strict sense without practical wisdom, nor practically wise without moral virtue' (*Ethics*, 6.1144.30).

[76] Dubay, *The Evidential Power Of Beauty*, pp. 243–4.

(e.g. Mk. 8:38; Lk. 9:26; Acts 10:22; Rev. 14:10). For a creature to be 'holy' means, in part, for it to display the opposite of multiplicity:

> Holiness is so named because it represents wholeness or unity of personality. God is eminently holy and His saints are holy to the degree they emulate Him ... Multiplicity is fragmentation, fractionalization, dispersion, dividedness. It is captured in the colloquial expression 'going to pieces.' Multiplicity in this sense also corresponds to the notion of diabolical, which literally means 'going off in opposite directions.'[77]

Integrity is necessary for a creature to be or become what it is intended to be by its creator. Its moral value is seen in the fact that 'Although we often lack integrity in ourselves, we are usually quick to recognize and denounce it in others ... We detest phoniness, hypocrisy, duplicity, double-dealing, and disingenuousness. We admire integrity, though we know that it often comes at a high price.'[78]

Objective goodness is objectively beautiful, and objective beauty is objectively good. To do a good or obligatory action is to do a beautiful action. In ancient Hebrew there is a linguistically enshrined recognition that goodness and beauty are intertwined. In the book of Genesis: 'God saw all that he had made, and it was very good.' (Gen. 1:31) The word translated here as 'good' 'may mean 'fitting' or 'beautiful' amongst a wide range of meanings.[79] God's affirmation of creation in Genesis might therefore be translated as: 'God saw all that he had made, and it was very beautiful.' Clearly, there is a priority of goodness over beauty that makes the 'very good' translation preferable; however, the full meaning of the text will be missed if we do not bear in mind that creation is affirmed as being both good *and* beautiful. In the Greek translation of the Old Testament the word *kalos* is used for the word we can translate as 'good' or 'beautiful'. The Authorised Version of the Bible usually translates *kalos* as 'good', and occasionally as 'honest' (e.g. Rom. 12:17; 2 Cor. 8:21). 'Honest' in this context is used in its Latin sense of *honestus*, meaning '*handsome, gracious, fair to look upon*'.[80] Cicero defined that which is *honestus* as being: 'such that even if its utility is taken away, and even if any rewards and fruits which come from it are removed, it can still be praised for its own sake'. That which is *honestus* (and by implication, that which is *kalos*) is an end in itself and not merely

---

[77] Donald Demarco, 'The Virtue of Integrity' @ < http://catholiceducation.org/articles/religion/re0352.html >

[78] Ibid.

[79] Forster and Marston, *Reason, Science And Faith*, p. 258.

[80] William Barclay, *New Testament Words* (London: SCM, 1964), p. 151.

a means to an end, intrinsically and not merely instrumentally good, and thereby beautiful. As G.E. Moore put it: 'the beautiful should be *defined as that of which the admiring contemplation is good in itself.*'[81]

It has been said that the modern word that comes nearest to *kalos* is the Scots word *bonnie*. In John's Gospel Jesus calls himself 'the good [*kalos*] shepherd' (Jn. 10:11). *kalos* describes the objective beauty of an objectively virtuous character and of the objectively good actions that spring from such a character: 'We may best of all see the meaning of *kalos*, if we contrast it with *agathos* which is the common Greek word for good ... When a thing or person is *agathos*, it or he is good in the moral and practical sense of the term, and in the result of its or his activity; but *kalos* adds to the idea of goodness the idea of beauty ...'[82] *agathos* refers to moral and instrumental goodness (instrumental goodness is being good for achieving a goal). The moral sense of *agathos* is employed in John's Gospel when a crowd is debating who Jesus is: 'Among the crowds there was widespread whispering about him. Some said, "He is a good [*agathos*] man" ' (Jn. 7:12). *kalos* regards the good not only as ethically or pragmatically good (*agathos*), but also as aesthetically good. For example, in talking about how a tree is known by its fruit, Jesus says: 'Make a tree good [*kalos*] and its fruit will be good [*kalos*], or make a tree bad and its fruit will be bad; for a tree is recognised by its fruit ... The good [*agathos*] man brings good things out of the good stored up in him, and the evil man brings evil things out of the evil stored up in him' (Mt. 12:33–35). It stands to reason that no one can be *agathos* in the moral sense without simultaneously being *kalos*, no one can be good without being, in respect of their goodness, beautiful. Angels must be both *agathos* and *kalos*, and Milton was right to write how:

> Abash'd the devil stood,
> and felt how awful goodness is, and saw
> Virtue in her shape how lovely.[83]

Colin McGinn notes that judgements of moral character are often expressed using aesthetic predicates, and interprets this 'as reflecting our implicit commitment to the view that goodness and badness of character

---

[81] G.E. Moore, *Principia Ethica* (Amhurst, New York: Prometheus, 1994). cf. Lewis, *The Abolition Of Man*.

[82] Barclay, *New Testament Words*, p. 145.

[83] *The Macmillan Dictionary Of Religious Quotations*, compiled by Margaret Pepper (London: Macmillan, 1996).

are allied to aesthetic qualities of the person'.[84] If one seeks goodness, one will also develop a beautiful soul: 'seek first his kingdom and his righteousness, and all these things [including inner beauty] will be given to you as well' (Mt. 6:33). Hence, McGinn concludes, 'virtues and vices *give rise* to aesthetic properties of the soul that bears them ... Virtue equals beauty plus the soul ... The particular kind of beauty proper to the soul is what virtue consists in.'[85] In the case of angels we can say that spirit plus virtue equals beauty. The aesthetic theory of virtue has a long Christian tradition: 'Hildegard [of Bingen] described a life of virtue as taking on the brilliant beauty of the stars ... throughout Hildegard's letters, books, and songs, the virtuous life always leads to beauty.'[86] Hildegard taught that: 'knowledge of eternal life is diffused by both [awe] and love of God, which reaches from a person's inner heart to his face.'[87] Perhaps this explains why angelic appearances are uniformly beautiful. Goodness of character equals beauty of spirit. A beautiful soul points to the truth of the good that formed its beauty. Thomas Dubay writes: 'The most beautiful men and women on earth, the saints, are what they are solely because of their complete Yes to the person, teaching, and grace of the crucified risen One. Each of the notes of the matchless symphony that is his doctrine and moral pattern of life is a tribute to the same Lord.'[88] Thus Angels are beautiful because of their complete 'Yes' to God and their beauty is a symphony of praise to the Lord of Hosts. Angels possess truth, knowledge, goodness and beauty in complete purity; an amazing concept that only leads us on to contemplate the fact that God possesses all these 'great making properties' *to the maximal possible degree*!

Satan and Other Demons

The term for an evil spirit, 'Demon', comes from the Greek *daimon*, which originally meant merely 'supernatural being' or 'spirit' and was used of any and all spiritual beings besides God. For example, the Greek philosopher Plato 'used *daimon* of divinity and fate, and regarded the *daimons* as intermediate beings'. [89] Indeed, 'Belief in demons is not

---

[84] Colin McGinn, *Ethics, Evil And Fiction* (Oxford: Clarendon Press, 1999).

[85] Ibid., p. 97.

[86] Goria Durka, *Praying With Hildegard Of Bingen* (Winona, Minnesota: Saint Mary's Press, 1991), pp. 53, 55.

[87] Ibid., p. 54.

[88] Dubay, *The Evidential Power Of Beauty*, p. 306.

[89] Peter G. Bolt, 'Jesus, the Daimons and the Dead' in Lane (ed.), *The Unseen World*, p. 79.

connected with any particular view of the cosmos. Demons have a very wide geographical and lengthy historical role as spiritual beings influencing man in his relationship to the sacred or holy.'[90] However, the New Testament uses *daimon* only of *evil* spiritual beings.

Peter Kreeft notes that believing in Satan 'means believing in (1) supernatural, (2) moral, (3) spiritual, (4) personal, (5) evil, and at least one of these five is usually denied'.[91] The reader should by now have a good idea of how all five elements of belief in the existence of Satan can be defended. None of the positions entailed by the rejection of these five elements is particularly appealing:

> (1) Some are naturalists who do not believe in moral evil (sin), only physical evil (pain). (2) Some are amoralists who have a phobia against judge-mentalism (i.e., moral law). (3) Most are Gnostics, who identify spirit with goodness (and thus, implicitly, matter with evil, though they no longer say that, as the original Gnostics did), so to them spiritual evil is an oxymoron. (4) Others are Marxists, Socialists, or other leftists who do not believe in personal evil but only evil social and economic systems and institutions (I wonder where they think these came from?). (5) Finally, and most desperately, cockeyed optimists do not believe in evil at all.[92]

As Kreeft goes on to say: 'The most influential man who ever lived did not fit into any of these five categories, so he was allowed to believe in the Devil. In fact, he not only believed in the Devil, He knew him quite personally from direct experience. Even more, He created him and watched him fall.'[93]

Satan's many names and descriptions give an insight into his nature. Satan (Job 1:6–12) means accuser, or adversary. *Abaddon* (Hebrew) or *Apollyon* (Greek) means the destroyer. Beelzebub (Greek *Beelzeboul*, cf. Mt. 12:24) means 'lord of the flies' and refers to 'the prince of demons'. *Belial* (2 Cor. 6:15) means worthless. Satan is also referred to as 'the ruler of the kingdom of the air' (Eph. 2:2), 'the prince of this world' (Jn. 12:31; 14:30), 'the god of this age' (2 Cor. 4:4), 'the tempter' (1 Thes. 3:5), 'a liar and the father of lies' (Jn. 8:44) and as being 'like a roaring lion' (1 Pet. 5:8). Satan is further described as presumptuous (Mt. 4:5–6), proud (1 Tim. 3:6), powerful (Eph. 2:2; 6:12), evil (1 Jn. 2:13), clever (2 Cor. 11:3), deceitful (2 Cor. 11:4; Eph. 6:11), fierce and

---

[90] < http://www.britannica.com >

[91] Peter Kreeft, 'Satan and the Millennium' @ < http://catholiceducation.org/ articles/religion/re0018.html >. Over half of Americans believe in Satan.

[92] Ibid.

[93] Ibid.

cruel (Lk. 8:29; 1 Pet. 5:8).[94] In contrast to Christ's *philanthropia*, his love of humanity, Satan appears among early church teachers (e.g. Basil of Caesarea) as the *misanthopos*, the hater of humanity. He is also the hater of beauty, *misokalos*.

Satan is not an equal but opposite god to God; he is an angel, created by God, who chose to rebel against God.

> To be bad, he [the devil] must exist and have intelligence and will. But existence, intelligence and will are in themselves good. Therefore he must be getting them from the Good Power ... And do you now begin to see why Christianity has always said that the devil is a fallen angel? That is not a mere story for the children. It is a real recognition of the fact that evil is a parasite, not an original thing. The powers which enable evil to carry on are powers given it by goodness. All the things which enable a bad man to be effectively bad are in themselves good things – resolution, cleverness, good looks, existence itself.[95]

Demons are not wholly evil as Angels are wholly good, for while it is possible to be wholly good (after all, God is), it is impossible to be *wholly* evil. Rather, demons are more bad than good, more ugly than beautiful, and thus bad and ugly *overall*.

Demons are both *like* Angels in being naturally un-embodied spirits, and *unlike* Angels in being confirmed, not in the grace of God, but in their sinful (divinely permitted but undesired) rejection of grace. Just as Angels are what they are by their 'Yes' to God, demons are what they are by their 'No' to God. As a result of their 'No' to God, demons are neither *kalos* nor *agathos*. Satan may be capable of masquerading as an angel of light (2 Cor. 11:14), but paedophiles are capable of masquerading as harmless boys or girls in Internet chat rooms. Demons lack integrity, being literally diabolical. They have no fidelity, no *emeth*. They are neither *pistos* (faithful) nor *alethes* (true). They do not love wisdom (*philo sophia*): demons are not philosophers!

---

94 Oropeza, *99 Answers To Questions About Angels*, pp. 80, 83. The Bible never associates Satan with 'Lucifer': 'A contextual reading of Isaiah 14 and Ezekiel 28 raises serious doubts about the reliability of the popular 'Lucifer is Satan' theory ... There is no assertion in the New Testament or in the apostolic fathers that Satan was once a beautiful angel named Lucifer. The Jewish traditions do not even make a clear connection between Satan and Isaiah 14 prior to about 100 C.E.' Ibid., pp. 80–83.

95 Lewis, *Mere Christianity*, p. 47. cf. Lewis's paper 'God and Evil' in *Christian Reunion And Other Essays* (London: Fount, 1990).

Like Angels, demons have the capacities of sensation, thought, belief, desire and will. However, the content of these capacities must be very different. For example, the desires of a demon are not to love and serve God like those of an Angel are! Where an Angel wills to do what is good in the eyes of God, a demon wills to do what is good in its own eyes. The intellectual life of demons cannot be characterized by the intellectual virtues. While a demon may be clever enough to be deceitful, they do not possess truth, knowledge, goodness or beauty in purity: far from it. Demons have a vicious moral character and consequently an intellectual life marred by arrogance, dishonesty, pride, rationalization, etc. The mental life of demons lacks *integrity*: 'There are plenty of truths [demons] would rather not know; plenty that [they] have no reason to want to know. Why should [they] not prefer to live in ignorance, or blind [themselves] with the realm of [demonically] constructed "truth"?'[96] A demon's intellectual life must be far poorer than that of the average Angel. Demons are consequently more fallible than Angels. As for how the intellect of the average demon compares with the intellectual life of the average human there is little data to go on, other than to note that the answer depends not just on moral factors, but on how low an angelic intellect must fall to equal that of a human! However, Gregory A. Boyd speculates: 'The "prince of darkness", it seems, is far more sophisticated than the demons he rules over, which perhaps also explains why Jesus engages in prolonged intellectual conversation with Satan in the Gospels (Mt. 4:1–11; Lk. 4:1–13), while his conversations with demons are only to get information and to then command them to leave.'[97]

God is more powerful and original than Satan and all the other demons put together; and the Bible assures us that God's side wins in the battle between good and evil:

> God has ordained *temporal* parameters around the freedom of angelic and human creatures, just as God has ordained parameters around the *scope* of this freedom ... Apparently out of integrity for the gift of freedom he has given, God endures for a time the wrath of these destructive rebels ... While the gift of life God gives to those who choose him is eternal, the gift of freedom to choose against him is apparently not ... In choosing against God, Satan and all who follow him are forever choosing against life and love. Nothing could possibly be worse.[98]

[96] Stephen L. Clark, *God, Religion And Reality* (London: SPCK, 1998), p. 43.
[97] Boyd, *God At War*, p. 374.
[98] Ibid, pp. 287–90. cf. *The Nature Of Hell: A Report By The Evangelical Alliance Commission On Unity And Truth Among Evangelicals* (Carlisle: Paternoster, 2000); Kreeft and Tacelli, *Handbook Of Christian Apologetics*;

The demons are an enemy already defeated by Jesus, now capable only of succeeding in minor skirmishes against the kingdom of God (1 Jn. 5:4–5; Mt. 25:31–46). Satan and his demons are fallen, finite beings, limited by their own sinfulness. They are no match for God, who has promised their eventual destruction (Mt. 25:41; Rev. 20:10). Alvin Plantinga speculates on the demonic state of mind:

> They know of God's power and know that they have no hope of winning any contest of power with him; nevertheless, they engage in just such a contest, perhaps in that familiar self-deceived condition of really knowing, in one sense, that they couldn't possibly win such a contest, while at some other level nevertheless refusing to accept this truth, or hiding it from themselves. Or perhaps ... knowing that they couldn't possibly win, they insist on fighting anyway, thinking of themselves ... as heroically contending against nearly insuperable odds, a condition, they point out, in which God never finds himself, and hence a way in which they can think of themselves as his moral superior. The devils also know of God's wonderful scheme for the salvation of human beings, but they find this scheme – with its mercy and suffering love – offensive and unworthy. No doubt they endorse Neitzsche's notion that Christian love (including the love displayed in incarnation and atonement) is weak, whining, resentful, servile, duplicitous ... and in general unappealing.[99]

What Demons Do

Elucidating what angels do helps to throw light on what angels are.

– Mortimer J. Adler[100]

Under Satan (Mt. 12:22–24; Mk. 3:23–26; Jn. 12:31) the demons war against the will of God (Rev. 16:12–16) and use their intelligence to deceive and discourage humans (2 Cor. 4:4; Eph. 6:11–12; 1 Thes. 2:18; 1 Tim. 4:1). This is something anyone involved with such occult practices as Ouija boards and spiritism should take seriously (Deut.

---

[98] (*continued*) C.S. Lewis, *The Problem Of Pain* (London: Fount, 1977). On who goes to Hell cf. Paul Copan, *'True For You But Not For Me': Deflating The Slogans That Leave Christians Speechless* (Minneapolis, Minnesota: Bethany House, 1998); Clark H. Pinnock (ed.), *The Grace Of God And The Will Of Man* (Minneapolis, Minnesota: Bethany House, 1989); John Sanders, *No Other Name: Can Only Christians Be Saved?* (London: SPCK, 1992).

[99] Plantinga, *Warranted Christian Belief*, p. 291.

[100] Adler, *The Angels And Us*, p. 69.

18:9–14).[101] Demons tempt us and seek to influence culture and society against God's ways. Demons also use their power to inflict suffering (Mt. 9:32–33). As Norman L. Geisler argues, 'Another argument in support of the reality of the Devil is that of demons who express a unified conspiracy against God, his plan, and his people. Without a leader the demonic forces would not manifest such an organized show of force against God.'[102]

The methodology of demonic warfare is hardly mysterious. It is easy enough to deduce that the demons have two obvious targets, two obvious allies, and three obvious strategies for attacking their targets. The two obvious targets are Christians and non-Christians. The object with non-Christians is surely first and foremost to hinder their becoming Christians. The object with Christians is surely either to stop them being Christians, or failing that, to hinder their effectiveness as Christians: 'Your enemy the devil prowls around like a roaring lion looking for someone to devour' (1 Pet. 5:8). The two obvious allies, which can be used for indirect attack, are 'the world' and 'the flesh' (human sinfulness). The obvious demonic strategies are to use direct and/or indirect methods to attack people's minds, attitudes and practices (the primary elements of spirituality, cf. Mt. 22:37; Mk. 12:30; Lk. 10:27). If the devil can lead a person to lack true beliefs, right attitudes, or spiritually healthy practices, one imagines that he would. It follows that the obvious strategy for Christian 'spiritual warfare' is to ally ourselves with God (and his angels) in reaching non-Christians with the gospel and in adopting true beliefs, godly attitudes and healthy spiritual practices! As Peter advised: 'Be self-controlled and alert. Your enemy the devil prowls around like a roaring lion looking for someone to devour. Resist him, standing firm in the faith …' (1 Pet. 5:8–9.)

During his house arrest in Rome in the early AD 60s, the apostle Paul was free to receive visitors and spread the gospel (cf. Acts 28:28–31). One of the ways he did this was by writing letters. The most famous biblical passage on the theme of how to resist the devil is in a letter Paul wrote during this time to the Christians in Ephesus.[103] Paul closes his

---

[101] cf. Josh McDowell and Don Stewart, *The Occult* (Wheaton, Illinois: Scripture Press, 1992).

[102] Geisler, *Baker Encyclopedia Of Christian Apologetics*, p. 684.

[103] 'Ephesus was the capital of the Roman province of Asia … Its population in the first century may have approached half a million … The fame of Ephesus was not only political and commercial: it was the centre for worship of the pagan goddess Artemis (Diana). It was also known as a centre of occult (magic) practices. The temple dedicated to Artemis was considered one of

letter with a famous analogy between Christians and Roman soldiers, between the tools of earthly warfare and those of *spiritual* warfare:

> Put on the full armour of God so that you can take your stand against the devil's schemes. For our struggle is not against flesh and blood, but against the rulers, against the authorities, against the powers of this dark world and against the spiritual forces of evil in the heavenly realms. Therefore put on the full armour of God, so that when the day of evil comes, you may be able to stand your ground, and after you have done everything, to stand. Stand firm then, with the belt of truth buckled round your waist, with the breast-plate of righteousness in place, and with your feet fitted with the readiness that comes from the gospel of peace. In addition to all this, take up the shield of faith, with which you can extinguish all the flaming arrows of the evil one. Take the helmet of salvation and the sword of the Spirit, which is the word of God. And pray in the Spirit on all occasions with all kinds of prayers and requests. With this in mind, be alert and always keep on praying for all the saints (Eph. 6:11–18).[104]

This passage has been summarized as an exhortation to make 'the right stand in the right strength'.[105]

Just as one human can find themselves under the power and influence of another human being, so people who don't make the right stand in the right strength can find themselves under the power of demons: we call it 'demon possession' or 'demonization'. Dr M. Scott Peck recounts the case of Hartley and Sarah (their names have been changed to preserve anonymity) in his fascinating book on the psychology of evil, *People of the Lie*.[106] Hartley was troubled by aggressive 'words' in his head that drove him to cut himself with his razor in a series of half-hearted suicide attempts. Hartley's wife, Sarah, was an overbearing woman who played the martyr, putting her husband down at every opportunity ('He's such a weakling,' 'Hartley's a worm of a man,' 'It would be much better for

---

[103] (*continued*) the seven wonders of the ancient world ... If religious life was dominated by emperor worship, idolatry, and the black arts of occultism and spiritism, moral life was typical of a Greco-Roman city: A large brothel stood at one of the major intersections.' Walter A. Elwell and Robert W. Yarbrough, *Encountering The New Testament* (Grand Rapids, Michigan: Baker, 1998), pp. 308–9. Life in Ephesus, if you swap the temples for shopping malls, doesn't sound too different than life in any modern Western city!

[104] For a detailed discussion of spiritual warfare and the armour of God visit my web site @ < http://www.peter-s-williams.co.uk/ >

[105] Elwell and Yarbrough, *Encountering The New Testament*.

[106] cf. M. Scott Peck, *People Of The Lie* (London: Arrow, 1990), pp. 122–35.

me if he didn't exist') and who freely admitted that Hartley hated her, but said that she was not afraid for herself since he 'wouldn't hurt a fly'.

> Sarah's comments that [Hartley's] mother was an alcoholic and his father as weak as he suggests that he came from a family in which his parents probably served as lazy role models and he probably failed to receive adequate fulfillment in his infantile needs. We can postulate that by the time he met Sarah he was already a profoundly lazy person, a child in adult's clothing who was unconsciously seeking the strong mother he had never had to take care of him. Sarah filled the bill perfectly, just as he undoubtedly met her requirements for a potential slave. Once the relationship was established, it became a vicious circle, naturally intensifying the sickness of each. Her dominion further encouraged his submissiveness, and his weakness further nourished her desire for power over someone.[107]

Vaguely aware that he was caught in a trap Hartley 'obsessed back and forth between the two easiest ways to extricate himself: to kill Sarah or to kill himself. But he was too lazy to even consider the one legitimate escape route open to him: the obvious, more difficult path of psychological independence.'[108] Peck observes:

> The theme of thralldom is not infrequent in fairy tales and myths in which princes and princesses … have become captive to the evil power of some wicked … demon … I was not able to rescue Hartley from his slavery. For it was a willing thralldom. He had voluntarily sold his soul into Sarah's keeping … Hartley was physically free to escape. Theoretically he could have just walked away from Sarah. But he had bound himself to her by chains of laziness and dependency …[109]

If such relationships of 'incestuous symbiosis' are not uncommon among humans, is it any wonder that such relationships can exist between humans and demons (cf. Chapter Four and Appendix I)?[110] Christians disagree about the role of human free will in demon possession. Some argue that people cannot become possessed without directly inviting this situation upon themselves, perhaps by meddling with the occult; others suggest that this view is naïve.

---

[107] Ibid, p. 133.
[108] Ibid.
[109] Ibid.
[110] I'm not suggesting this is *the* way to conceive demonization, but presenting what may plausibly be taken as an analogous case.

There is a very real 'world in between' in which reside conscious, free beings who, like human beings, possess power to influence others, for better or for worse ... They can therefore fight with each other and victimize human beings ... In other words, just as evil adults can and do sometimes victimize children against their will and God's will, just as rapists victimize women against their will and God's will ... so demonic spirits can apparently sometimes victimize people against their will – and against God's will ... This is the price we pay, or at least risk paying, for a cosmos composed of a vast multiplicity of free, morally responsible agents.[111]

Of course, even if it is possible to become an unwitting victim, it is only wise to avoid 'tempting fate'. It may be going too far to say that a human (especially a non-Christian) *cannot* be possessed against their will, but contemporary experience seems to suggest that such cases are the exception rather than the rule. Either way, Jesus has an amply demonstrated ability to break-up demonic relationships (cf. Appendix I), and has given Christians the authority to deal with demons in his name.

What Angels Do

Angels worship God. This does not mean that they play harps.[112] Rebecca Merrill Groothuis defines and describes 'worship':

> Worship is both vocation and celebration. It is daily work done as unto the Lord for his glory; this is continual, living worship. Then there is also the conscious acting-out of this attitude in a kind of ritual celebration; this outward enactment of inward faith and conviction serves to strengthen that conviction ... Worship by its definition means to glorify God and enjoy him forever ...Worship of God is the organizing principle, the chief occupation, of the citizens in heaven.[113]

Worship is what Angels are for, it is their purpose (their *telos*) and it is what they do *continually*. It is their vocation and their joy to worship God. Angels worshipfully serve the will of God (Heb. 1:7; Ps. 103:20) and as part of that service they serve Christ's body, the church: 'Are not

---

[111] Boyd, *God At War*, p. 199–200. cf. Liesl Alexander, *Free To Live* (Chichester: New Wine Press, 1988).

[112] There's nothing to say that an angel can't play a harp with an assumed body, or can't play one without using a body, or play one 'in its mind', although I fancy they prefer electric guitar these days!

[113] Rebecca Merrill Groothuis, 'Putting Worship in the Worship Service', in Groothuis, *Christianity That Counts*, pp. 73–4.

all angels ministering spirits sent to serve those who will inherit salvation?' (Heb. 1:14). Angels 'are God's messengers whose chief business is to carry out His orders in the world'.[114] Angels are not at our beck and call, but God's. Angels strengthen us (1 Kgs. 19:5–8), give us insight (Dan. 9:22), protect us (Ps. 34:7, 91:10) and rejoice when we repent (Lk. 15:7). The Bible says that one or more Angels acted to carry out God's will on the following occasions:

1. Passover and the crossing of the Red Sea (Ex. 12, 14:19).
2. Appeared to Gideon (Judg. 6:12).
3. Appeared to Samson's parents (Judg. 13:3–21).
4. Appeared to Elijah (1 Kgs. 19:5).
5. Rescued Elisha (2 Kgs. 6:16ff.).
6. Defeated Sennacherib's army (Isa. 37:36). This is an extraordinary example of angelic power recorded in no less than six sources, both biblical and non-biblical (IV Kings 19:35, Tobit 1:21, Ecclesiasticus 48:24, Isa. 37:36, Josephus and Herodotus).
7. Delivered Daniel from Lions (Dan. 6:22).
8. Appeared to Zechariah (Lk. 1:11).
9. Appeared to Joseph (Mt. 1:20).
10. Appeared to Mary (Lk. 1:26ff.).
11. Appeared to the shepherds (Lk. 2:8–14).
12. Rescued Peter from prison (Acts 12:7ff.).
13. Appeared to Paul on a ship (Acts 27:23).
14. Appeared to John on Patmos (Rev. 1:1).
15. Ministered to Jesus after his temptation in the wilderness (Mt. 4:11).
16. Ministered to Jesus in the garden of Gethsemane (Lk. 22:43).[115]

Why does God sometimes act through Angels instead of directly? After all, God is present to everywhere, all-knowing and almighty, so what need does he have of messengers? God has no need of anything he creates; it is simply a good thing that he creates and that his creation includes creatures able to participate in his will by their own free choice. We know that God often acts through humans (think of the prophets, the disciples; indeed, think of the church as the body of Christ!), so *why not* Angels? It is simply an observable part of God's character to delegate where possible. God is not a control freak.

---

[114] Billy Graham, *Angels* (London: Hodder & Stoughton, 1976), p. 28.
[115] cf. Kendall, *Understanding Theology* vol. I, p. 254.

Guardian Angels?

On the question of whether or not each adult individual (or each Christian at least) has his or her own guardian Angel, I am currently agnostic. Catholics traditionally answer this question in the affirmative.[116] For example, F. Suarez SJ says: 'Even though Scripture does not affirm explicitly the existence of Guardian Angels, nor has the Church defined its truth, it is nevertheless universally admitted, and it is so firmly based upon Scripture as interpreted by the Fathers, that its denial would be a very great rashness and practically an error.'[117] Here it is admitted that neither the Bible nor even the Catholic Church explicitly teaches the existence of guardian Angels. Rather, the argument is one based on the consent and authority of the early church fathers, who interpreted the scriptures to imply the existence of such guardians. We may be well advised to adhere to a tradition that does not contradict scripture in the absence of good reason to doubt its trustworthiness. Then again, why would children receive angelic guardianship (Mt. 18:10) and adults not? Thus Pascal Parente argues: 'The Divine Providence that protected their tender bodies in childhood will certainly not abandon them to the fury of their enemies [i.e. demons] now that their immortal soul, with their body, is exposed to far greater dangers ...'[118] The logic of this argument does not, however, necessitate *Angelic* protection. One might assume that the fellowship of God (including the indwelling of His Holy Spirit) and of other Christians might be sufficient to the job in hand. Of course, we have already conceded that God apparently likes to delegate where possible, so perhaps the Christian enjoys the company both of God *and* Angel. However, one might think there is something implausible in the belief that each person has their assigned guardian given the facts that the number of living Christians is constantly increasing and that the number of available angels is finite. These arguments for and against guardian Angels for adults seem to me to be quite evenly matched.[119]

Peter Kreeft argues that angels, guardian or otherwise, cannot make us good, 'But angels can help, just as human friends can. They can be

---

[116] As do 46 per cent of those polled by *Time* magazine.

[117] F. Suarez SJ, *De Angelis*, VI, 17.

[118] Parente, *The Angels*, p. 109.

[119] However, Bible teacher Kenneth Hagin sr claims that in 1963 Jesus appeared to him, together with an Angel that Jesus specifically assured him was his guardian Angel. The Angel delivered a message from God about an important ministry decision and promised the arrival of specific financial support, which arrived within the specified time period. cf. Terry Law, *The Truth About Angels* (Lake Mary, Florida: Creation House, 1994), pp. 72–3.

God's instruments. But we must use, or play, the instrument – just as we must accept and use human help.'[120] Thus Angels 'can't put judgements in your mind or choices in your will, but they can put images in your imagination ...'[121] Ultimately, all such inspiration comes from God, whether directly or indirectly. In addition to their ministerial function, Angels 'will occasionally perform miracles on matter, because matter is passive and unfree'[122] (cf. Acts 12:7ff.). Hence Angels occasionally help people in physical danger, although as Kreeft says, this is rare 'and not to be counted on (especially when driving!)'.[123] It seems reasonable to suppose that Angels are primarily concerned not with 'our light and momentary troubles' (2 Cor. 4:17) but with the spiritual warfare of 'soul making'. Angelic intervention is, I assume, usually a bonus rather than a necessity.

An Aristotelian Assay

Aristotle pointed out that there are four distinct types of explanation. For example, if we are to give a comprehensive explanation for the existence of a house we must appeal to the existence of the stuff the house is made out of (its material cause), explain the arrangement of that stuff (its formal cause), explain how that stuff came to be in that form (its efficient cause) and finally, we must provide the reason why the house exists, the goal (or *telos*) that this arrangement of matter serves (its final or *teleological* cause – to provide shelter). Applying Aristotle's four causes to angels we see that: 1) as spirits, angels have no material cause in the above sense. Angels are not made out of any pre-existing substance as is a house (but then, matter itself has no material cause, so it is hardly surprising that spirit likewise has no 'material' cause), nor are they composed of matter in the modern sense of the term (physical substance). However, we can ask after the ontological nature of angels and discover that angels are composed of spirit (*ruach* or 'personal power'). 2) The angelic spirit has the *form* of a person (the only form a spirit can take is personal, just as matter is by nature impersonal), a rational creature made in the image of God; thus an angel is a spirit (*ruach*) in the sense of *non-physical 'energy'* with the capacity to *think, value* and *will*. 3) The *efficient cause* of an angel is a basic and free act of creation on the part of God. 4) The *telos* of an angel is to worship God.

---

[120] Kreeft, *Angels (And Demons)*, p. 94.
[121] Ibid., p. 96.
[122] Ibid., p. 94.
[123] Ibid., p. 100.

Just as there are good houses and bad houses, so there are good and bad angels. However, while the house has no say in its value, the character of an angel is the character it has freely chosen. That an angel has the freedom to make this choice is a good thing, because it is a pre-condition of the value of freely choosing to love God and fulfil its *telos*. However, the exercise of angelic free will to reject God is a bad thing, a frustration of the angelic *telos* that results in that corruption of the intended angelic nature that is called 'demonic'; a nature the moral and aesthetic value of which is so low as to be an objectively evil and ugly thing, a thing whose self-imposed and fitting destination is hell.

Conclusion

The above angelic assay is a conjecture based on philosophical presuppositions, the data of scriptural revelation and personal experience. Such conjecture at least shows that while angels may be beyond imagination, they are not beyond conception. We can construct an angelic assay which is not only logically coherent but, given certain background information, quite plausible. Angels are not merely possible (weakly conceivable); they are plausible (strongly conceivable).

Chapter Four

Angelic Actuality

Given the assumption of a creator God I find it entirely plausible that we are not alone as rational beings; and scripture and the writings of the saints offer evidence for the existence of angels – pure spiritual beings, not the androgynous chorus line of popular culture.

– J.J. Haldane[1]

Although this chapter will focus on marshalling evidence for the existence of angels, I want to begin by defending the proposition that it may be rational to believe in angels *without evidential justification*. Christian philosophers who adhere to 'Reformed Epistemology' (e.g. Kelly James Clark, Alvin Plantinga and Nicholas Wolterstorff) argue that belief in God can be 'basic' in the same way that trust in the general reliability of our memory and other cognitive systems is 'basic'.[2] It is worth our while to consider this approach because it has consequences for the rationality of belief in angels.

> Man has an innate, natural capacity to apprehend God's existence even as he has a natural capacity to accept truths of perception … Given the appropriate circumstances – such as moments of guilt, gratitude, or a sense of God's handiwork in nature – man naturally apprehends God's existence … God has so constructed us that we naturally form the belief in his existence under appropriate circumstances.[3]

---

[1] J.J. Haldane in Smart and Haldane, *Atheism & Theism*, p. 210.

[2] cf. Alvin Plantinga, 'Intellectual Sophistication and Basic Belief in God' @ < http://www.leaderu.com/truth/3truth03.html >; Clark, *Return To Reason*. Reformed epistemology echoes William James' argument for 'the right to believe' without evidence in certain carefully defined circumstances (cf. Williams, *The Case For God*).

[3] William Lane Craig, *Reasonable Faith* (Wheaton, Illinois: Crossway, 1994), p. 29.

Belief in angels is surely *rationally permissible* for anyone with such a 'basic' belief in God. I am convinced that arguments are not necessary for belief (whether in God or angels) to be rational. Suppose you judged the evidence each way to balance out (or suppose you are unable to judge the evidence), you surely wouldn't be *irrational* in following a gut instinct either to believe or to disbelieve. Arguing that 'we should never believe something without evidence' lands one in an infinite regress.[4]

Alvin Plantinga distinguishes between *de jure* and *de facto* challenges to Christian belief: 'The *de jure* challenge to Christian (or theistic) belief ... is the claim that such belief is, irrational ... or unjustifiable ... [and] contrasts with the *de facto* challenge, according to which the belief in question is false.'[5] Atheists often complain that Christian belief is *irrational*. However, as Plantinga points out: 'What you properly take to be rational ... depends on what sort of metaphysical and religious stance you adopt. It depends on what kind of beings you think human beings are, and what sort of beliefs you think their noetic faculties will produce when they are functioning properly ...'[6] In other words, your views about what sort of creature a human is will determine or at least heavily influence your opinion as to whether theistic belief is rational or not. If you think that humans are the result of blind and unintended evolutionary forces, then you might be inclined to view belief in God as an illusion 'properly traced to wishful thinking or some other cognitive mechanism not aimed at truth ... (Freud) or to a sort of disease or dysfunction on the part of the individual or society (Marx).'[7] On the other hand, if you think that humans are created by God, and that he has given us a natural tendency to believe in his existence (at least in certain situations), then you won't think that belief in God is typically the result of an intellectual defect or a belief producing mechanism that isn't aimed at truth. Plantinga argues against all *de jure* objections: 'If the *warrant* enjoyed by belief in God is related in this way to the *truth* of that belief, then the question whether theistic belief has *warrant* is not after all independent of the question whether theistic belief is *true*.'[8] This being so, 'the dispute as to whether theistic belief is ... [warranted] can't be

---

[4] cf. Peter van Inwagen, 'Is It Wrong, Everywhere, Always, and for Anyone, to Believe' @ < http://www.faithquest.com/home.cfm?main=docs/philosophers /vaninwagen/clifford.cfm >

[5] Alvin Plantinga, 'Warranted Belief in God', *Philosophy Of Religion: The Big Questions* (Oxford: Blackwell, 1999).

[6] Ibid.

[7] Ibid.

[8] Ibid.

settled just by attending to [*de jure*] epistemological considerations.'[9] That is, *de jure* objections to theism are guilty of begging-the-question. The upshot of all this is that 'a successful atheological objection will have to be to the truth of theism, not to its rationality, or justification, or intellectual respectability'.[10]

Plantinga's line of thought has important consequences for angelology, in that if belief in angels is even *possibly* the result of a divinely intended properly functioning cognitive system, then his anti-*de jure* argument can be applied to belief in angels. If this is the case, *de jure* objections to belief in angels beg-the-question, not directly (as in the case of *de jure* objections to belief in God), but as to whether God exists and might have given humanity a natural disposition to believe in angels, at least in certain circumstances. Those circumstances might most plausibly be thought to include reading God's literary revelation, the Bible. Plantinga argues that the Holy Spirit participates in a cognitive process that endorses Christian belief in at least the main outlines of the Christian worldview and gospel, especially in conjunction with reading scripture: 'the beliefs thus produced in us meet the conditions necessary and sufficient for warrant; they are produced by cognitive processes functioning properly (in accord with their design plan) in an appropriate epistemic environment ... according to a design plan successfully aimed at truth ...'[11] Any beliefs formed through this process, *including beliefs about angels*, may be thought to enjoy justification, rationality, and warrant. Indeed, as Plantinga says, 'if they are held with sufficient firmness, these beliefs qualify as *knowledge*...'[12] To the extent that a person's belief in angels plausibly qualifies for such warrant, to such an extent is their belief in angels both rationally permissible and immune to *de jure* criticism. However, while belief in angels may not need evidential justification, this isn't to say that belief in angels lacks evidential justification. In fact, I believe that there is a strong evidential case for the existence of angels.

Arguing for Angels

Harold J. Berman writes that 'to search for truth is to be open to the possibility that some discovered truth will lay claim to one's

[9] Ibid.
[10] Ibid.
[11] Plantinga, *Warranted Christian Belief*, p. 206.
[12] Ibid.

allegiance'.[13] What does it mean to say that something has such a claim on one's allegiance? After all, not all beliefs are equally obligatory: 'Some are very, very reasonable (7+5=12); some are very, very unreasonable (George Bush is a Martian); and others fall somewhere between these extremes.'[14] I would think it safe to say that *belief in angels falls somewhere between the extremes of rationality, being neither certainly true nor certainly false.* Consider the following eleven-point spectrum of rationality:

0)	Certainly false (e.g. 7+5=2)
0.1)	False beyond a reasonable doubt
0.2)	Very improbable
0.3)	Improbable
0.4)	More improbable than not
0.5)	Counterbalanced – no preponderance of evidence either way
0.6)	More probable than not
0.7)	Probable
0.8)	Very probable
0.9)	True beyond a reasonable doubt
1)	Certainly true (e.g. 7+5=12)

In terms of the above spectrum, a belief is rationally *permissible* if it is counterbalanced. My argument so far has been to show that belief in angels is at least rationally permissible. For a belief to be rationally *obligatory* it must be the case that we ought to assign it an epistemic value of *more* than counterbalanced. That is, an argument for a hypothesis need not provide certainty for our belief to be rationally compelled.

The discussion thus far has omitted an important distinction. As Habermas and Moreland note: 'Often a particular belief is a part of a larger system of beliefs, and it gains rational support from its role in that system. In cases like these, it is less rational to accept the belief if it is evaluated on its own, apart from its supporting web of beliefs, assuming, of course, that the system itself is reasonable.'[15] The rationality of belief in angels is certainly an instance of a belief that gains support from its role as part of a system of belief, namely Christian theism; a system which I hold to be demonstrably reasonable. Some of the arguments for

---

[13] Harold J. Berman, 'Judeo-Christian Versus Pagan Scholarship' in Kelly Monroe (ed.), *Finding God At Harvard* (Grand Rapids, Michigan: Zondervan, 1996), p. 295.

[14] Habermas and Moreland, *Beyond Death*, p. 16.

[15] Ibid.

angels can stand alone, but other arguments, as will be seen, depend on one or more facets of the Christian system being true. For example, *if* the Bible is the word of God, and *if* the Bible teaches the existence of angels, then this is a very strong reason to believe in angels. Of course, that the Bible is the word of God is a premise that some would dispute. Arguments can be advanced to support the claim that the Bible is the word of God; but these arguments are most convincing when approached with the belief in hand that God exists. Again, this is a belief that some would question, but for which a rational defence can be mounted. Hence, the arguments for angels that draw upon the web of Christian belief will carry weight with those who accept, or can be brought to accept, that 'the system itself is reasonable'. (Sceptics should begin by taking into account the failure of the 'problem of evil' discussed in Chapter One, Plantinga's defence of belief in God as properly basic and immune to *de jure* criticism, and the cumulative positive case for God outlined in Chapter Two. For more on these topics see the Bibliography.) In presenting arguments for belief in the existence of angels I will therefore make a distinction between 'independent' and 'non-independent' arguments.

Suppose a naturalist were to seriously consider the evidential case for angels. I would hardly think it likely that the arguments could be expected to do more than to convince them that it is *rationally permissible* to believe in angels, or that it is rationally obligatory to believe in angels *if one accepts beliefs such as*: 'God exists,' 'The Bible is the word of God' or 'Jesus is the Son of God.' The naturalist may think that these beliefs are false and even irrational (just as Christians think naturalism is false and even irrational), but it is surely reasonable to expect naturalists to concede that belief in angels is rational and/or obligatory *for someone who holds the appropriate background beliefs*. The question would then be whether or not those background beliefs were reasonable. I doubt that the independent evidence for angels is sufficient on its own to make belief in naturalism irrational. On the other hand I think that the independent evidence might make belief in angels rationally *permissible* and that the total evidence makes belief in angels rationally obligatory *for anyone who accepts premises such as* 'God exists,' etc. Moreover, I think that the evidence for the existence of God, and the evidence for Jesus and the Bible being respectively the incarnate and literary word of God, is sufficiently strong to convince the open-minded, humble seeker after truth. This being so, I think it follows that, *absolutely speaking*, belief in angels is also rationally obligatory. Stephen T. Davis argues: 'There can be no such thing as a subjectively fool-proof [theistic proof] … We should not expect that there will be a [theistic proof] that convinces every atheist ... Rather, successful [theistic proofs] *should* convince atheists that God exists.'[16] The same point applies to argument for angels, whether or not they depend in turn upon the theistic or Christian 'system'.

It is now received wisdom that the arguments for God are cumulative, or, at least, are best approached cumulatively. That is, the weight of evidence for God accumulates as one adds arguments to an overall case that doesn't rest on any one piece of evidence. Individual arguments are like strands in a rope. Those individual strands may be of differing strength, but when they are twined together the result is stronger than any of the strands on its own; the whole is stronger than the sum of its parts, due to the mutual coherence of those parts. Another good way to describe this argumentative procedure is by the court analogy. Isolated pieces of evidence may be insufficient on their own to warrant convicting someone 'beyond reasonable doubt', but taken together the evidence does warrant conviction. It is invalid to argue that as none of the evidence warrants conviction no conviction is warranted. Likewise with the case for angels: individual arguments for the existence of angels may be insufficient to warrant the conviction that angels exist, but presented with a cumulative case, the court may have to decide that angels exists.

All of the following arguments give reason to think that angels exist. Some of the following evidence is directly related to the existence of Angels, while other evidence directly relates to the existence of demons (and even to the existence of one demon in particular, namely Satan).

Independent arguments for angels

1) Common Consent

Over 65 per cent of the current world population believe in the existence of finite spirit beings. A poll conducted by *Time* magazine discovered that 69 per cent of Americans believe in angels (by way of comparison, only 25 per cent of Americans believe in ghosts).[17]

The fact that a lot of people believe something *is* evidence for its truth, because it means that many people have made judgements about the belief in question and have lived by that judgement – testing their belief in the arena of life, including intellectual life. Such evidence may be weak, but it *is* evidence. As Joshua Hoffman and Gary S. Rosenkrantz affirm: 'if entities of a certain kind belong to folk ontology [the ontological

---

[16] Davis, *God, Reason And Theistic Proofs*, p. 191.
[17] Nancy Gibbs, 'Angels Among Us', *Time*, 27 December 1993, p. 56.

presumptions of our common-sense worldview], then there is prima facie presumption in favour of their reality ... Those who deny their existence assume the burden of proof.'[18] One can categorize believers in angels in various ways, by numbers (the majority of people past and present believe in angels or 'daemons'), by intellectual ability, as scientists or philosophers, as martyrs or saints. In all of these categories, the majority of people have surely been believers in angels. Is it likely that they were all wrong? As the saying goes, a million French men can be wrong, but it is less likely than a hundred French men being wrong!

Peter Kreeft reports that 'just about all religions teach that there exists something like angels: spirits superior to man but inferior to God.'[19] Although they have divergent understandings of such spiritual beings, Zoroastrian, Buddhist, Taoist, Jewish, Christian, Muslim, New Age, Animist, traditional Chinese and Japanese believers all recognize the existence of finite supernatural agents. Belief in angels is a constant factor across many different cultures: 'Angels appear in almost every culture and religion in the world, from ancient Sumeria, Egypt and Assyria to contemporary civilizations.'[20] Biblical belief in and teaching about demons is foreshadowed in the mythology of many nations and religions: 'Belief in demons is not connected with any particular view of the cosmos. Demons have a very wide geographical and lengthy historical role as spiritual beings influencing man in his relationship to the sacred or holy ... The ancient Assyrian demon *rabisu* apparently is a classic prototype of a supernatural being ...'[21] Belief in finite spiritual beings besides the gods, both good and bad, can be traced back to ancient Indo-Iranian religion from which evolved early Zoroastrianism with its malevolent *devas*, and early Hinduism (as reflected in the Vedas) with its benevolent *devas* and malevolent *asuras* (evil lords). Chinese religion includes belief in the demonic *kuei-shen* who are manifested in all aspects of nature: 'the Chinese who were influenced by Taoism and folk religions used bonfires, firecrackers, and torches to ward off the *kuei*.'[22]

> In India, the Raksava represented every hostile force. They appeared either in horrible guises or in a very beguiling form. It was said that they entered abandoned corpses, ate the flesh and then made them obey their will, in

---

[18] Joshua Hoffman and Gary S. Rosenkrantz, *Substance: Its Nature And Existence* (London: Routledge, 1997), p. 7.

[19] Kreeft, *Angels (And Demons)*, p. 103.

[20] Oropeza, *99 Answers To Questions About Angels*, p. 13.

[21] < http://www.britannica.com >

[22] Ibid.

order to spread evil all around them. The Raksava's leader was Ravana, the enemy of Rama. He was the head of a kingdom which was always in conflict with the gods and the work of the devout.[23]

Indeed, 'It is interesting that demonology in various religions tends to centre in the belief in one dominant power of evil.'[24] There were also Babylonian demons (such as the man-crushing *Alu*, the murdering *Gallu*, the baby-attacking *Lamast* and the mountain-trembling *Pazuzu*). Pagan religion includes 'evil spirits in nature … the *narakas* (creatures of hell) of Jainism, [and] the *oni* (attendants of the gods of the underworld) in Japanese religions …'[25]

A straw poll of what G.K. Chesterton called 'the democracy of the dead' would thus find overwhelming support for the existence of angels and demons. As Carl Sagan admitted: 'Despite successive waves of rationalist, Persian, Jewish, Christian and Muslim worldviews, despite revolutionary social, political and philosophical ferment, the existence, much of the character, and even the name of demons remained unchanged from Hesiod to the Crusades.'[26] Either this majority of past and present humanity is right (in general, if not in the specific detail of their angelology), or deluded. If it is less plausible to believe that they are deluded than that they are correct, then it is more plausible to believe that angels exist than to deny their existence. At the very least, common consent adds *some* weight to the cumulative case for angels.

2) Authority

Wesley C. Salmon writes: 'It would be a … mistake to suppose that every appeal to authority is illegitimate, for a proper use of authority plays an

---

[23] Fernand Comte, *The Wordsworth Dictionary Of Mythology* (Ware, Hertfordshire: Wordsworth, 1994), p. 73.

[24] Lewis, *Philosophy Of Religion*, p. 191.

[25] < http://www.britannica.com >

[26] Carl Sagan, *The Demon-Haunted World* (London: Hodder Headline, 1996), p. 110. Aside from tarring belief in demons by association with the stranger forms such belief has taken, Sagan provides a naturalistic explanation of demonic phenomena in psychological and physiological terms which he suggests may also account for purported alien abduction experiences. However, Sagan's explanation fails to match the accounts of demon possession in the Bible and in certain contemporary reports, and therefore only serves to strengthen belief in demons. Christians could accept Sagan's explanation for some reports of demonic activity while retaining a belief in demons to explain those reports that his naturalistic explanation seems unable to cover. Sagan pays no attention to angels.

indispensable role in the accumulation and application of knowledge ...
The appeal to reliable authority is legitimate, for the testimony of a
reliable authority *is* evidence for the conclusion.'[27] Authority is right,
not might; it means 'having the right to say'. If anyone has the right to
say whether or not immaterial beings exist, it is surely philosophers
(not scientists!). The majority of the universally acknowledged great
philosophers have believed in the existence of immaterial agents.
Aristotle argued that immaterial beings are responsible for the motion of
the heavens (*Metaphysics* 12:8). Plotinus affirmed the existence of
'guardian spirits' (*Enneads* 3:4). Indeed, the list of philosophers (past
and present) who believe in angels also includes: Mortimer J. Adler,
Anselm, Aquinas, Augustine, Bonaventure, William Lane Craig,
Stephen T. Davis, William A. Dembski, Austin Farrer, Paul D. Feinberg,
Norman L. Geisler, Etienne Gilson, Douglas Groothuis, Gary R.
Habermas, J.J. Haldane, Peter Kreeft, Leibniz, C.S. Lewis, John Locke,
Peter Lombard, Justin Martyr, Terry L. Miethe, J.P. Moreland, Occam,
Stephen E. Parrish, Pascal, Alvin Plantinga, Scott B. Rae, Duns Scotus,
Richard Swinburne, Ronald K. Tacelli and Dallas Willard.

3) Occam's Razor and the occult
The existence of demons would provide a simple, single, unifying
explanation for naturalistically unexplained paranormal phenomena,
which (assuming the reality of such phenomena) is therefore to be
preferred by Occam's Razor over the proposal of multiple, less simple,
or less adequate explanations.[28]

4) Experience
One can argue that since people have encountered angels and demons,
such beings must exist. This is the most persuasive independent evidence,
the evidence that should give naturalists most pause for thought.

Notorious arguments against the believability of reported miracles,
and by extension any reported supernatural event (such as meeting an
angel), have been advanced by the likes of David Hume and Immanuel
Kant; but as Stephen T. Davis reports: 'the vast majority of philosophers
today, whether theists or non-theists, are of the opinion that the relevant
arguments of Hume and Kant are seriously defective. At the very least,

---

[27] Wesley C. Salmon, *Logic* (Englewood Cliffs, New Jersey: Prentice Hall, 1963).

[28] cf. Habermas and Moreland, 'Reincarnation: Is It True?', *Beyond Death* ch. 11; McDowell and Stewart, *The Occult*; Perry (ed.), *Deliverance: Psychic Disturbance And Occult Involvement*; White, *The Science Of The X-Files*.

rather devastating critiques of the relevant views of both philosophers have appeared in the past forty years ... You cannot rule out a priori the possibility of miracles or rational belief in miracles.'[29] The real question is how strong the evidence is. While the evidence may or may not convince the naturalist that belief in angels is rationally obligatory, I think it does demonstrate the rational permissibility of belief in angels. As Hope Price discovered: 'Hundreds, possibly thousands, of men and women living today in Britain are quite certain they have seen angels.'[30] A *Time* magazine poll discovered that 13 per cent of Americans believe they have seen or sensed the presence of an angel (10 per cent claim to have been in the presence of a ghost, but ghosts can be explained by reference to the demonic – cf. argument 3).[31] This means that over thirty-seven million Americans would claim to have been in the presence of an angel. Is it really *likely* that each and every one of over 37 million people are lying or deluded in this matter? If not, then it is *likely* that angels exist. And remember, that's only Americans. Even if we assume a lower 10 per cent claim on the part of the world population we can estimate that some 610 million people think they have encountered an angel. And this is only to count people who are alive today!

It is hugely implausible to question the reality of so much experience; the only question is how best to interpret it. The 'principle of credulity' encourages us to take experience at face value unless we have reason for doubt. Things that might incline us towards doubting the validity of angelic encounters include judgements about the mental or moral unreliability of the witnesses, the availability of simpler but equally adequate interpretations of the experiences in question, or the presumption of naturalism. The first of these possibilities is implausible relative to the number of people involved. The presumption of naturalism is a question-begging presumption, and one there is ample reason to reject. As to the remaining reason for doubt, we must take each report on a case-by-case basis and draw our conclusions. From my own reading of purported angelic and demonic encounters I would say that while many strike me as being open to question, there is nevertheless a hard core of

---

[29] Stephen T. Davis in Paul Copan and Ronald Tacelli (eds), *Jesus' Resurrection: Fact Or Figment?* (Downers Grove, Illinois, IVP, 2000), p. 72. cf. Geivett and Habermas (eds), *In Defence Of Miracles*.

[30] Hope Price, *Angels* (London: Pan, 1995), p. 2.

[31] Gibbs, 'Angels Among Us', p. 56. For the record, I am minded to give ghosts some kind of natural explanation (cf. White, *The Science Of The X-Files*), or to attribute them to demonic forces, as seems most appropriate on a case-by-case study.

reports by otherwise sober-minded, sane and intelligent people that seem to be best explained by the angelic hypothesis. (Of course, the fact that an experience is 'open to question' does not mean that an alternative, naturalistic explanation must be true.) As Peter Kreeft argues, there are only two groups of people who would disagree with the conclusion that *some reported experiences of angels and demons are true*: '(1) the materialists, who claim to know that there are no spirits and thus believe *no* angel stories, and (2) people who even believe the National Enquirer and thus believe *all* angel stories.'[32]

Some testimony to the existence of finite spiritual beings is more impressive than others. Particularly impressive is the testimony of a reasonable man convinced against his prior beliefs on a matter falling within his field of professional expertise. The following description of demon possession comes from Christian psychologist and pastor David Instone Brewer.

> I once went to interview a patient but found that he was asleep. He was lying on his bed, facing the wall, and he did not turn around or respond when I walked in. I sat in his room for a while thinking that he might wake up, and after a while I thought I might pray for him. I started to pray silently for him but I was immediately interrupted because he sat bolt upright, looked at me fiercely and said in a voice which was not characteristic of him: 'leave him alone – he belongs to us.'
>
> Startled, I wasn't sure how to respond, so we just sat and stared at each other for a while. Then I remembered my fundamentalist past and decided to pray silently against what appeared to be an evil spirit ... because I was aware that an hysterical disorder could mimic demon possession. If the person felt that I was treating them as if they were possessed, this would exacerbate the condition and confirm in his mind that he really was possessed. I also prayed silently in case I was making a fool of myself. I can't remember exactly what I prayed but probably rebuked the spirit in the name of Jesus. Immediately I did so, I got another very hostile outburst along the same lines ... I realised then that I was in very deep water and continued to pray, though still silently.
>
> An onlooker would have seen a kind of one-sided conversation. I prayed silently and the person retorted very loudly and emphatically. Eventually (I can't remember what was said or what I prayed) the person cried out with a scream and collapsed on his bed. He woke up a little later, unaware of what had happened. I was still trying to act the role of a medic, so I did not tell him anything about what had happened. His behaviour after waking was quite striking in its normality. He no longer heard any of the oppressive voices

---

[32] Kreeft, *Angels (And Demons)*, p. 102.

which had been making him feel cut off and depressed, and his suicidal urges had gone.[33]

Brewer (a research librarian at Tyndale House, Cambridge) is a trained psychologist who, until this event took place, felt 'fairly satisfied that the Gospel accounts of demonization can be dealt with in terms of modern psychiatry or medicine'. His account is presented 'with much hesitation ... because I realise that they sound very unreasonable in this modern age'. He is careful to distinguish between what he can and can't remember, and his report bears all the marks of a trained observer giving a careful account of something surprising. He wasn't expecting these events. Nor does he leap to conclusions:

> I have personally been persuaded away from [a sceptical viewpoint] by a series of events which occurred while I was studying psychiatry, and during my time in pastoral work ... When I was dealing with the strange personalities which spoke out of [a] person I was always careful to speak silently, even if the person appeared to be asleep. If these personalities were part of a multiple personality syndrome or an hysterical reaction, it would have been counter-productive to speak out loud anything which might make him believe that these personalities were distinct from himself.
>
> These voices answered specific questions such as What is your name?, When did you come? This gradually convinced me that I was not dealing with a purely psychiatric disorder. After such 'conversations', which often involved much shouting, rage and abuse ... the person usually had no memory of any of these disturbing events.[34]

I think we may quickly dismiss the suggestion that Brewer is lying; it is obvious that he is telling us things as he believes they happened. Besides, his experience finds corroboration in the experience of other educated and rational people:

> Reading back to myself what I have written above, it seems like the rambling of a rabid fundamentalist or the paranoia of someone who needs urgent psychiatric help. I can only invite you to assess this in the way in which I present it – as a report of experiences which I have been reluctant to air in public in case they provoke ridicule or condemnation. I have heard similar stories (though not in such detail) from other ministers who are also reluctant to mention such things in public.[35]

---

[33] David Instone Brewer, 'Jesus and the Psychiatrists' in Lane (ed.), *The Unseen World*.
[34] Ibid.
[35] Ibid.

Personally, I am prepared to take Brewer at his word. Given that his experiences cannot easily be given a naturalistic explanation (and if one were possible it seems that Brewer would have known it and have preferred it) then a supernatural interpretation becomes a plausible response to his testimony.

Psychiatrist M. Scott Peck relates his involvement with two cases of possession (both apparently Satanic possession) in his best-selling book *People of The Lie*. Having come to a point of belief in God and in the reality of human evil, Dr Peck says he 'was left facing an obvious intellectual question: Is there such a thing as evil spirit?'[36] He says: 'I thought not ... Still priding myself on being an open-minded scientist, I felt I had to examine the evidence that might challenge my inclination in the matter ...'[37] Peck made it known that he was interested in observing cases of purported possession for evaluation

> The first two cases turned out to be suffering from standard psychiatric disorders, as I had suspected, and I began making marks on my scientific pistol. The third case turned out to be the real thing. Since then I have also been deeply involved with another case of genuine possession. In both cases I was privileged to be present at their successful exorcisms ... As a hard-headed scientist – which I assume myself to be – I can explain 95 percent of what went on in these two cases by traditional psychiatric dynamics ... But I am left with a critical five percent I cannot explain in such ways. I am left with the supernatural – or better yet, subnatural.[38]

Peck argues that while people like to ask whether a patient is possessed or mentally ill, this is an invalid question, for 'As far as I can currently understand these matters, there has to be a significant emotional problem for the possession to occur in the first place. Then the possession itself will both enhance that problem and create new ones. The proper question is: "Is the patient just mentally ill or is he or she mentally ill and possessed?" '[39] Peck affirms the importance of free will in both possession and exorcism:

> Possession appears to be a gradual process in which the possessed person repeatedly sells out for one reason or another ... Free will is basic. It takes precedence over healing. Even God cannot heal a person who does not want to be healed. At the moment of expulsion both these patients voluntarily

---

[36] Peck, *People Of The Lie*, p. 208.
[37] Ibid., pp. 208–9.
[38] Ibid., pp. 209, 224.
[39] Ibid., p. 219.

took the crucifix, held it to their chests and prayed for deliverance. Both chose that moment to cast their lots with God. Ultimately it is the patient himself or herself who is the exorcist.[40]

Peck concludes: 'Given the severity of their psychopathology before their exorcisms, the rapidity of their progress to health is not explainable in terms of what we know about the ordinary psychotherapeutic process.'[41]

Walter Martin reports several cases of demon possession, including an instance involving a non-believing psychologist caused to change his mind by the weight of personal experience.

I had a psychologist friend who was present with me at an exorcism in Newport Beach, California. Before we entered the room he said, 'I want you to know I do not believe in demonic possession. This girl is mentally disturbed.' I said, 'That may well be. We'll find out very soon.' As we went into the room and closed the door, the girl's supernatural strength was soon revealed. Suddenly from her body a totally foreign voice said quietly, with a smirk on the face (she was unconscious – the psychologist testified to that), 'We will outlast you.' The psychologist looked at me and said, 'What was that?' 'That is what you don't believe in,' I said. We spent about 3½ hours exorcising what the psychologist didn't believe in! At the end of the exorcism he was not only a devout believer in the personality of the devil, but in demonic possession and biblical exorcism as well.[42]

So, we have several cases of scientifically minded men, all trained in matters of mental illness (in psychology and psychiatry), convinced, against the grain of their initial scepticism, of the reality of demon possession.

The Revd James LeBarr, as *Time* magazine recently reported, 'is chaplain at a psychiatric hospital and is well aware of the danger of mistaking psychological symptoms for spiritual ones'. Hence he calls in a psychiatrist and a medical doctor before any exorcism, but notes: 'there comes a point, when somebody is climbing up the wall or floating on the ceiling or talking a language they've never studied, when it's harder to put it in the "psychological-problem" bin.'[43] Other

[40] Ibid., pp. 217, 225.

[41] Ibid., p. 227.

[42] Walter Martin, *Exorcism: Fact Or Fable* (Santa Ana, California: Vision House, 1975), p. 21.

[43] James LeBarr quoted in 'If You Liked The Movie …' by David Van Biema, *Time Magazine* @ < http://www.time.com/time/magazine/articles/0,3266,557 22,00.html > To respond to LeBarr's report of someone 'floating on the ceiling'

psychologists and psychiatrists agree that possession is sometimes the best explanation. According to Dr Gary R. Collins, 'Whereas twenty-five years ago the suggestion of demonic activity would have been immediately dismissed, many psychologists are beginning to recognize that maybe there are more things in heaven and earth than our philosophies can account for.'[44]

Consider two cases of possession recorded by the Christian Deliverance Study Group (an Anglican group that helps train those who advise Anglican bishops in this area).

A twenty-four-year-old girl was admitted to a psychiatric clinic, claiming that she was possessed. She was showing some of the traditional signs of possession, for example the ability to speak in a foreign language of which she had no previous knowledge, and an unusual knowledge of events. The psychiatrists were divided as to whether she was suffering from a neurotic or psychotic condition, but agreed that a priest should be involved in the case.

---

[43] (*continued*) (assuming he means this literally) that 'Levitation can't happen so this can't be a real possession' would be question begging. Professor Main, head of physics at the University of Nottingham, worked on a project to levitate a frog using an effect called diamagnetism: 'By changing the energy of electrons whizzing around in the nuclei of atoms, you create a force that acts on a molecular level. "In our experiment, we actually levitated the frog by acting upon its molecules," says Main. The trick lies in balancing the force of gravity against the force of magnetism ... you need exactly the same field to levitate a human as a frog, just a much bigger magnet' (*Focus* no. 109, December 2001, p. 70.) Isn't it conceivable that a demon could replicate this effect by acting directly upon the electrons in a body? Being open to the evidence doesn't mean believing every supernatural claim, but it must mean being ready to accept *sufficient* evidence as warranting a supernatural explanation. Empirical evidence for demons is necessarily evidence for unusual phenomena. Someone keeping their feet on the ground hardly constitutes evidence of possession; whereas someone defying gravity without the use of a very large and expensive magnet might well do! Perhaps a contemporary eye-witness report by the chaplain of an American psychiatric hospital isn't sufficient to warrant belief in a supernatural occurrence. If it isn't, this doesn't disprove levitation or demon possession.

[44] Gary R. Collins in Lee Strobel, *The Case For Christ: A Journalist's Personal Investigation Of The Evidence For Jesus* (Grand Rapids, Michigan: Zondervan, 1998), p. 153. After writing her PhD thesis on Angel Experiences, agnostic Emma Heathcote-James nevertheless admits: 'psychological and medical theories have not provided answers that could explain away every experience I have investigated'. *Seeing Angels* (London: John Blake, 2001), p. 15.

The priest saw the patient interviewed by two psychiatrists and then he interviewed the patient himself. When the priest entered the room, the patient (without knowing of his visit) knew his name and where he was from and that he was an exorcist. It was agreed that the rite of exorcism should be carried out. During this, the patient convulsed and spoke in the voices of three different men, claiming to be Lust, Greed and Death [notice the judicious 'claiming to be']. These spirits were exorcised one at a time, after which the girl collapsed and lost consciousness for a short while. On gaining consciousness, she asked for something to eat, and appeared to be quite normal.[45]

The exorcist was called in by the relatives of the possessed woman, who had been for many years a member of a witch coven centred in the country village in which she had lived all her life. The possessed was a middle-aged woman of limited intelligence and working-class status. She had never left the isolated village in her life except for shopping in the neighbouring market town. *Immediately* the exorcist entered the room, she started calling out details of his past life which he thought he had forgotten and which were relevant to a wild youth. The second priest in the team had served for many years in the Middle East and was an Arabic scholar. He questioned the woman in various Arabic dialects, and she replied in those dialects. Neither the past of the exorcist nor the dialects could have been known to this woman by any rational process. After exorcism she lost these extrasensory powers and renounced her witchcraft.[46]

Of course, not all encounters with angels are encounters with fallen angels. Consider the occasion of the apostle Peter being sprung out of jail by an Angel, as reported in Acts 12. Peter was arrested and placed in prison, guarded 'by four squads of four soldiers each' (Acts 12:4): 'Peter was sleeping between two soldiers, bound with two chains, and sentries stood guard at the entrance. Suddenly an angel of the Lord appeared and a light shone in the cell. He struck Peter on the side and woke him up. "Quick, get up!" he said, and the chains fell off Peter's wrists' (Acts 12:6–7). The Angel tells Peter to dress and to follow him. Peter does so and is led out of the prison: 'but he had no idea that what the angel was doing was really happening; he thought he was seeing a vision' (Acts 12:9). Passing by the guards the iron prison gate opens for them 'by itself' (Acts 12:10) and they make their exit: 'Then Peter came to himself and said, "Now I know without a doubt that the Lord sent his angel and rescued me from Herod's clutches" ' (Acts 12:11). Realizing that he was

---

[45] Perry (ed.), *Deliverance: Psychic Disturbance And Occult Involvement*, p. 125.

[46] Ibid., p. 126.

indeed free, Peter 'went to the house of Mary the mother of John, also called Mark, where many people had gathered and were praying' (Acts 12:12). Peter knocks at the door, but when a servant girl answers it and recognizes Peter's voice she is so excited that she forgets to let him in and runs to tell everyone that Peter is at the door; but they don't believe her. (This is the sort of real-to-life incident of which C.S. Lewis comments, 'there are only two possible views. Either this is reportage … [or else the writer] without known predecessors or successors, suddenly anticipated the whole technique of modern, novelistic, realistic narrative. If it is untrue, it must be narrative of that kind. The reader who doesn't see this has simply not learned to read.')[47] However:

> Peter kept on knocking, and when they opened the door and saw him, they were astonished. Peter motioned with his hand for them to be quiet and described how the Lord had brought him out of prison … In the morning [after Peter has fled to a safe location], there was no small commotion among the soldiers as to what had become of Peter. After Herod had a thorough search made for him and did not find him, he cross-examined the guards and ordered that they be executed (Acts 12:16–19).

Here we have an incident recorded (around about AD 62) by a contemporary, Luke, who is acknowledged to be a careful and reliable historian. Luke writes that the detail of Peter's escape from prison *came from Peter himself*: 'Peter … described how the Lord had brought him out of prison' (Acts 12:17). Luke's account includes plenty of detail in matters of public record (e.g. the guards were executed by Herod), including people's names (Mary the mother of James, also called Mark), that would have been open to falsification by interested parties at the time. This indicates that Luke is confident of his facts. Another indication of authenticity in this account is the incredulity of the Christians involved. Peter does not realize that his escape is actually happening until it is over; and the Christians at Mary's house demonstrate their lack of faith by refusing to believe that their prayers for Peter have been answered. The account specifically rules out any subjective, psychological interpretation. Peter initially thought he was seeing a vision, but then realized that his experience was real. What convinced him of the reality of his experience was obviously the fact that he was no longer within the prison, sleeping chained by the wrists between two soldiers, as he would be had his experience been merely subjective! So what explanation best

---

[47] C.S. Lewis, 'Fern-Seed and Elephants', *Fern-Seed And Elephants* (Glasgow: Fount, 1989), p. 108.

accounts for Peter's escape from Herod's clutches? Is it likely that Peter managed to escape his chains and his guards, the sentries and the prison itself, under his own steam? And if he did, is it likely that this disciple of the world's greatest moral teacher, Jesus – and a man who was in prison for his faith, then proceeded to lie to his fellow believers, spinning them a tall tale about an Angel? No one but a dogmatic naturalist would accept such an unlikely explanation; but this would seem to be the only alternative to accepting the explanation Luke endorses: that an Angel delivered Peter from Herod's jail.

Denver-based Bible teacher Marilyn Hickey relates the story of a man known to her who, like Peter, was released from prison by an Angel. This man (she calls him Louis in her book) was imprisoned in his own country and fellow Christians were praying for him. One night a man in the uniform of a military police officer unlocked the door to Louis's cell and told Louis to follow him. Doing so, Louis noticed that, although this 'officer' had unlocked his cell, he didn't unlock any of the other doors before them. They simply popped open. When they got outside the prison, the 'officer' told Louis to 'go home,' and then he disappeared.[48]

In 1929 Frank Laubach was a missionary in the Philippine Islands. Seeking for a quiet place to pray one day he made a solo walk up to a hilltop on Mindanao, unaware that he was being followed by Moro head-hunters intent on killing him. However, as the head-hunters later told Laubach, they did not attack *because they were afraid of the big man who walked beside him*! Laubach's prayers on the hilltop resulted in his missionary and literacy work with impoverished people that affected almost a million people.[49] Billy Graham relates a similar story of deliverance:

> The Reverend John G. Paton, a missionary in the New Hebrides Islands, tells a thrilling story involving the protective care of angels. Hostile natives surrounded his mission headquarters one night, intent on burning the Patons out and killing them. When daylight came they were amazed to see the attackers unaccountably leave. They thanked God for delivering them.
>
> A year later, the chief of the tribe was converted to Jesus Christ, and Mr. Paton, remembering what had happened, asked the chief what had kept him and his men from burning down the house and killing them. The chief replied in surprise, 'Who were all those men you had with you there?' The missionary answered, 'There were no men there; just my wife and I.' The chief argued that they had seen many men standing guard – hundreds of

---

[48] Law, *The Truth About Angels*, p. 74. cf. Marilyn Hickey, *Angels All Around* (Denver, Colorado: Marilyn Hickey Ministries, 1991), pp. 45–7.

[49] Law, *The Truth About Angels*, p. 71.

big men in shining garments with drawn swords in their hands. They seemed
to circle the mission station so that the natives were afraid to attack. Only
then did Mr Paton realise that God had sent His angels to protect them. The
chief agreed that there was no other explanation.[50]

Non-independent arguments

5) *Scripture teaches the existence of angels and demons (including
    particular Angels and Satan)*
As Peter Kreeft and Ronald Tacelli aver, 'It is clearly and constantly
taught throughout Scripture that God works through these spiritual
intermediaries. Expunge them as inessential and you seem to be left with
a document in tatters.'[51] Norman L. Geisler likewise argues that: 'Those
who take the Bible seriously are obliged to believe in Satan's existence,
since the Bible unmistakably refers to the demonic … Once the authenticity and divine origin of the Bible are established … the existence of
Satan follows.'[52]

There are many reasons for believing that the Bible is God's word:

(i) Confirmation by archaeology.
'Besides the general outline of New Testament history confirmed by
secular sources close to Christ, there is specific confirmation of specific
facts of New Testament history from archaeology.'[53] When a text is reliable in matters that can and have been tested, we should gain confidence
in its reliability in matters that have not or cannot be tested.

*(ii) Scripture has a common message, including the common witness of
     the New Testament writers to the teaching and deeds of Jesus.*
For all its diversity, the Bible contains an amazing unity considering that
it is a collection of material written by so many different authors over
such a swathe of human history. A single source of inspiration would
explain this unity.

*(iii) The human author's conviction that they spoke with God's
      authority.*
Peter wrote in a letter that: 'We did not follow cleverly invented stories
when we told you about the power and coming of our Lord Jesus Christ,

---

[50] Graham, *Angels*, p. 15.
[51] Kreeft and Tacelli, *Handbook Of Christian Apologetics*, p. 116.
[52] Geisler, *Baker Encyclopedia Of Christian Apologetics*, p. 683.
[53] Geisler, *Christian Apologetics*, p. 325.

but we were eye-witnesses of his majesty' (2 Pet. 1:16). Luke begins his Gospel with the assertion that: 'since I myself have carefully investigated everything from the beginning, it seemed good also to me to write an orderly account for you, most excellent Theophilus, so that you may know the certainty of the things you have been taught' (Lk. 1:3–4). Timothy wrote that: 'All Scripture is inspired by God and useful for teaching the truth, rebuking error, correcting faults, and giving instruction for right living ...' (2 Tim. 3:16–17 GNB). These men are either lying, or delusional, or telling the truth. If they are neither lying nor deceived then they are telling the truth. Given the high moral standards of these men and the nature of their writings, which option is most rational? I submit that it is the last option.

(iv) The Bible's indestructibility.
The indestructibility of the Bible lends some support to the idea of its divine preservation. In spite of facing determined and aggressive assaults, the Bible has not only survived, but has consistently triumphed. The Bible has been likened to an anvil that has worn out the hammers of countless opponents.

(v) The long and constant witness of the church.
This is really an argument from common consent and authority. There is an uninterrupted testimony, stretching over three millennia, from the great and the good, from all over the world, to the mark of divinity born by the Bible. If a book impresses itself upon impressive minds it had better impress us as well.

(vi) The power of the Bible's teaching.
It is my experience that in so far as I follow the teaching of the Bible about things such as personal relationships, those relationships work and are the best sort of relationships I can imagine. When I don't do what the Bible says, things don't work so well. Just as the fact that when I follow the correct instruction manual my Word for Windows package works, so the fact that the Bible's teachings work is some indication that it is, as it were, the correct instruction manual. If the biblical teaching is the best teaching about how to live the best life, who should I suspect wrote it? People who were just having a guess, who only had a lifetime's experience to draw upon, who were drawing upon the accumulated wisdom of a historical community, or who really knew what they were talking about? Obviously, people who really knew what they were talking about. The 'right by luck' suggestion is totally implausible. The

'humanly experienced' suggestions are more plausible, but then one would expect other books to give equally good advice.

The Bible's ethical teaching is an outworking of its theological teaching, and is there to protect and guide us as to how life is best lived. If you ignore the maker's instructions – for example, by putting Guinness in the petrol tank of your car – you don't find freedom and happiness, you find yourself going nowhere and faced with a mechanic's bill! So it is, in my experience, with the Bible. If the manual really helps you run the car well, you'd suspect the car's manufacturer was at least in the background of the manual's creation. Likewise, if the Bible really works in my life, then I'm going to suspect that the author of life is, at the very least, in the background somewhere.

(vii) The fulfilment of biblical prophecy.

Fulfilled prophecy is evidence in which some apologists invest far too much, and with inadequate care. Nevertheless, it seems to me that there are at least some genuinely predictive prophecies. As Norman L. Geisler reports of Isaiah 53:

> In Old Testament times, the Jewish rabbis *did* consider this to be a prophecy concerning the Messiah. That's the opinion that's really relevant. Only later, after Christians pointed out this was obviously referring to Jesus, did they begin saying it was really about the suffering Jewish nation. But clearly that's wrong. Isaiah customarily refers to the Jewish people in the first-person-plural ... but he always refers to the Messiah in the third-person singular ... and that's what he did in Isaiah 53. Plus, anyone who reads it for themselves will readily see it's referring to Jesus.[54]

Isaiah lays down the following challenge: 'Bring in your idols to tell us what is going to happen ... declare to us the things to come, tell us what the future holds, so that we may know that you are gods' (Isa. 41:22–23). Isaiah clearly sets up a distinction between idols who cannot and so do not reveal the future, and God, who can and does: 'Underlying all the prophetic writings, and also in a sense the whole of the Old Testament, there is an atmosphere of expectation, a looking-forward to a climax of history or a fulfillment of God's sovereign purpose ...'[55] Robert C. Newman writes:

> Fulfilled predictions are one type of miracle that can be tested centuries after the event took place. All we need is good evidence (1) that the text clearly

---

[54] Norman L. Geisler in Strobel, *The Case For Faith*, p. 132.
[55] Ibid., p. 199.

envisions the sort of event alleged to be the fulfillment, (2) that the prophecy was made well in advance of the event predicted, (3) that the prediction actually came true and (4) that the event predicted could not have been staged [or infallibly known in advance] by anyone but God. The strength of the evidence is greatly enhanced if (5) the event itself is so unusual that the apparent fulfillment cannot be plausibly explained as a good guess.[56]

When these criteria are met fulfilled prophecies are instances of specified complexity, meriting a design inference. For example, the book of Ezekiel, completed *c.* 565 BC,[57] provides an elaborate prediction about the fate of the powerful seaport city state of Tyre (cf. Ezek. 26ff.). This particular prophecy dates from 586 BC, the eleventh year of the reign of Jehoiakim. The sixth-century BC dating of Ezekiel has been confirmed by archaeology: 'Stone tablets have been found with a nearly complete text of the book of Ezekiel dating from 600–500 BC (the time of Ezekiel). This verifies the existence of the prophecy long before its fulfillment.'[58] Ezekiel prophesies that 'many nations' will come against Tyre, tearing down its walls and towers; its rubble will be scraped away and it will become a bare rock, they will 'throw your stones, timber and rubble into the sea'; 'Out at sea she will become a place to spread fishnets' and it 'will never be rebuilt'. What happened? Tyre was besieged for thirteen years by Nebuchadnezzar, who took the mainland portion of Tyre in 573 BC. In the course of the siege the citizens of Tyre relocated to an island about a half-mile offshore 'and Nebuchadnezzar's troops had to settle for little plunder'.[59] About 250 years later (*c.* 322 BC), Alexander the Great attacked this island city.

> Having no navy, he used the rubble from the old mainland city and slave labor from the surrounding nations to build a causeway out to the island to capture the city. To obtain enough material for the causeway, the mainland site was scrapped clean. Though the island city later recovered, a substantial

---

[56] Robert C. Newman, 'Fulfilled Prophecy as Miracle' in Geivett and Habermas (eds), *In Defence Of Miracles*, p. 214.

[57] cf. John Stephen Jauchen (ed.), *NIV Thompson Student Bible* (Indianapolis, Indiana: Kirkbride Bible Company, 1999).

[58] Ralph O. Muncaster, *Does The Bible Predict The Future?* (Eugene, Oregon: Harvest House, 2000), p. 40. 'Study of the specific form of Hebrew used in the inscriptions indicates the tablets were written during the time of Ezekiel – 600 to 500 BC.' Ralph O. Muncaster, *Can Archaeology Prove The Old Testament?* (Eugene, Oregon: Harvest House, 2000), p. 43.

[59] Robert C. Newman, 'Fulfilled Prophecy as Miracle' in Geivett and Habermas (eds), *In Defence Of Miracles*, p. 214.

village now occupying the northern part of the former island, the mainland site has never been restored. Moreover, parts of the former island are used even today for spreading fishnets.[60]

I agree with Newman that: 'The specifications about Tyre are sufficiently unusual to make coincidence unlikely. They were fulfilled by such actors over such a time span as to rule out the plausibility of intentional human fulfillment.'[61]

In a passage read every year at Christmas carol services throughout the world, Isaiah writes:

> Therefore the Lord himself will give you a sign: The virgin will be with child and will give birth to a son, and will call him Immanuel ... For to us a child is born, to us a son is given, and the government will be upon his shoulders. And he will be called Wonderful Counsellor, Mighty God, Everlasting Father, Prince of Peace. Of the increase of his government and peace there will be no end. He will reign on David's throne and over his kingdom, establishing it and upholding it with justice and righteousness from that time on and for ever. The zeal of the Lord Almighty will accomplish this (Isa. 7:14, 9:6–7).

According to Robert D. Culver: 'Here we have the opening and closing words of a single prophetic oracle. The majority of scholars, both liberal and conservative, agree in this. Too often expositors have sought to explain one portion of the prophecy without the other.'[62] It has been questioned whether 'virgin' is the best translation here (although the Greek translation of the Old Testament used a word meaning virgin); some suggest that 'young woman' would be a better rendering. One wonders how the birth of a son to a young woman would be much of 'a sign' from God; but even putting this question aside, there is more here to examine, for 'Immanuel' means 'God with us'. According to Isaiah then, God promises (1) a son (not a daughter), born (2) to a young woman/virgin, who (3) is to be equated with God and who will reign (4) in the line of king David with (5) 'no end', 'forever' (something no merely human king could accomplish). Jesus *was*: (1) a son; (2) born of a young woman (a virgin); (3) equated with God; (4) of David's line[63] (Mt. 1:1); and (5) people ever since *have* counted him as their Lord and king.

---

[60] Ibid.

[61] Ibid.

[62] Robert D. Culver, 'Were the Old Testament Prophecies Really Prophetic?' in Howard F. Vos (ed.), *Can I Trust The Bible?* (Chicago, Illinois: Moody Press, 1971), p. 104.

[63] In 1993 a fragment of a stone monument was discovered at Tel Dan, near the

Many other prophetic passages are fulfilled in the person of Jesus (e.g. Ps. 22, where the parallels with Jesus' 'passion' are striking). It might be objected that some events may have been humanly manipulated so as to fulfil prophecy and give the appearance of Jesus being the Messiah. But there are many fulfilled prophecies over which Jesus could, humanly speaking, have had no control, such as: the time of his birth (Dan. 9), the place of his birth (Mic. 5:2), and the circumstances of his death (Ps. 22). Nor can these fulfilled prophecies be plausibly explained away as 'flukes of history'. The odds against one man fulfilling the conditions of all the relevant prophecies by luck are phenomenal.[64] Besides, would God allow prophecy to be fulfilled by mistake, or by the wrong person? Fulfilled prophecy thus appears to be a case where the miraculous activity of God can be offered as 'a best causal explanation … when naturalistic processes seem incapable [or unlikely] of producing the *explanandum* effect, and when intelligence is known to be capable of producing it and thought to be more likely to have produced it.'[65] As Robert D. Culver concludes:

> Even by using the most extreme tactics it is impossible to date a large number of the Old Testament prophecies so late that they may be considered mere historical accounts rather than predictions. And once we conclude that many of these prophecies are truly prophetic, the whole narrative of human history becomes a vast account of their fulfilment and a vast demonstration of the power and foreknowledge of God and the truth of His Word.[66]

(viii) The authority of Christ.
This is the argument closest to the core of Christian belief: Jesus guarantees the authority of scripture. Jesus held the Old Testament in high regard: 'I tell you the truth, until heaven and earth disappear, not the smallest letter, not the least stroke of a pen, will by any means disappear

---

[63] (*continued*) border of Israel and Syria, that mentions King David and the 'House of David'. cf. Muncaster, *Can Archaeology Prove The Old Testament?*, p. 33.

[64] Peter Stoner, former chair of the Mathematics and Astronomy Department at Pasadena City College, and later chair of the Department of Science at Westmont, analysed 48 specific predictions about the Messiah fulfilled by Jesus and concluded that the chances of anyone fulfilling them by chance was 1 in 10 to the power of 157! cf. 'Prophecy Proves The Bible' @ < http://www.geocities.com/Athens/Aegean/8830/prophecy.html >

[65] Meyer, *The Creation Hypothesis*, p. 97.

[66] Culver, 'Were the Old Testament Prophecies Really Prophetic?' in Vos (ed.), *Can I Trust The Bible?*, pp. 115–16.

from the Law until everything is accomplished' (Mt. 5:18). He quoted scripture as an authority, often using the phrase 'It is written ...' He spoke of himself and of events surrounding him as being a fulfilment of the Old Testament, i.e. 'The Law' (Lk. 24:25–27). Most emphatically, he said: 'The Scripture [i.e. The Old Testament] cannot be broken' (Jn. 10:35). Jesus is recorded as giving authority to his disciples to 'go and make disciples of all nations' (Mt. 28:19). Writing the Gospels and letters that make up the New Testament is fairly obviously an integral part of that project. Jesus promised that he would send the Holy Spirit, '[the one] my Father has promised' (Lk. 24:49), who would lead them 'into all truth' (Jn. 16:13). Jesus said to his disciples that the Holy Spirit would teach them all things and remind them of all he had said to them (Jn. 14:26). In other words, 'Jesus not only confirmed the divine authority of the Old Testament but he also guaranteed the inspiration of the New Testament.'[67] This line of thought has been accused of arguing in a circle, using the Bible to prove the Bible. But this objection merely reveals a lack of attention on the part of the critic. From the premise that the New Testament writings that attribute the relevant sayings to Jesus are historically reliable it is argued, on the basis of the claims recorded in those documents, that Jesus is divine, and concluded that what Jesus says, including what he says about scripture, is therefore authoritative. Allow me to briefly validate this important argument.

Premise One: The New Testament is a well-attested, generally reliable source of historical information about Jesus: The New Testament Gospels and letters were written within the lifetime of eyewitnesses. Many of these documents were written by eyewitnesses and/or with the collaboration of eyewitnesses; eyewitnesses who, moreover, were often martyred for refusing to renounce the truth of their accounts. Scholars are agreed that all four Gospels were written within sixty or so years of Jesus' death. More 'conservative' scholars think all or most of the Gospels were written within thirty or so years of Jesus' death. According to F.F. Bruce, 'even with the later dates, the situation is encouraging from the historian's point of view, for the first three Gospels were written at a time when many were alive who could remember the things that Jesus said and did, and some at least would still be alive when the fourth Gospel was written.'[68] Nevertheless, 'in recent years, there has been a trend in New Testament studies towards dating the Gospels

---

[67] Geisler, *Christian Apologetics*, p. 368.

[68] F.F. Bruce, *The New Testament Documents: Are They Reliable?* (Leicester: IVP, 2000), p. 17.

earlier.'[69] The texts as we have them are better attested than any other piece of ancient literature. As theologian John A.T. Robinson states: 'the wealth of manuscripts, and above all the narrow interval of time between the writing and the earliest extant copies, make it by far the best attested text of any ancient writing in the world.'[70] If you want to deny the historicity of the New Testament you must deny the whole of ancient history. As Professor Craig L. Blomberg concludes: 'on sheer historical grounds alone there is substantial reason to believe in the general trustworthiness of the Gospel tradition.'[71] (For more on the historical reliability of the New Testament, see Appendix I.)

Premise Two: The New Testament validates the hypothesis that Jesus is divine: While Jesus didn't exactly go around saying 'I'm God,' he *did* lay claim to divinity in a host of *implicit* ways that are more or less explicit.[72] You can't get much more explicit than claiming, as Jesus did, the authority to forgive sin or the right to sit on God's judgement throne! As William Lane Craig reports, 'the majority of New Testament critics today agree that the historical Jesus deliberately stood and spoke in the place of God himself.'[73] Jesus' claim to divinity forces us to ask, 'Was he sincere or was he lying?' If he wasn't lying, then he must have been sincere. If he was sincere, he was either right or wrong. If he was wrong, then he was sincerely deluded about his very selfhood in such a fundamental way that it could only be described as madness. Therefore, if Jesus was neither lying nor mad, he was both sincere and correct.[74]

Fulfilled prophecy (see above) and Jesus' resurrection act as a divine seal of approval upon Jesus' claims. Gary R. Habermas argues that any conclusion about the historicity of the resurrection must accommodate the minimal set of facts acknowledged by the majority of critical scholars.

Virtually no one doubts Jesus' death by crucifixion. It is also recognized that the disciples despaired ... As well recognized as any New Testament fact is

---

[69] Moreland, *Scaling The Secular City*, p. 151.

[70] John A.T. Robinson, *Can We Trust The New Testament?* (Grand Rapids, Michigan: Eerdmans, 1977), p. 36.

[71] Craig L. Blomberg, *Jesus And The Gospels: An Introduction And Survey* (Leicester: Apollos, 1997), p. 381. For more on the reliability of the New Testament, see Appendix I.

[72] cf. Bibliography.

[73] William Lane Craig, *Will The Real Jesus Please Stand Up?* (Grand Rapids, Michigan: Baker, 1999), p. 25.

[74] cf. Bibliography.

that, shortly after Jesus' death, these followers had experiences that they believed were appearances of the risen Jesus. As a result, they were transformed from being in a state of fear to being willing to die for their faith. Very soon afterwards, the disciples proclaimed Jesus' death and resurrection as their central message in Jerusalem and the surrounding area, and the church was born. Two skeptics, Jesus' brother James and Saul (Paul) became believers after they also believed that Jesus had appeared to them.[75]

Stephen T. Davis writes: 'no one who denies that Jesus was raised from the dead or who offers reductive theories of the resurrection has yet been able to account adequately for these widely accepted facts. Though many have tried, no one who rejects belief in the resurrection of Jesus has been able to tell a convincing story of what occurred in the days following the crucifixion.'[76] Occam's Razor enjoins us to pick the simplest adequate hypothesis to explain the known data, and adequacy is more important than simplicity. Therefore, we should accept the resurrection as the simplest *adequate* explanation of the facts (indeed, as the only adequate explanation). C.S. Lewis hit the nail on the head when he said: 'The question is, I suppose, whether any hypothesis covers the facts so well as the Christian hypothesis.'[77] With Lewis, I think the evidence clearly supports 'the Christian hypothesis': 'The alternative hypothesis is not legend, nor exaggeration, nor the apparitions of a ghost. It is either lunacy or lies. Unless one can take the ... alternative (and I can't) one turns to the Christian theory.'[78]

Conclusion: What Jesus teaches about scripture is true: 'a demonstration of the general historical trustworthiness of the [New Testament], particularly of the Gospels and Acts, impels one to respond to the claims of Christ which confront us on almost every page. And if one accepts the [New Testament's] portrait of who Jesus is, then one ought to believe his teachings, not least with respect to his high view of Scriptures.'[79]

---

[75] Gary R. Habermas in Cowan (ed.) *Five Views On Apologetics*, p. 115.

[76] Stephen T. Davis, *Risen Indeed* (London: SPCK, 1993), pp. 180–81.

[77] Lewis, 'God in the Dock', *God In The Dock*, p. 83.

[78] Ibid.

[79] Craig L. Blomberg, 'The Historical Reliability of the New Testament' in Craig, *Reasonable Faith*, p. 203. However, we shouldn't simply hand angelology over to a supposedly simple process of compiling proof texts. The Bible is not a work of systematic or philosophical theology. We cannot evade the task of paying attention to hermeneutical issues, or that of seeking to integrate the voices of Christian tradition, experience, theology and philosophy.

Once you accept the reliability of the relevant texts, and the divinity of Jesus, the authority of the biblical record becomes inescapable, because that authority is established by the authoritative testimony of God transmitted through a historically reliable text.

6) Jesus taught the existence of angels

Jesus clearly thought that angels and demons were real, but 'To be a disciple of Jesus means, among other things, to trust what he said.'[80] Jesus' attitude to Angels and demons in the New Testament is surely hard to discount as an accommodation to unsophisticated times:

> Belief in angels was not universal in Jesus' day. The Sadducees, for example, disbelieved in angels as well as the resurrection. Jesus went out of his way to side against them on the reality of angels as well (see Mk 12:25). His teaching about angels was unprecedented in the ancient world; he said 'these little ones' – that is, children, and perhaps the uneducated – have angels who 'continually see the face of my father in heaven' (Mt 18:10). No Jew had ever taught that angels behold the face of God – even the seraphim must shield their eyes from his glory (Isa. 6:2). If angels do not exist, then Jesus was *wrong* when he taught these things. And if he was wrong, then he was not a fully trustworthy teacher. Is any Christian ready to believe that?[81]

Therefore, disciples of Jesus ought to believe in the existence of Angels and demons.

7) Christian tradition teaches the existence of angels

'As a part of formulating a biblical and systematic theology ... the main contours of church history should be consulted, and a burden of proof should be placed on any view that is at odds with what the majority of great thinkers have held throughout church history.'[82] This principle does not suggest 'that the voice of church history is univocal or infallible',[83] but simply that 'the teachings of the great intellectual leaders of the past provide insights that should be taken seriously.'[84] As Stephen T. Davis writes: 'Respect for Christian tradition must (or so I would argue) grant great weight to views held by virtually all the fathers of the church unless there is serious reason to depart from what they say.'[85] After all,

---

[80] Habermas and Moreland, *Beyond Death*, p. 66.
[81] Kreeft and Tacelli, *Handbook Of Christian Apologetics*, p. 116.
[82] Moreland and Rae, *Body & Soul*, p. 43.
[83] Ibid.
[84] Ibid.
[85] Ibid., pp. 43–4.

the voice of a Christian thinker should carry more prima facie weight for the Christian than the voice of a secular thinker; not only because the secular thinker inevitably operates within a system of presuppositions antithetical to the Christian worldview (and hence to the truth), but because the office of teacher is recognized in scripture as a gift of the Holy Spirit. The existence of angels is clearly taught by the church fathers and the majority of great thinkers throughout church history. Therefore Christians ought to believe in angels unless they have good reason not to do so. However, as the previous chapter demonstrated, there is no good reason to disbelieve in angels – certainly not if one accepts, as Christians should accept, the existence of God and the human soul. Therefore the authority of Christian tradition is good reason for the Christian to believe in angels.

8) *Demons have a role to play in theodicy, and this fact provides*
　　theists with some support for the hypothesis that demons exist
Arguments for the conclusion that God and evil are logically compatible do not need (and generally do not claim) to be *plausible* explanations of *how it is* that God and evil are compatible. This is the task assumed by *theodicy*. Rather, as Kelly James Clark writes, 'All the theist needs to do, to refute the logical problem of evil, is to specify a possible way or a possible state of affairs for evil and God to consistently coexist.'[86] Alvin Plantinga famously pointed out that referring natural evil to demons extends the free will defence, thereby proving that God and evil are not logically incompatible. It is implausible to think that *all* natural evil is in fact due to demons, but in a logical *defence* plausibility is irrelevant. However, the fact that demons could explain some evil not attributable to human free will, thereby providing a partial explanation of *how it is* that the co-existence of God and evil is not a contradictory state of affairs, provides anyone who believes in God with *some* warrant for believing that fallen angels exist. And if fallen angels exist, unfallen angels are a distinct possibility.

　　This is admittedly a fairly weak argument since, as Swinburne notes, there is little independent evidence to show that demons have very much power.[87] Nevertheless, as part of the cumulative evidence for angelic beings, this evidence has a part to play. Indeed, the fallen angel hypothesis is a thoroughly plausible and non-*ad hoc* element of Christian theodicy:

---

[86] Clark, *Return To Reason*, pp. 65–6.
[87] However, consider reports of demonic levitation.

Auschwitz, Hiroshima, Bataan, the Gulag, the Ukraine, Rwanda, the 'killing-fields' of Pol Pot's Cambodia, Mao's 'Great Leap Forward' – is this evil natural or supernatural? Is it not the Marquis de Sade writ large and multiplied by millions? A telling a chilling sign that these evils are from the Devil, not the world or the flesh, is the total absence of remorse that followed, in every case, on the part of the perpetrators. No one who actually experienced these atrocities could believe that human nature alone was responsible for such unlimited and deliberate malice. To have no remorse for having macheted pregnant women, bayoneted babies like melons, or systematically gassed six million Jews only because they were Jews is not human. The demon, having done his work through his human instruments, departs, and the killer feels no guilt, as if he had not been there, as if the deed had been done by someone else. Alas, this is precisely the case. Even the agnostic humanist, meeting such evil, approves the sentiment that this could not have been merely human. For if it were, the humanist would have to believe an even more misanthropic anthropology than that of the 'Original Sin Conservative' he despises.[88]

Whether we are considering moral or apparently natural evil, the theist has good reason to adopt belief in fallen angels.

9) *Extrapolation*

Finally, the theist can argue by extrapolation (as Mendeleev argued in constructing the periodic table of elements). Since nature seems to contain life at every possible level, and since there is an obvious gap between the infinite, immaterial God and finite, embodied human beings, one would expect the existence of finite but immaterial beings. Following in the footsteps of Aquinas, John Locke argued just so in his *Essay Concerning Human Understanding* (Book III, Chapter VI, Section 12 and Book IV, Chapter XVI, Section 12). As F.C. Copleston summarizes the argument:

> We can discern the ascending order or ranks of forms from the forms of inorganic substances, through vegetative forms, the irrational sensitive forms of animals; the rational soul of man, to the infinite … God: but there is a gap in the hierarchy. The rational soul of man is created, finite and embodied, while God is uncreated, infinite and pure spirit; it is only reasonable, then, to suppose that between the human soul and God there are finite and created spiritual forms which are without body.[89]

---

[88] Peter Kreeft, < http://catholiceducation.org/articles/religion/re0018.html >
[89] F.C. Copleston, *History Of Philosophy: Medieval Philosophy* (London: Search Press, 1979), p. 329.

The argument from extrapolation can be seen as an extension into metaphysics of the scientific principle of plenitude. Physicist Paul Davies writes: 'It has generally been the experience of scientists that there are few rules or processes consistent with the laws of nature that fail to be instantiated somewhere in nature ... Physicists find that if there is a place for the description of a certain sort of particle in [the mathematics of particle physics], then the actual physical particle is found to exist in suitable circumstances.'[90] Given that 'nature' is the creation of God, this principle of plenitude gives us reason for thinking that God is not 'minimalist' in his creative tastes. There seems to be no reason to think that God's taste suddenly changes at the limits of the natural world. This being so, we have reason to expect that God has created in the realm of the purely supernatural.

Conclusion

Angelology employs a typically scientific mode of argumentation, namely, argument to best explanation: 'Suppose we have a set of items xi through xn that stand in need of explanation and we offer some explanans E as an adequate or even best explanation of the explanda. In such a case, E explains xi through xn and this fact provides some degree of confirmation for E.'[91] Here is a set of proposed explanda:

(1) The majority of humanity believes in angels.
(2) The majority of philosophers believe in angels.
(3) There are various paranormal phenomena that would be coherently and economically explained if demons exist.
(4) There are multiple historical and contemporary reports by evidently honest and intelligent eyewitnesses (including psychologists, psychiatrists and clergy) to the reality of Angels and demonic possession (including Satanic possession).
(5) The Bible teaches that Angels and demons (including Gabriel, Michael and Satan) exist (and we have good reason to trust what the Bible teaches).
(6) Jesus teaches that Angels and demons (including Satan) exist (and we have good reason to trust what Jesus teaches).
(7) Christian tradition teaches that Angels and demons (including Satan) exist.

---

[90] Paul Davies, *Are We Alone?* (London: Penguin, 1995), pp. 15–16.

[91] J.P. Moreland, @ < http://capo.org/premise/96/april/p960406.html >, p. 2.

(8) The hypothesis that demons exist provides a partial explanation of *how it is* that God and evil are compatible realities.

(9) Given the existence of God, there is a continuous pattern of hierarchy in creation that seems to come to a unique, aesthetically abrupt and unexpected end, unless angels exist.

I offer the existence of angels as the most reasonable hypothesis given these nine explanda.[92]

Philosophers of science 'have proposed three criteria that must be satisfied for [a hypothesis] to constitute the best explanation of [the evidence]'.[93] First, the hypothesis must be *consonant* with the evidence. Instead of injecting discord into our understanding of the evidence, the hypothesis must harmonize with it and with the network of beliefs of which the evidence is a part. Consonance is more than a requirement of logical coherence: 'Consonance involves both goodness of fit and aesthetic or theoretical judgement.'[94] Second, the hypothesis must *contribute* to explaining the evidence. This is done by solving problems or answering questions pertinent to the evidence 'which could not be handled otherwise'.[95] This requirement 'is a corollary of Occam's razor, ensuring that adding [the hypothesis] to our stock of beliefs will not be superfluous'.[96] Third, as the best explanation, the hypothesis in question must have a comparative advantage over its rivals; it 'must simply do a better job of explaining [the evidence] than any of its current competitors'.[97] What results when we apply these three criteria to the hypothesis that angels exist?

First, the hypothesis of angels is clearly *consonant* with the evidence. Instead of injecting discord into our understanding of the above evidence, the angelic hypothesis harmonizes with it and, particularly in the case of the 'non-independent arguments', with the network of beliefs (theism and/or Christianity) of which the evidence is a part. Indeed, the angelic hypothesis has a particularly good theoretical and aesthetic 'fit' with the theistic/Christian worldview. Second, the angelic hypothesis certainly contributes to explaining the evidence. If angels did exist, then

---

[92] For a more technical account of how these explanda support the existence of angels, cf. Appendix II.

[93] William A. Dembski and Stephen C. Meyer, *Science And Evidence For Design In The Universe* (San Francisco: Ignatius, 2000), p. 227.

[94] Ibid.

[95] Ibid.

[96] Ibid.

[97] Ibid., p. 228.

many otherwise unexpected things (Jesus teaching their existence, people apparently meeting them, etc.) would be a matter of course. Or to put it another way, the existence of angels would coherently explain a wide range of phenomena. For example, anyone who believes in God and the immateriality of the human mind but not angels owe those who believe in all three an explanation of why God's observed pattern of creativity would come to the abrupt and aesthetically jarring halt the non-existence of angels causes. Third, the angelic hypothesis has a comparative advantage over its rivals. For example, consider the evidence of demonic possession. The principal rival to the angelic hypothesis in this instance is (an admittedly simpler) naturalistic explanation in terms of some sort of natural mental disorder. However, the psychological explanation loses out to the angelic explanation on two counts. For one thing, the psychological explanation is inadequate. While a psychological explanation of purported possession may sometimes (or even mainly) be the best explanation, there do seem to be cases where it isn't up to the task. There are several cases where initially sceptical trained psychologists or psychiatrists have become convinced that some instances of possession are genuine. The psychological explanation cannot account for as wide a range of data as the angelic hypothesis (it can't account for Peter's escape from prison, etc). On all three criteria then, the existence of angels is the best explanation.

If one considers *only the independent evidence* (1–4) I would estimate that the arguments given above make belief in angels rationally *permissible*, as long as one does not begin with a dogmatic belief in naturalism (a belief against which I believe there is a sufficient weight of evidence to prove false). This means that belief in angels is, subjectively speaking, rationally *permissible* not only for Christians, but for people of various other worldviews (including Jews, Muslims, New Age believers and agnostics). The argument from experience is surely the hardest evidence to discount here, but we should not forget that one's assessment of the evidence depends upon what background knowledge one allows. For example, the initial plausibility of angels is lower for the agnostic than for the philosophical theist. On the other hand, if one additionally takes into consideration *the non-independent evidence* (5–9) then, presuming one accepts the relevant background knowledge, belief in angels is surely rationally *obligatory*. Certainly, consideration of the cumulative force of the total evidence makes belief in angels not only rationally *permissible* but also rationally *obligatory* for Christians, and perhaps for philosophical theists and members of other theistic religions.

These conclusions should teach Christians not to disparage New Age belief in angels *per se*, but to concentrate on showing them how belief in angels is rendered more compelling, secure and specific by acceptance of the Christian system, and to providing a loving critique of New Age angelology and worldview from the Christian perspective. It also teaches us that in discussion with someone who is a naturalist or a Christian non-believer the Christian believer should concentrate on defending the rationally obligatory nature of belief in angels *given that the Christian worldview is true* (or at least, given that God exists). With the naturalist, the Christian believer should aim to highlight the importance of presuppositions so that the debate can be moved to a discussion of naturalism versus theism. In all these cases fruitful debate is possible. The intellectual goal of such debates should primarily be to encourage an awareness of the crucial role played by worldview presuppositions and the susceptibility of such presuppositions to rational, truth orientated inquiry, so that ultimately both parties might share in the truth. Of course, such debates should have more than an intellectual goal. Other goals in debate are as important, if not more important, than intellectual goals. For example, the goal of fostering friendly mutual respect for the persons involved as individuals.

I conclude that angels are not only weakly conceivable (possible), not only strongly conceivable (plausible), but that they are actual. Angels exist.

Appendix I

New Testament Criticism and Jesus the Exorcist

What do you want with us, Jesus of Nazareth? Have you come to destroy us? I know who you are – the Holy One of God!

> – Anonymous demon (Mk. 1:24)

The New Testament presents Jesus as, among other things, 'an exorcist *par excellence*'.[1] Is the acceptance of this claim historically plausible in the light of New Testament criticism? I will argue that it is.

John's Gospel ignores the already well-trod subject of exorcism: 'John's Gospel does not record any exorcisms. The author chose to use a selection of signs to enforce his teaching and it may be that the exorcisms did not achieve his purposes.'[2] We will therefore concentrate upon the so-called synoptic Gospels of Matthew, Mark and Luke, as well as Luke's sequel to his Gospel, Acts.

It is common today to divide Jesus' miracles into three categories: healings, exorcisms and nature miracles. 'It may be surprising that the community of critical scholars appears to have adjusted its stance toward at least the first two divisions,' says Gary R. Habermas, but this is indeed the case: 'A majority of recent scholars believe that Jesus was at least a healer and an exorcist.'[3] According to Craig L. Blomberg, 'Jesus was most certainly an exorcist.'[4] Even as liberal a scholar as 'Jesus Seminar' member Marcus Borg concludes: 'it is virtually indisputable that Jesus was a healer and exorcist.'[5] Fellow Jesus Seminar member

---

[1] Brewer, 'Jesus and the Psychiatrists' in Lane (ed.), *The Unseen World*, p. 148.
[2] Keith Warrington, *Jesus The Healer* (Carlisle: Paternoster, 2000).
[3] Gary R. Habermas, *Why I Am A Christian* (Grand Rapids, Michigan: Baker, 2001), p. 117.
[4] Craig L. Blomberg, *The Historical Reliability Of The Gospels* (Leicester: IVP, 1987), p. 90.
[5] Quoted by Habermas, *Why I Am A Christian*.

John Dominic Crossan likewise affirms: 'You cannot ignore the healings and exorcisms,' and adds that: 'throughout his life Jesus performed healings and exorcisms for ordinary people.'[6] Rudolf Bultmann concurs that there is 'no doubt' Jesus really 'healed the sick and expelled demons'.[7] A.M. Hunter's statement on the matter is carefully worded: 'No Christian with a respect for his intellectual integrity need doubt that Jesus ... cured those thought to be possessed by evil spirits ...'[8] As Habermas concedes of this scholarly acceptance of Jesus' healings and exorcisms: 'Usually, these are recognized as historical and explained cognitively. Both sick individuals as well as those who thought they were possessed by demons get better when they *believed* they were well.'[9] In other words, many scholars accept that Jesus cured apparently possessed people, but attempt to explain away the supernatural reality of both the problem and solution as Jesus and the biblical writers understood it. Hunter's judicious affirmation is compatible with acceptance or denial of genuine demon possession and exorcism. The question remains: Do the Gospels understandably but falsely portray Jesus as successfully exorcising real demons, or is the portrait of Jesus exorcising demons correct? Can an investigation of the historical data lead us towards a more definite conclusion either way? One's answer to that question will be primarily determined by a priori philosophical beliefs; but it may also be affected by the evidence. As Habermas writes:

> Scholars sometimes speak as if the factual data can be divorced from worldview concerns ... Yet it is undeniable that everyone generally operates within his or her own concept of reality ... Having said this, however, the factual data are still equally crucial ... We do need to be informed by the data we receive. And sometimes this is precisely what happens – the evidence on a subject convinces us against our indecisiveness or even contrary to our former position.[10]

An historical event and its metaphysical interpretation are often separate issues, but they are not unrelated. If one accepts that Jesus and his contemporaries thought that he performed successful exorcisms, one can go on to ask how best to interpret this data metaphysically speaking;

---

[6] Quoted by Gary R. Habermas, 'Did Jesus Perform Miracles?', *Jesus Under Fire* (Carlisle: Paternoster, 1996), p. 124.
[7] Ibid.
[8] Ibid.
[9] Ibid., p. 114.
[10] Habermas, *Jesus Under Fire*, p. 126.

and *the data itself must play a role in this process*. With this in mind, let us begin by considering the status of the data, historically speaking.

General Evidence

What sort of literature are the synoptic Gospels? Discussion of the genre of 'Gospel' has been dominated by an unfortunate dichotomy between viewing them as essentially 'accurate records of the life of Jesus'[11] (a view associated with seeing the Gospels as biography) or viewing them as proclamation 'and not in any sense "records" of the past'.[12] This dichotomy is clearly false. Something can be both an essentially accurate record *and* a passionate proclamation. The assumption of some critics that 'the early church was so taken up with its proclamation of the Risen Christ that it was not interested at all in the past of Jesus'[13] is just that: an assumption. It is, moreover, a highly implausible assumption, in that the earliest Christian proclamation is tied directly to the past historical reality of Jesus (as well as to the *present* reality of Jesus). That past reality includes Jesus' exorcisms, and it is this past reality that informs the present reality of a continuing Christian ministry of exorcism *in the name of Jesus*.

While the Gospels are clearly not biographies in the modern sense, when the above false dichotomy is rejected 'it becomes clear that the evangelists are concerned with the *story* as well as the *significance* of Jesus.'[14] The only reasonable justification for the denial that essentially accurate historical data and significance are combined in the Gospels is the claim that the Gospels are *not* essentially accurate. According to Graham N. Stanton, 'Many readers of the Gospels have assumed that they are intended to be accurate records of the life of Jesus, perhaps from eyewitnesses. They are then very puzzled by the differing accounts of the same incident in two or more Gospels.'[15] In general terms, this is a view of the Gospels that I share; but I think that the puzzlement Stanton talks of can be handled by good hermeneutics. As Craig L. Blomberg concludes: 'The Gospels may be accepted as trustworthy accounts of what Jesus did and said ... other conclusions, widespread though they are, seem not to stem from even-handed historical analysis but from

---

[11] Graham N. Stanton, *The Gospels And Jesus*, (Oxford: Oxford University Press, 1993).

[12] Ibid.

[13] Ibid.

[14] Ibid.

[15] Ibid.

religious or philosophical prejudice.'[16] Accepting this conclusion does not require one to view the Gospels as straightforward biography, or as a set of disinterested historical accounts.

The Gospels are perhaps closer in genre to ancient biography, although comparison is difficult (Matthew and Luke are perhaps a little closer than Mark to ancient biography): 'To readers familiar with the Old Testament or with later Jewish writings, or with Greco-Roman writings of the period, the Gospels would recall either some of the elements of a biography, or of a theological treatise, or perhaps even of a tragedy. But the Gospels do not fit easily and naturally into any of these categories.'[17] Journalist William Proctor (perhaps unsurprisingly) suggests that 'the accounts of the Resurrection in the New Testament seem to fit rather nicely into [the] journalistic genre – either as stand alone investigative articles, or as part of a longer, book-length journalistic treatment of the early Christian movement.'[18] After all:

> Like modern-day journalists, the New Testament writers reported occurrences and encounters involving relatively recent or ongoing current events ... Like reporters today – and unlike most historians – the resurrection reporters wrote soon after the events they described ... Also, the techniques and sources the reporters used in putting together the resurrection narratives are similar to the approach used in modern-day news media. It is clear, for instance, the reports are based on eye-witness interviews, first-person observations, and backup written materials.[19]

Gospel means 'good news', a description that entails a combination of journalism and proclamation. In the end, the Gospels are perhaps best assigned a genre of their own: *journalistic proclamation*. As such, I contend that the Gospels are, at the very least, a *well-attested, generally reliable* source of information about Jesus. As Cambridge theologian David Ford writes: 'The mainstream position has never been that every detail of the biblical records need to be precisely accurate ... Rather, the emphasis has been on trusting the stories to give a testimony good enough to know Jesus and what he did and suffered, and to relate to him.'[20]

---

[16] Blomberg, *The Historical Reliability Of The Gospels*.

[17] Stanton, *The Gospels And Jesus*.

[18] William Proctor, *The Resurrection Report* (Nashville, Tennessee: Broadman & Holman, 1998), p. 7.

[19] Ibid., p. 5.

[20] David Ford, *Theology: A Very Short Introduction* (Oxford: Oxford University Press, 1999), p. 47.

We know that the New Testament texts as we have them are *better attested than any other piece of ancient literature*. The gap between the events and their being recorded, and between their being recorded and the earliest surviving manuscripts, is extremely favourable compared with other historical documents. Consider the number of New Testament manuscripts compared to other ancient works: The writings of Plato survive in 7 manuscripts. The work of the Roman historian Livy comes to us through 10 manuscripts. Homer's *Iliad* is the closest comparison, with 643 surviving manuscripts. The New Testament comes to us through over 24,000 manuscripts (including some 5,000 Greek manuscripts). Consider the time between the original writing and the earliest surviving manuscript fragments. Between Aristotle's philosophy and our earliest copy lie 1,450 years. Between Herodotus and our copies lie 1,300 years. Between Pliny the Younger and our copies lie 750 years. Between Homer and our earliest copy (again, this is the closest comparison) lies 500 years. Between the New Testament and the earliest surviving fragment lies 100 years *at most*. In short: 'No other ancient document equals the New Testament when it comes to the preservation of manuscripts, both in terms of number and closeness in time to the original autographs.'[21]

The New Testament Gospels were all written within the lifetime of eyewitnesses. J.P. Moreland affirms: 'a strong case could be made for the fact that much of the New Testament, including the Gospels and the sources behind them, was written by eyewitnesses.'[22] Walter A. Elwell and Robert W. Yarbrough point out that: 'according to the best evidence available from the early years of the church, three of the four Gospels are directly linked to the apostles; the fourth, Luke, by his own testimony (Lk. 1:1–4), was dependent on eyewitnesses and those who had known Jesus from the beginning.'[23] Moreover, most of these eyewitnesses were martyred for refusing to renounce the truth of their accounts.[24] On the authorship of the Gospels R.T. France notes:

> Luke, the doctor who was a companion of Paul (Col. 4:14; 2 Tim. 4:11; Phlm. 24) is the most widely accepted, as the author of both the third Gospel and its sequel, the Acts of the Apostles. Mark, similarly a colleague of Paul (Acts 12:25; 15:37–41; Col. 4:10; 2 Tim. 4:11; Phlm 24), but also, if the

---

[21] Corduan, *No Doubt About It*, p. 193.

[22] Moreland, *Scaling The Secular City*, p. 137.

[23] Elwell and Yarbrough, *Encountering The New Testament*, p. 75.

[24] cf. Josh McDowell and Bill Wilson, *He Walked Among Us* (Carlisle: Paternoster, 2000), pp. 118–19.

same Mark is intended, a companion of Peter (1 Pet. 5:13), is accepted by many as at least a possible author of the second Gospel ... There are in fact weighty defenders today of the traditional authorship of all four Gospels ... Personally I find all four traditional ascriptions at least plausible.[25]

According to Irenaeus (*c.* AD 130–200):

> Matthew published ... the Gospel among the Hebrews in their own dialect, while Peter and Paul were preaching the gospel in Rome and founding the church. After their departure, Mark, the disciple and interpreter of Peter, he too handed down to us in writing the things preached by Peter. Luke also, the follower of Paul, put down in a book the gospel preached by that one. Afterwards, John, the disciple of the Lord who also leaned upon his breast, he too published a Gospel while residing in Ephesus.[26]

Tertullian (*c.* AD 160–225) testifies that: 'of Apostles, John and Matthew instill us with faith; of Apostolic men [i.e. *disciples of Apostles*], Luke and Mark renew it ...' Let's review the evidence for authorship of the synoptic Gospels, book by book (in probable chronological order).

Mark: 'The only author ever attached to the second Gospel is ... Mark. There is an unbroken testimony that includes Papias, Irenaeus ... Clement of Alexandria, Tertullian, Origen, Jerome, and Eusebius the church historian ... The question then arises as to who this Mark is. Here, again, only one suggestion was ever made by the early believers, and that was John Mark, one who worked so closely with Peter as to be called his "son" (1 Pet. 5:13). He was a cousin of Barnabas (Col. 4:10), a traveler with Paul and Barnabas (Acts 13:5), and the son of a wealthy family in Jerusalem (Acts 12:12–14) ...'[27] According to Papias (as quoted by Eusebius), the early second-century Bishop of Hierapolis in Phrygia:

> the presbyter [John the apostle] used to say this: 'Mark became Peter's inter-preter and wrote accurately all that he remembered, not indeed in order of the things said or done by the Lord. For he had not heard the Lord, nor had he

---

[25] R.T. France, *The Evidence For Jesus* (London: Hodder & Stoughton, 1986), pp. 122, 124.

[26] This testimony does not necessarily bear upon the question of what order these Gospels were *written* in, since it talks about when the Gospels were *received* by Irenaeus.

[27] Elwell and Yarbrough, *Encountering The New Testament*, pp. 88–9, my italics.

followed him, but later on, as I said, followed Peter, who used to give teaching as necessity demanded but not making, as it were, an arrangement of the Lord's oracles, so that Mark did nothing wrong in writing down single points as he remembered them. For to one thing he gave attention, to leave out nothing of what he had heard and to make no false statements in them.[28]

Here we have a direct link to the testimony of John the apostle as to the authorship, the authority (derived from the apostle Peter upon whom Mark relied for his information) and the episodic, unchronological nature, of Mark's Gospel.

Matthew: 'The only person ever suggested as the author of the first Gospel until recent times was the apostle Matthew. Among the Church Fathers, Irenaeus, Origen, and Eusebius, quoting earlier sources, all attest to this ... Those who were closest and knew best named the apostle Matthew as the author. There is no compelling reason their testimony should be rejected ...'[29]

Luke: 'All of the early evidence, including Irenaeus, Clement of Alexandria, Tertullian, Origen, Eusebius, and Jerome, states that Luke, the traveling-companion of the apostle Paul, was the author of this two part work (Luke–Acts). Even the early opponent of the church, Marcion, affirmed this.'[30] As Irenaeus testified in AD 180: 'Luke, also who was a follower of Paul, put down in a book the Gospel that was preached by him.'[31] Luke was an educated Gentile, a doctor and a close friend of Paul (Col. 4:14). He travelled with Paul towards the end of his life (2 Tim. 4:11): 'The sections from the Book of Acts where Luke becomes part of his own narrative can be easily identified, because Luke switches from 'they' to 'we', including himself in the group ...'[32] Luke's professed purpose is clear:

> Many have undertaken to draw up an account of the things that have been fulfilled among us, just as they were handed down to us by those who from the first were eye-witnesses and servants of the word. Therefore, since I myself have carefully investigated everything from the beginning, it seemed good also to me to write an orderly account for you, most excellent

---

[28] Eusebius, quoting Papias, a second century bishop. Ibid., p. 88.
[29] Ibid.
[30] Ibid., p. 98.
[31] Irenaeus, quoted by Walter A. Elwell and Robert W. Yarbrough, *Encountering The New Testament* (Grand Rapids, Michigan: Baker, 1998), p. 82.
[32] Elwell and Yarbrough, *Encountering The New Testament*, p. 99.

Theophilus, so that you may know the certainty of the things you have been taught (Lk. 1:1–4).

Hence, as Craig L. Blomberg writes: 'a good case can still be made for Matthew, Mark, Luke, and John as the authors of the Gospels that have traditionally been attributed to them.'[33] After all, 'Why would Christians ... ascribe these otherwise anonymous Gospels to three such unlikely candidates if they did not in fact write them? Mark and Luke, after all, were not among Jesus' twelve apostles ... Though an apostle, Matthew is best known for a negative characteristic, his unscrupulous past as a practitioner of a trade [tax collecting] Jews considered traitorous to their nation (Mt. 9:9–11).'[34] This being so, one would expect the Gospels to date from reasonably close to the events they record. Is this the case? It is. The following table lists the general range of (minority) 'conservative' and (majority) 'liberal' dates proposed for the writing of the Gospels (in probable chronological order).

Gospel	Conservative date	Liberal date
Mark	40s – mid 50s	late 60s–70s
Matthew	40s – early 60s	80s–90s
Luke	50s – early 60s	80s–90s
John	mid 60s – mid 90s	90s

The scholarly debate between these two 'camps' only concerns about a twenty- to thirty-year difference in dating. The majority of scholars are agreed that *all four Gospels were written within about sixty years of Jesus' death* (in *c.* AD 30). The 'liberal' majority place Mark *within about forty years of Jesus' death*. More 'conservative' scholars think that all or most of the Gospels (i.e. the synoptic Gospels) were written *within thirty or so years of Jesus' death* and that Mark's Gospel was written *within about ten to twenty years of Jesus' death*. According to F.F. Bruce, 'even with the later dates, the situation is encouraging from the historian's point of view, for the first three Gospels were written at a time when many were alive who could remember the things that Jesus said and did,

---

[33] Blomberg, *Jesus And The Gospels*, p. 365.
[34] Craig L. Blomberg, 'Where Do We Start Studying Jesus?', *Jesus Under Fire*, p. 28.

and some at least would still be alive when the fourth Gospel was written.'[35] However: 'in recent years, there has been a trend in New Testament studies towards dating the Gospels earlier.'[36] As Carsten Peter Thiede reports: 'those who argue for early dates of authentic Gospels as sources of information about an historical Jesus ... are no longer the conservative or fundamentalist outsiders.'[37]

According to Stanton, it is widely accepted that Mark was 'the first Gospel to have been written' and that it is 'therefore the Gospel with the highest claims to be accepted as a reliable historical source'.[38] While the second part of Stanton's claim does not necessarily follow from the first, since there are other factors besides historical proximity to consider in weighing the historical reliability of a report, such proximity is an important factor in weighing historical evidence. Several arguments are advanced for Marcan priority, from the fact that Matthew and Luke contain most of the material found in Mark.

(1) It is easy to see why Matthew and Luke might want to expand Mark's Gospel with their own material, but less obvious why the reverse process would occur: 'If an early Christian writer knew both Matthew and Luke, it is difficult to see why he would ever want to write ... Mark's Gospel.'[39]

(2) 'Matthew and Luke frequently modify or omit redundant phrases or unusual words found in Mark, and improve his rather unsophisticated literary style.'[40]

(3) 'A number of Marcan passages which seem to place Jesus in a bad light have been modified by Matthew and Luke.'[41] For example, 'Mark 3:21 notes that some people were saying that Jesus was "out of his mind". Neither Matthew nor Luke includes this strongly critical comment.'[42] It may be plausible to think that a latter Matthew and Luke 'tidy up' Mark in this way; but it is also possible that a later Mark simply has an author with a more open approach to reporting potentially embarrassing events if they happened, as shown by his even-handed portrayal of the disciples.

---

[35] Bruce, *The New Testament Documents*, p. 17.
[36] Moreland, *Scaling The Secular City*, p. 151.
[37] Carsten Peter Thiede, *Jesus: Life Or Legend?* (Oxford: Lion, 1990), p. 9.
[38] Stanton, *The Gospels And Jesus*, p. 35.
[39] Ibid., p. 38.
[40] Ibid., p. 36.
[41] Ibid., p. 37.
[42] Ibid.

(4) 'Matthew and Luke never agree in order against Mark: they seem to have made occasional changes to Mark's order quite independently. But it is now generally accepted that while this observation does support Marcan priority strongly, it can also be used to support rival hypotheses.'[43]

In sum, of these four arguments the first two offer the best evidence for Marcan priority, while the last two offer evidence that is more ambiguous. Nevertheless, this evidence is sufficient to warrant the inductive conclusion that Mark was written first and that it was used by both Matthew and Luke as one of their sources.

A point worth making in this context is that just because Luke, for example, copied some material from Mark, doesn't automatically mean Luke's report can't count as a separate source to Mark, because Luke (and Matthew for that matter) presumably cross-checked the accuracy of Mark as source material with other sources where possible. After all, Luke himself writes that: 'I myself have carefully investigated everything from the beginning ...' (Lk. 1:3).

The book of Acts, the second half of a two-part work by Luke, a physician and companion of Paul, ends with Paul in prison (*c*. AD 62). That nothing is said about Paul's trial indicates that Acts was written before it took place. This in turn means that Luke should not be dated later than Acts. Given Marcan priority (with Luke being written after Matthew and Matthew after Mark), it would seem that all three 'synoptic' Gospels were written *within thirty years of Jesus' death*. Other evidence supports this conclusion: 'In particular, various passages in Matthew refer to details of temple worship, which would be unnecessary anachronisms after AD 70, and one passage (Mt. 17:24–27) would be positively misleading since it approves the payment of the temple tax, which after AD 70 was diverted to the upkeep of the temple of Jupiter in Rome!'[44]

While the majority of scholars still advocate the later composition dates for the Gospels (i.e. AD 60s–90s), their arguments often rely upon naturalistic assumptions that more 'conservative' scholars do not share. As a case in point: 'all the Gospels record Jesus prophesying the destruction of Jerusalem. Now, liberal scholars who don't believe anything supernatural can occur, argue that this shows that the Gospels must be written after the fall of Jerusalem [in AD 70] (a main reason they date the Gospels late).'[45] To adopt such an approach is to beg the question. It is

---

[43] Ibid., p. 36.
[44] Ibid., p. 121.
[45] Gregory A. Boyd, *Letters From A Skeptic* (Eastbourne: Kingsway, 2000), p. 95.

no less question begging to conclude that Jesus' exorcisms must have purely naturalistic explanations because one assumes that demons cannot, or do not, exist.

I conclude that the synoptic Gospels were probably all written by the people whose name they bare *within thirty-five years of the crucifixion*; in the order of Mark (40s – mid-50s), Matthew (mid-50s – early 60s) and Luke (late-50s – early 60s). R.T. France testifies: 'It is ... probable that some ... of the Gospels were written in substantially their present form within thirty years of the events, and that much of the material was already collected and written a decade or two before that.'[46] We can additionally note that: 'Many Gospel critics will accept the earlier existence of a written collection of Jesus' sayings (usually called 'Q') on which both Matthew and Luke drew ...'[47] This 'source', material absent from Mark but common to Matthew and Luke, would have to date from the mid-50s *or earlier*.

A.N. Sherwin-White, the Oxford scholar of ancient Roman and Greek history, studied the rate at which legend accumulated in the ancient world, using Herodotus as a test case. He concluded that a span of two generations is not sufficient for legend to wipe out a solid core of historical facts. But as J.P. Moreland writes: 'The picture of Jesus in the New Testament was established well within that length of time.'[48] Hence I agree with Craig L. Blomberg's conclusion that: 'Whatever else one may or may not believe by faith, on sheer historical grounds alone there is substantial reason to believe in the *general* trustworthiness of the Gospel tradition.'[49] As R.T. France says:

> At the level of their literary and historical character we have good reason to treat the Gospels seriously ... Indeed, many ancient historians would count themselves fortunate to have four such responsible accounts written within a generation or two of the events and preserved in such a wealth of manuscript evidence ... Beyond that point, the decision as to how far a scholar is willing to accept the record they offer is likely to be influenced more by his openness to a 'supernaturalist' world-view than by strictly historical considerations.[50]

---

[46] France, *The Evidence For Jesus*, p. 121.
[47] Ibid., p. 101.
[48] Moreland, *Scaling The Secular City*, p. 156.
[49] Blomberg, *Jesus And The Gospels*, p. 381.
[50] R.T. France, 'The Gospels as Historical Sources for Jesus, the Founder of Christianity', *Truth* 1 (1985): 86.

Specific Evidence

Aside from the general trustworthiness of the Gospels and Acts examined above, what specific historical warrant do we have for taking the claim that Jesus was an exorcist seriously? In answering this question I will deploy some tools of New Testament scholarship, a set of criteria that serve to highlight those parts deserving particular esteem historically speaking. This is not to say that anything that does not trigger identification by one or more of these criteria is unreliable. The proper critical rule is 'innocent until proven guilty'; besides, we have all of the general historical warrant mentioned above. Rather, the triggering of one of these 'marks of authenticity' indicates that the text in question is to be considered *especially reliable from a purely historical point of view*. In addition to drawing heavily on Mark as the earliest Gospel, the standard criteria I will use are:

(1) *Multiple source attestation:* (the more sources, and the more independent they are, the better).
(2) *Dissimilarity:* (anything that differs from first-century Judaism is likely to be authentic).
(3) *Embarrassment:* (anything embarrassing to the church would hardly be made up by them!).
(4) *Admissions by antagonistic witnesses:* (anything admitted by the enemies of the church is probably authentic).

Graham Twelftree notes several marks of authenticity in Jesus' exorcisms, unusual facts about his mode of operation that cannot have been borrowed from the common practice of the day and thereby pass the criterion of dissimilarity: Jesus used no material devices (in contrast to other ancient cases), neither did he require departing demons to give proof of their exit, nor did he use common formulas such as 'I bind you'. Finally, Jesus did not pray to remove the evil spirits or invoke any authority beyond his own: '"Be quiet!" said Jesus sternly. "Come out of him!" The evil spirit shook the man violently and came out of him with a shriek. The people were all so amazed that they asked each other, "What is this? A new teaching – and with authority! He even gives orders to evil spirits and they obey him" ' (Mk. 1:25–27, cf. Lk. 4:31–37). Mark's account stresses Jesus' spiritual power, in that Jesus commands the demon to depart *by his own authority, without the use of material or magical devices* and *without requiring proof of exit* (thus showing his confidence in his own authority). As Keith Warrington writes: 'The amazement of the people may have been due to the fact that Jesus dealt with the demon by a word, without resorting to magic.'[51] It also high-lights the fact that the inauguration of God's kingdom through Jesus would entail, and be evinced by, the waning of demonic power. This authoritative exorcism serves to validate the authority of Jesus' teaching: 'new teaching – and with authority!'

Twelftree examined the world of thought contemporary to Jesus' exorcisms and concluded that people 'were not uncritical in their acceptance of a report of a miracle ... Not everyone believed in demons and exorcism ... People in the New Testament world [were able] to discriminate between those sicknesses which were and those which were not thought to be caused by demons.'[52] For example, 'All three synoptic Gospels record that, during the evening of the day on which Peter's mother-in-law was healed, many who were sick and demonised were brought to Jesus for ministry, each category of affliction kept separate in the accounts.'[53] Again, compare the cures of deaf, dumb and blind persons in Mark 7 and 8, where there is no exorcism (despite Mark's interest in such events) with the similar cases in Matthew 9 and 12, where dumb and blind people *are* exorcised: 'There must have been some diagnosis or discernment by Jesus at the time, whereby he was able to tell which cases required the casting-out of evil spirits and which did not.'[54] What symptoms might Jesus have used for diagnosis? In New Testament times there were: 'well-established maladies like fever, leprosy and paralysis it was not thought necessary to attribute either to Satan or to demons (Mk. 1:29–31, 40–44, 2:1–12). [Rather] the idea of demon-possession was reserved for conditions where the individual seemed to be totally in the grip of an evil power (using his vocal chords, Mk. 1:24, 5:7, 9; Acts 16:16; convulsing him, Mk. 1:26, 9:20–22, 26; superhuman strength, Mk. 5:3–4; Acts 19:16).'[55] Some of these symptoms can, it is true, be given psychiatric explanations. However, 'The presence of a diagnosable psychiatric disorder does not ... invalidate a possible spiritual basis or trigger for the disturbance itself ...'[56] As psychiatrist M. Scott Peck concludes: 'there has to be a significant emotional problem for the possession to occur in the first place. Then

---

[51] Warrington, *Jesus The Healer*, p. 104.
[52] Graham Twelftree, *Christ Triumphant* (London: Hodder & Stoughton, 1985), p. 169.
[53] Warrington, *Jesus The Healer*, p. 45.
[54] Perry (ed.), *Deliverance: Psychic Disturbance And Occult Involvement*, p. 146.
[55] Ibid.
[56] Ernest Lucas (ed.), *Christian Healing* (London: Lynx, 1997), p. 148.

the possession itself will both enhance that problem and create new ones. The proper question is: "Is the patient just mentally ill or is he or she mentally ill and possessed?" [57] Psychiatric explanations do not contradict spiritual explanations. Then again, a face-to-face diagnosis can include more intuitive factors than a listing of symptoms. The Christian is quite within their epistemic rights to assume that Jesus' discernment in such matters was more than merely human.

Nor is all the evidence amenable to psychiatric explanation. For example, in the story of the Gerasene demonic (Mk. 5:1–20, Mt. 8:28–34, Lk. 8:26–39), signs of possession include not only great strength (Mk. 5:3) and a disregard for pain (Mk. 5:5), but a stampede of local pigs into whom the demons beg to flee: 'the evil spirits came out and went into the pigs. The herd, about two thousand in number, rushed down the steep bank into the lake and were drowned.' (Mk. 5:13.) Gregory A. Boyd comments: 'Ancient people generally associated particular demons with particular regions (especially around tombs and desert regions, Lk. 8:27, 29; 11:24), and this seems to be reflected in this passage ... The demons' desperate plea to remain in the area by entering a local herd of swine ... makes it appear that these degenerate spirits somehow needed to remain in this region, as though (perhaps) this were some sort of geographical assignment they had received from their chief and had to obey.' [58] However, the demons' ruse goes wrong: 'for instead of finding a permanent abode that would allow them to stay in the region, the pigs immediately rush headlong over a cliff and drown ... Where they went after that ... is not clear. But it is clear that they did not get what they wanted, which seems to have been Jesus' plan all along.' [59] This event caused public uproar:

> Those tending the pigs ran off and reported this in the town and countryside, and the people went out to see what had happened. When they came to Jesus, they saw the man who had been possessed by the legion of demons, sitting there, dressed and in his right mind; and they were afraid. Those who had seen it told the people what had happened to the demon-possessed man – and told about the pigs as well. Then the people began to plead with Jesus to leave their region (Mk. 5:14–16).

The people's disquiet probably reflects either the false assumption that Jesus' power over the demonic came from the prince of demons himself, or the simple realization that someone stronger than the demons was in

---

[57] Peck, *People Of The Lie*, p. 219.
[58] Boyd, *God At War*, p. 195.
[59] Ibid., pp. 193–4.

their midst. As for the previously possessed man himself, he 'went away and began to tell in the Decapolis [ten cities] how much Jesus had done for him. And all the people were amazed' (Mk. 5:20). It is interesting to note Jesus departing in this instance from his usual practice of requiring those he healed not to tell other people about him. This was Jesus' practice because he did not want to cause the sort of sensation that would re-enforce the popular Jewish misunderstanding of the Messiah as a political and military saviour who would restore the past glories of Israel. One can explain Jesus' deviation from his normal secrecy by the fact that he is in Gentile territory, as shown by the fact that pigs were being herded and by reference to the Gentile name for the 'ten cities' (Decapolis) in the area.

Matthew's account of this exorcism, although clearly an account of the same event (pigs and all), differs from the earlier Mark and the later Luke in mentioning *two* possessed men. It would seem that either Mark left out the second man as extraneous to his purpose (a not uncommon practice in the ancient world) or that his source did the same, and that Matthew (a probable eyewitness) gave the full details in his report. Assuming that Luke knew both preceding Gospels, he clearly followed Mark's omission. Keith Warrington notes: 'Matthew records that Jesus delivers two demoniacs, though both Mark and Luke refer to only one. The similarities between the accounts suggest strongly that they are reflecting one and the same historical event, the difference in numbers being no hindrance to understanding of the passage.'[60] Although Matthew's account is thus more accurate by modern reporting standards, it does not contradict Mark or Luke *when one accounts for the reporting conventions of the time*. As Craig L. Blomberg writes: 'It is more natural to suggest that there really were two characters present ... but that one acted as spokesman for the two and dominated the scene in such a way that left the other easily ignored in narratives which so regularly omitted non-essential details.'[61] Indeed, the fact that we have two different and therefore *independent* accounts of this exorcism actually adds to the historical justification for accepting the reliability of the story. Moreover, to lay claim to widespread public knowledge of a particular exorcism and its results, and to do so within a generation of its advent, is no way to make up a story! One can only conclude that the story wasn't made up (the same point about the widespread knowledge of non-Christian witnesses applies to the deliverance recorded in Mk. 1:23–28 and Lk. 4:31–37).

---

[60] Warrington, *Jesus The Healer*, p. 47.
[61] Blomberg, *The Historical Reliability Of The Gospels*, p. 151.

All three synoptic Gospels recount Jesus' healing of the boy suffer-ing demonically caused epilepsy (Mt. 17:14–21, Mk. 9:14–29, Lk. 9:37–43). Jesus' disciples fail to exorcise this demon, although they have recently been given authority by Jesus to do just that (Mt. 10:1, Lk. 9:1): 'Their incapacity is to be interpreted in the light of their not appropriating the authority that has been delegated to them.'[62] Matthew and Mark record the disciples asking Jesus to explain their failure and Matthew records that it was due to their lack of faith (Mt. 21:21ff, cf. Lk. 12:5ff.). Keith Warrington observes: 'Their trust and confidence in God's power available to them have for some reason deserted them.'[63] The crucial point is that this episode is not only reported by all three synoptic Gospels, but that it is highly *embarrassing* to Jesus' disciples. There are therefore excellent historical grounds for thinking that this incident happened; the only question is how to interpret it. Was the boy suffering from *nothing but* epilepsy? The fact that Jesus healed the boy through exorcism might be thought to indicate that there was more to the incident than that:

> liberal New Testament scholars have attempted to explain cases of demonization and exorcism such as the one in Mark 9 as merely primitive ways of describing and dealing with epilepsy or similar disorders ... But if one grants that this account in the Gospels is at least minimally rooted in actual history – and few today deny it – this explanation must be judged inadequate, for it does not fully explain what transpired.
>
> This exclusively naturalistic explanation fails to account for why the boy fell into convulsions when he saw Jesus or for why the seizures involved sui-cidal behaviour. Nor does it account for why Jesus' exorcism worked, why the demon 'shrieked' when it left (though the boy had been mute), or how Jesus, the Son of God, could have misdiagnosed the body's condition (while still getting the cure right).[64]

The New Testament records that strangers used the name of Jesus to perform exorcism: ' "Teacher", said John, "we saw a man driving out demons in your name and we told him to stop, because he was not one of us." "Do not stop him," Jesus said. "No one who does a miracle in my name can in the next moment say anything bad about me" ' (Mk. 9:38–39, cf. Lk. 9:49). This triggers the criterion of embarrass-ment, since it calls into question any claim of the church to be the sole purveyor of Jesus' power and teaching, 'especially as Jesus does not

---

[62] Ibid., p. 88.
[63] Ibid.
[64] Boyd, *God At War*, p. 198.

condemn the practice'.[65] This story also embarrasses the disciple John. And why would strangers use Jesus' name in exorcism unless Jesus was well known as a powerful exorcist? Again, we find some Jews experimenting with Jesus' name as an authority in exorcism, although without success, in Acts 19:13–17:

> Some Jews who went around driving out evil spirits tried to invoke the name of the Lord Jesus over those who were demon-possessed. They would say, 'In the name of Jesus, whom Paul preaches, I command you to come out.' Seven sons of Sceva, a Jewish chief priest, were doing this. One day the evil spirit answered them, 'Jesus I know, and I know about Paul, but who are you?' Then the man who had the evil spirit jumped on them and over-powered them all. He gave them such a beating that they ran out of the house naked and bleeding.

It is unlikely that anyone could have simply invented such a story, involving as it does the sons of such a prominent a member of society in such a publicly embarrassing situation. Jewish writers would hardly want to lampoon themselves with such a tale, and Luke would hardly have made up a story that important contemporaries would have been in a position to deny. It is also interesting to note that the possessed man was able to overpower, beat and strip naked seven men!

Graham Stanton reports: 'it was very easy to "write off" miracle workers in first century Palestine. Exorcisms could be readily explained as the result of possession by the prince of demons ...'[66] This is just what some of Jesus' contemporaries did do, a fact attested by the earliest Gospel (Mk. 3:22) and by Q: 'It is only by Beelzebub, the prince of demons, that this fellow drives out demons' (Mt. 12:24); 'By Beelzebub, the prince of demons, he is driving out demons' (Lk. 11:15). Here we have multiple attestation to an important admission by antagonistic witnesses: 'All three Synoptists record Jesus exploring the folly of the Pharisees' claim that he operates in the power of Beelzebub, noting that a divided kingdom is doomed ...'[67] The important thing is that *Jesus' enemies did not attempt to refute the fact of his exorcisms*. Instead, they merely sought to reinterpret those facts to suit their own worldview (which is exactly the response made by modern day sceptics). Hence Jesus' critics unwittingly testify to the fact that Jesus did indeed engage in successful exorcism.

---

[65] Brewer, 'Jesus and the Psychiatrists' in Lane (ed.), *The Unseen World*, p. 147.
[66] Stanton, *The Gospels And Jesus*, p. 217.
[67] Warrington, *Jesus The Healer*, p. 77.

David Instone Brewer, whose approach to these matters is formed both by an understanding of modern psychiatric thinking *and* personal experience of exorcism, says that while a psychiatrist might suggest reinterpreting biblical accounts of exorcism in terms of various psychiatric disorders, such an approach has 'only limited value as explanations of what is described in the Gospels'.[68] For example, psychiatry cannot explain the insight that many of the demonized have into Jesus' identity: 'The man in the synagogue shouted out that Jesus was the Holy One of God (Mk. 1:24/Lk. 4:34). The mad man of Gadera called him Son of the Most High God (Mk. 5:7/Mt. 8:29/Lk. 8:28.) Many other demonised people are also recorded as shouting that he was the Son of God, and having to be silenced (Mk. 1:34; 3:11; Lk. 4:41). This insight into Jesus' character cannot be explained in psychiatric terms.'[69] One explanation for the demon's actions is that they are disturbed by the mere presence of Jesus and vocalize their discomfort, a pattern recognizable from contemporary accounts of possession. Gregory Boyd thinks that, given the power invested in names by ancient cultures, the demons are attempting (and failing) to gain power over Jesus by the use of his name. Keith Warrington suggests that the demons attempted to complicate life for Jesus by proclaiming his status at an inopportune time, but that 'Jesus refused to allow any slowing down of his ministry and saw through the unsubtle (at least to him) strategy of the demons.'[70]

Conclusion

There is good historical warrant, both general and specific, for believing that Jesus performed genuine and successful exorcisms. Aside from the evidence for the general reliability of the synoptic Gospels and Acts, several relevant facts are additionally supported by the criteria of *multiple source attestation, dissimilarity, embarrassment*, and *admission by antagonistic witnesses*. This data is not only compatible with a literal understanding of possession and exorcism, but includes several facts (Jesus' exorcisms actually healed people; one very public exorcism resulted in a drowned herd of pigs; the possessed knew of Jesus' status) that are difficult to account for in purely naturalistic terms.

---

[68] Brewer, 'Jesus and the Psychiatrists' in Lane (ed.), *The Unseen World*, p. 135.
[69] Ibid., p. 138.
[70] Warrington, *Jesus The Healer*, p. 45.

Appendix II

Bayes' Theorem and the Evidence for Angels

Bayes' Theorem, named after its inventor Thomas Bayes (1701–61) is 'one of the most important theorems of probability theory'.[1] Bayes' Theorem depends on the fact that 'a given hypothesis h is probable if the evidence that we encounter is what we would expect to encounter if h were true.'[2] In other words, 'a hypothesis h is confirmed by evidence e if and only if that evidence is more likely to occur if the hypothesis is true than if it is false.'[3] In evaluating any hypothesis we have certain items of background knowledge (call this background knowledge k): 'On the basis of k, h will have a certain prior probability, that is, probability before we investigate the available evidence …'[4] As Richard Swinburne explains: '$P(h/k)$, the prior probability of h, depends … on the internal simplicity of h … and also on how well h fits in with our general background knowledge of the world contained in k.'[5] Bayes' Theorem therefore states that: 'Where k is our general background knowledge of what there is in the world and how it works, e is our phenomena to be explained … and h is our hypothesis, $P(h/e.k)$ is a function of the prior probability of h, $P(h/k)$; and of its explanatory power with respect to e.'[6] In symbolic notation Bayes' Theorem looks like this:

$$P(h/e.k) = \frac{P(h/k) \times P(e/h.k)}{P(e/k)}$$

---

[1] Davis, *God, Reason And Theistic Proofs*, p. 116. Explanations of Bayes' Theorem can be found in Davis, *God, Reason And Theistic Proofs*; Moreland, *Christianity And The Nature Of Science*; and Swinburne, *The Existence Of God*.

[2] Davis, *God, Reason And Theistic Proofs*, p. 116.

[3] Swinburne, *The Existence Of God*, p. 64.

[4] Davis, *God, Reason And Theistic Proofs*, p. 116.

[5] Swinburne, *The Existence Of God*, p. 64.

[6] Ibid.

This means that the probability of hypothesis *h* given the evidence *e* and background knowledge *k* is equal to the prior probability of hypothesis *h* given background knowledge *k*, multiplied by the probability of evidence *e* given the truth of hypothesis *h* and background knowledge *k*, divided by the probability of evidence *e* on background knowledge *k* alone. If we apply Bayes' Theorem to the cumulative case for angels, we find that the posterior probability of the hypothesis that angels exist (call this hypothesis *a*) given the evidence (*e*) and our background knowledge (*k*) equals the prior probability of *a* given *k*, multiplied by the probability of *e* given *a* and *k*, divided by the prior probability of *e* given *k*. That is:

$$P(a/e.k) = \frac{P(a/k) \times P(e/a.k)}{P(e/k)}$$

- P(*a*/*e*.*k*) = the posterior probability of *a* given *e* and our background knowledge *k*. This term 'is what we are trying to derive; it is the overall probability of *h* given *e* and *k*'.[7]
- P(*a*/*k*) = the prior probability of *a* (given our background knowledge) quite apart from *e*.
- P(*e*/*a*.*k*) = a measure of *a*'s predictive power, of how likely the evidential phenomena *e* are if *a* is true. In other words, 'how strong is the connection between *a* and *e*? If we accept *a*, does that make *e* 100 percent likely (1), or does it just make *e* more probable than not?'[8]
- P(*e*/*k*) = the probability of *e* apart from *a* (called 'the expectedness of *e*').

If the probability that *a* is true given *e* and *k* is greater than the probability that *a* is true without *e* – if P(*a*/*e*.*k*)>P(*a*/*k*) – then the evidence *e* offers positive support for *a*. The Bayesian form of the case for angels thus says that P(*a*/*e*.*k*) – the posterior probability of *a* given *e* & *k* – is equal to:

(i) P(*a*/*k*) – the prior probability of angels existing considered on the basis of our background knowledge apart from the specific evidence for *a*, *multiplied by*

(ii) P(*e*/*a*.*k*) – the probability that the evidence would occur given the existence of angels, *divided by*

(iii) P(*e*/*k*) – the probability that the evidence *e* will obtain given that angels don't exist.

---

[7] Davis, *God, Reason And Theistic Proofs*, p. 117.
[8] Habermas and Moreland, *Beyond Death*.

What sort of values should we assign to (i)–(iii)? What is the prior probability of *a*? I have sought to establish the *possibility* that angels exist, especially given the existence of God and/or the immateriality of the human mind (this effort can be considered as contributing to the contents of *k*). Given that angels are *possible* we cannot assign them a prior probability of 0 (since 0 indicates that something has no probability, like a square circle). So what value should we assign? We must of course take into consideration the advice of Occam's Razor not to multiply entities beyond necessity. Including angels in our worldview makes it more complicated than not including them does. Angels are fairly complex entities. Therefore, the advocate of belief in angels should assume a burden of proof and assign angels a probability value of *more than 0 but less than 0.5*. This said, *a* would seem to have quite a good natural fit with *k*, so P(*a/k*) can't be all *that* improbable.

What is the probability that the evidence would occur given the existence of angels: P(*e/a.k*)? What is *a*'s predictive power? How strong is the connection between *e* and *a*? In some cases (e.g. consent, authority, the argument from the occult) it seems perhaps only slightly more probable than not that the evidence would exist given *a*. In other cases it seems quite probable that the evidence would exist given *a*. For example, the probability that experiences of demonic possession or angelic encounters would sometimes (even if rarely) occur given *a* seem quite high (perhaps as high as the probability that some people would on occasion see an endangered, rare species of animal). The probability that God's word (both scripture and Jesus) would teach the existence of angels given their existence and involvement in revelation would seem to be quite high. The probability that the evidence would occur given the existence of angels is certainly greater than 0.5.

Finally, what is the expectedness of *e*, the prior probability of the evidence occurring given that angels *do not* exist? Again, the answer to this question varies across the different arguments given above, but when we take into account the cumulative force of these arguments, I think that the likelihood of the total body of evidence occurring given that angels do *not* exist is quite low, and hence < 0.5.

Even erring on the side of caution it seems that angels are at least *possible*, so the prior probability of angels existing considered against our background knowledge – P(*a/k*) – must be greater than zero (perhaps 0.2). On the basis of the criteria for good explanations examined in Chapter Four, I would judge P(*e/a.k*), the probability of the total evidence occurring given *a* and *k*, as being quite likely (perhaps 0.7). I further judge that P(*e/k*), the existence of the total evidence given that angels *don't* exist, is very unlikely (perhaps around 0.2). In particular, it seems highly unlikely that Jesus and the Bible would teach that angels exist, as is quite clearly the case, if they did not exist (even more improbable than that they would not teach their existence if they did exist). Hence:

$$P(a/e.k) = \frac{P(a/k) > 0 \times P(e/a.k) > 0.5}{P(e/k) < 0.5}$$

and $P(a/e.k) = > 0.5$. Bayes' Theorem thus confirms that the probability of angels existing, given all of the available evidence, while not incontrovertible, is high (in the range of 0.7–0.9). Indeed, if the case for angels were being tried in court, I believe the case would have to be declared proven 'beyond reasonable doubt'.

Appendix III

The Argument for God from the Existence of Angels

The reasonable supposition here is that evidence of the existence of angels is indirect evidence for theism. As far as I know, the existence of angels has not been formally advanced as an argument for the existence of God before. This argument is, however, the only one for which I can claim any originality!

As we have seen, there are several independent arguments for the existence of angels. If these arguments are, when taken together, judged to count in favour of the existence of angels, then this also lends some credence to the existence of God. (One cannot, of course, use the *dependent* arguments for angels in any argument for God without begging the question.) There are four reasons to think this.

First of all, the existence of finite supernatural personal beings makes the supposition that there exists an infinite supernatural personal being more acceptable. Once you have opened the door to the supernatural even a crack, it is hard to deny the plausibility of 'going the whole hog' and letting God have a look in.

Second, it seems reasonable to suppose that angels are contingent, dependent supernatural beings whose existence therefore implies the existence of a necessary and independent supernatural being. As supernatural entities, angels cannot be thought to have a natural origin or explanation.

Third, the existence of angels surely gives a measure of credence to those religions in which their existence is taught, and hence lends credence to the other truth claims of those religions, including God's existence. We are rationally disposed to place a greater degree of trust in someone's testimony when they have been proved correct on previous occasions. If theistic religions teach that there exist finite spiritual beings created by God, and we verify the existence of finite spiritual beings, this surely lends some support to the claim, made by the same source, that God exists. This is analogous to the support given to an entire scientific hypothesis if even one of its predictions is verified. While it is true that this argument would also confer *some* support to non-theistic religions that teach the existence of spiritual beings (e.g. New Ageism), if one takes into account the fine detail of the evidence for angels, one will find that it actually gives greatest support to Christian theism. Consider, for example, the verified power of the name of Jesus over cases of demon possession.

Finally, if the hypothesis of angels is shown to have a 'natural fit' within a theistic worldview via the argument from extrapolation, then reason to believe in angels is indirect reason to believe in the theistic worldview into which such beings naturally fit. This can be simply illustrated. The hypothesis 'there are burglars' gives one a priori reason to expect otherwise inexplicable fingerprints in some houses. Thus, a posteriori experience of unexplained fingerprints in some houses supports the hypothesis 'there are burglars'. Likewise with God and angels. The hypothesis 'God exists' gives one a priori reason to expect the existence of angels (via the extrapolation argument). Thus a posteriori experience of angels supports the hypothesis that God exists.

Appendix IV

Who's Who – Introducing some Christian Philosophers and Apologists

Adler, Mortimer J.
Dr Adler, who *Time* magazine dubbed America's 'philosopher for everyman', authored many books including *Aristotle For Everybody* (New York: Simon & Schuster, 1997); *Truth In Religion: The Plurality Of Religions And The Unity Of Truth* (New York: Collier, 1990); and *The Angels And Us* (New York: Collier, 1982). Adler was Chair of the Board of Editors of the *Encyclopaedia Britannica*, Director of the Institute for Philosophical Research, an Honorary Trustee of the Aspen Institute and Honorary Chairman and Cofounder of the Center for the Study of Great Ideas. In 1976 Adler wrote of his recognition that religious commitment 'would require a radical change in my way of life', and acknowledged: 'The simple truth of the matter is that I did not wish to live up to being a genuinely religious person' (*Philosopher At Large* [London: Macmillan, 1977]). In 1980 Adler published *How To Think About God* (New York: Collier, 1991), in which he argued for God's existence. He later wrote that the thinking he did in writing *How To Think About God* 'was influential in my becoming a Christian in 1984' (*Adler's Philosophical Dictionary* [New York: Scribner, 1995], p. 186), cf. < http://www.radicalacademy.com/adlerdirectory.htm >

Alston, William P.
Professor of Philosophy Emeritus at Syracuse University, Alston is noted for his work on the epistemology of theistic religious experience. cf. 'The Experiential Basis of Theism' @ < http://www.leaderu.com/ truth/3truth04.html >; 'Why I am a Christian' @ < http://www.leaderu .com/truth/1truth23.html >; *A Realist Conception Of Truth* (Ithaca, New York: Cornell University Press, 1996); *Perceiving God: The Epistem-ology Of Religious Experience* (Ithaca, New York: Cornell University Press, 1993); 'Perceiving God' in Kelly James Clark (ed.),

Readings In The Philosophy Of Religion (Peterborough, Ontario: Broadview Press, 2000).

Aquinas, Thomas
The most celebrated Christian theologian, philosopher and apologist of the medieval period, the hugely productive Aquinas (*c.* 1225–74) continues to be an influential voice in theology and philosophy. Born in Italy, Aquinas took early schooling at the Benedictine Abbey of Monte Cassino before studying liberal arts and philosophy at the University of Naples, after which he joined the Dominican order. Making known his intention to go to Paris for further studies as a Dominican, Aquinas was forcibly detained by his family for about a year (they locked him in his room!). After his family relented, Aquinas did go to Paris, where he worked under Albertus Magnus and became a lecturer (as a Bachelor and then a Master) in theology. Philosophers who model their own thought after that of Aquinas – like Jacques Maritain, Etienne Gilson, J.J. Haldane and Norman L. Geisler – are called 'Thomists'. Aquinas was particularly important for employing a Christianized Aristotelianism in the defence and elucidation of Christianity.

Major works include *De Anima* (on the soul), *De Veritate* (on truth), the apologetics work *Summa Contra Gentiles*, and by far his most important and influential work, *Summa Theologica* (summary of theology), which was still unfinished at his death. The best-known section of *Summa Theologica* are the 'Five Ways' Aquinas gives to demonstrate the existence of God: 1) from motion to an unmoved mover, 2) from effect to first cause, 3) from contingent to necessary being, 4) from degrees of perfection to a most perfect being, and 5) from purpose in nature to a purposer of nature. Aquinas' work was declared to be the official teaching of the Roman Catholic Church by Pope Leo XIII in 1879. cf. Thomas Aquinas Links @ < http://www.mother.com/~flindahl/calendar/st046e.htm >;
'*Lux Veritatis*' @ < http://www.geocities.com/Athens/Academy/6591/index.html >;
Thomistic Philosophy @ < http://www.aquinasonline.com >;
Timothy McDermot, *Aquinas: Selected Philosophical Writings* (Oxford: Oxford University Press, 1998); Ralph McInery (ed. and trans), *Thomas Aquinas: Selected Readings* (London: Penguin Classics, 1998); G.K. Chesterton, *Thomas Aquinas* (London: Hodder & Stoughton, 1933); F.C. Copleston, *Aquinas* (Harmondsworth, Middlesex: Pelican, 1957).

Clark, Kelly James
Clark, like Alvin Plantinga, under whom he studied, is a 'reformed episte-
mologist'. He is Assistant Professor of Philosophy at Calvin College,
Grand Rapids, Michigan. cf. Kelly James Clark, *Return To Reason*
(Grand Rapids, Michigan: Eerdmans, 1990); (ed.), *Readings In The
Philosophy Of Religion* (Peterborough, Ontario: Broadview, 2000); 'I
Believe in God, the Father, Almighty' @ < http://www.calvin.edu/aca
demic/philosophy/writings/ibig.htm >; Kelly James Clark, 'Plantinga vs.
Oliphint: and the Winner is ... ' @ < http://www.homestead.com/philo
freligion/files/KClarkPaper.htm >.

Craig, William Lane
A leading evangelical Christian philosopher and classical apologist, Dr
William Lane Craig became a Christian at the age of sixteen. Craig
pursued undergraduate studies at Wheaton College (BA, 1971) and
graduate studies at Trinity Evangelical Divinity School (MA, 1974; MA,
1975), as well as at the University of Birmingham in the UK (PhD, 1977)
and the University of Munich (DTheol, 1984). From 1980–86 he taught
Philosophy of Religion at Trinity. After seven years at the University of
Louvain in Brussels, the Craigs moved back to the USA where Bill is now
Research Professor of Philosophy at Talbot School of Theology in
La Mirada, California. Craig often engages non-Christians in public
debates, and is the leading modern proponent of the 'Kalam' cosmo-
logical argument (i.e. everything with a beginning has a cause, the
universe had a beginning, therefore the universe has a cause: God).
For Craig's exposition and defence of this argument see his web site:
< http://www.leaderu.com/offices/billcraig/ >; 'Why I Believe God Exists'
in Norman L. Geisler and Paul K. Hoffman (eds), *Why I Am A Christian*
(Grand Rapids, Michigan: Baker, 2001); or Craig's *Reasonable Faith*
(Wheaton, Illinois: Crossway, 1994). For a critique see Peter S.
Williams, *The Case For God* (Crowborough, East Sussex: Monarch,
1999). Craig is also well known for defending the historical resurrection
of Jesus, and for the attention his natural theology pays to physics. In
addition, Craig defends the moral argument for God's existence, advocates the view that God is eternal rather than atemporal, and writes
about God's omniscience in relation to contemporary science, human
freedom and divine foreknowledge (for all this and more, see Craig's
web site: < http://www.leaderu.com/offices/billcraig/ >). Craig is the
author, co-author, or editor of over twenty books and numerous papers.
cf. 'The Virtual office of Dr. William Lane Craig' @ < http://www.
leaderu.com/offices/billcraig/menus/index.html >;

'Cosmos and Creator' @ < http://www.arn.org/docs/odesign/od172/cos mos_172.htm >; William Lane Craig (ed.), *Philosophy Of Religion: A Reader And Guide* (Edinburgh: Edinburgh University Press, 2002); Paul Copan and Craig A. Evans (eds), *Who Was Jesus? A Jewish–Christian Dialogue* (Louisville, Kentucky: Westminster John Knox Press, 2001); *Time And Eternity: Exploring God's Relationship To Time* (Wheaton, Illinois: Crossway, 2001); 'Why I Believe God Exists' in Norman L. Geisler and Paul K. Hoffman (eds), *Why I Am A Christian* (Grand Rapids, Michigan: Baker, 2001); Paul Copan and Ronald K. Tacelli (eds), *Jesus' Resurrection: Fact Or Figment? A Debate Between William Lane Craig And Gerd Ludemann* (Downers Grove, Illinois: IVP, 2000); 'Design and the Cosmological Argument' in William A. Dembski (ed.), *Mere Creation: Science, Faith & Intelligent Design* (Downers Grove, Illinois: IVP, 1998); Paul Copan (ed.), *Will The Real Jesus Please Stand Up: A Debate Between William Lane Craig And John Dominic Crossan* (Grand Rapids, Michigan: Baker, 1998); 'The Empty Tomb of Jesus' in R. Douglas Geivett and Gary R. Habermas (eds), *In Defence Of Miracles* (Leicester: Apollos, 1997); 'Did Jesus Rise from the Dead?' in J.P. Moreland and Gary R. Habermas (eds), *Jesus Under Fire* (Carlisle: Paternoster, 1995); William Lane Craig and Quentin Smith, *Theism, Atheism And Big Bang Cosmology* (Oxford: Oxford University Press, 1995); *Reasonable Belief* (Wheaton, Illinois: Crossway, 1994); *The Son Rises: The Historical Evidence For The Resurrection Of Jesus* (Chicago, Illinois: Moody Press, 1981).

Davis, Stephen T.
Stephen T. Davis (PhD, Claremont Graduate School) is Professor of Philosophy at Claremont McKenna College. cf. < http://www.faithquest .com/home.cfm?main=docs/philosophers/davis/index.cfm >; *God, Reason And Theistic Proofs* (Edinburgh: Edinburgh University Press, 1997); *Risen Indeed: Making Sense Of The Resurrection* (London: SPCK, 1993); *Logic And The Nature Of God* (London: Macmillan, 1983); 'God's Actions' in R. Douglas Geivett and Gary R. Habermas (eds), *In Defence Of Miracles* (Leicester: Apollos, 1997).

Dembski, William A.
Holding a PhD in mathematics from the University of Chicago and a PhD in philosophy from the University of Illinois at Chicago, as well as degrees in theology and psychology, Dembski is a leading light of the Intelligent Design Movement. The recipient of two fellowships from the National Science Foundation, Dembski is a senior fellow of the Discovery Institute Center for the Renewal of Science and Culture.

Dembski has written numerous articles and has authored, edited and/or contributed to a clutch of books including: *No Free Lunch: Why Specified Complexity Cannot Be Purchased Without Intelligence* (Lanham, Maryland: Rowman & Littlefield, 2001); *The Design Inference* (Cambridge: Cambridge University Press, 1999); *Intelligent Design: The Bridge Between Science & Theology* (Downers Grove, Illinois: IVP, 1999); (ed.), *Mere Creation: Science, Faith & Intelligent Design* (Downers Grove, Illinois: IVP, 1998); with Michael J. Behe and Stephen C. Meyer, *Science And Evidence For Design In The Universe* (San Francisco: Ignatius, 2000); (ed.) with James M. Kurshiner, *Signs Of Intelligence: Understanding Intelligent Design* (Grand Rapids, Michigan: Baker, 2001); with John Mark Reynalds (eds), *Three Views On Creation And Evolution* (Grand Rapids, Michigan: Zondervan, 1999). cf. < http://www.arn.org/dembski/wdhome.htm >; < http://www.leaderu.com/offices/dembski/menus/articles.html >.

Geisler, Norman L.
Dr Norman L. Geisler is a prolific evangelical classical apologist and ethicist (having authored or co-authored over fifty books). He is Dean and Professor of Theology and Apologetics at Dallas Theological Seminary. Geisler, a Thomist, is a founder of the Evangelical Philosophy Society. Geisler notably advocates the classical model of God as atemporal; the existence of absolute, objective truth, goodness and beauty; the compatibility of libertarian freedom and divine omniscience; and the historical resurrection of Jesus. Geisler's best book is probably the scrupulously methodical *Christian Apologetics* (Grand Rapids, Michigan: Baker, 1976). cf. < http://www.normgeisler.com >; *Options In Contemporary Christian Ethics* (Grand Rapids, Michigan: Baker, 1981); with Winfried Corduan, *Philosophy Of Religion* (Grand Rapids, Michigan: Baker, 1988); with Paul D. Feinberg, *Introduction To Philosophy: A Christian Perspective* (Grand Rapids, Michigan: Baker, 1997); with Josh McDowell, *Love Is Always Right: A Defence Of The One Moral Absolute* (Dallas, Texas: Word, 1996); with Paul K. Hoffman (eds), *Why I Am A Christian: Leading Thinkers Explain Why They Believe* (Grand Rapids, Michigan: Baker, 2001). See also the weighty culmination of his career that is the *Baker Encyclopedia Of Christian Apologetics* (Grand Rapids, Michigan: Baker, 1999).

Groothuis, Douglas R.
Dr Groothuis is Associate Professor of Philosophy at Denver Seminary and is author of *Truth Decay: Defending Christianity Against The Challenges Of Postmodernism* (Downers Grove, Illinois: IVP, 2000);

Christianity That Counts: Being A Christian In A Non-Christian World (Grand Rapids, Michigan: Baker, 1994); *Unmasking The New Age* (Downers Grove, Illinois: IVP, 1986); *Confronting The New Age* (Downers Grove, Illinois: IVP, 1988); and *Revealing The New Age Jesus* (Downers Grove, Illinois: IVP, 1990). cf. < http://www.denverseminary .edu/catalog/0103/faculty/groothuis.php >; < http://www.arn.org/groot huis/dghome.htm >.

Habermas, Gary R.

Dr Habermas (PhD, Michigan State University; DD, Emmanuel College, Oxford) holds the title of Distinguished Professor of Philosophy and is Chair of the Department of Philosophy and Theology at Liberty University in America. Habermas is one of the foremost apologists on the subject of Jesus' resurrection (for example, he debated the resurrection with atheist philosopher Anthony Flew, and was judged the winner by both a panel of debate judges *and* a panel of philosophers). Habermas also argues for mind–body dualism. Books authored, co-authored, edited and/or contributed to by Habermas include: *The Resurrection Of Jesus* (Grand Rapids, Michigan: Baker, 1980); *Ancient Evidence For The Life Of Jesus: Historical Records Of His Death And Resurrection* (Nashville, Tennessee: Thomas Nelson, 1984); *The Verdict Of History* (Nashville, Tennessee: Thomas Nelson, 1988); *The Historical Jesus: Ancient Evidence For The Life Of Christ* (Joplin, Missouri: College Press, 1996); debate with Anthony Flew, *Did Jesus Rise From The Dead? The Resurrection Debate*, Terry L. Miethe (ed.), (San Francisco: Harper & Rowe, 1987); Gary R. Habermas and J.P. Moreland, *Beyond Death: Exploring The Evidence For Immortality* (Wheaton, Illinois: Crossway, 1998); R. Douglas Geivett and Gary R. Habermas (eds), *In Defence Of Miracles* (Leicester: Apollos, 1997); his contribution to Lee Strobel, *The Case For Christ* (Grand Rapids, Michigan: Zondervan, 1998); 'Did Jesus Perform Miracles?' in Michael J. Wilkins and J.P. Moreland (eds), *Jesus Under Fire* (Carlisle: Paternoster, 1995); 'Why I Believe the Miracles of Jesus Actually Happened' and 'Why I Believe the New Testament is Historically Reliable' in Norman L. Geisler and Paul K. Hoffman (eds), *Why I Am A Christian: Leading Thinkers Explain Why They Believe* (Grand Rapids, Michigan: Baker, 2001).

Kreeft, Peter

Professor Kreeft is a popular American Catholic writer who lectures in philosophy at Boston College. Kreeft received his PhD from Fordham University. Francis X. Maier, editor of the *National Catholic Register*, is justifiably fulsome in his praise: 'Lots of writers have the gift of irony, or humour, or logic, or common sense. Very few combine all these gifts in one talent and put it at the service of truth. Peter Kreeft is simply the best, the most engaging, Christian apologist at work today.' Kreeft's writing is a joy to read: it is accessible, witty and wise. He often employs a dialogue form, making philosophical ideas clearly relevant. He is notable for his engaging defence of objective truth, goodness and beauty and the vital importance of these 'permanent things' to the individual and to society. Kreeft (the name is Dutch for 'lobster'!) is a leading interpreter and proponent of the thought of C.S. Lewis. cf. *C.S. Lewis: A Critical Essay* (Front Royal, Virginia: Christendom College Press, 1988); *C.S. Lewis For The Third Millennium: Six Essays On The Abolition of Man* (San Francisco: Ignatius, 1994); *Between Heaven & Hell: A Dialog Somewhere Beyond Death With John F. Kennedy, C.S. Lewis & Aldous Huxley* (Downers Grove, Illinois: IVP, 1982); 'The Achievement of C.S. Lewis: A Millennial Assessment' @ < http://www.discovery.org/viewDB/index.php3?command=view&id=511&program=CS%20Lewis%20and%20Public%20Life >. Kreeft's other published work include: *The Best Things In Life* (Downers Grove, Illinois: IVP, 1984); *Three Philosophies Of Life* (San Francisco: Ignatius, 1989); *Heaven: The Heart's Deepest Longing* (San Francisco: Ignatius, 1989), which is perhaps the best book on heaven; *The Journey* (Downers Grove, Illinois: IVP, 1996); with Ronald K. Tacelli, *The Handbook Of Christian Apologetics* (Downers Grove, Illinois: IVP, 1994), which deserves status as a classic introduction to the field; and 'Why I Believe Jesus is the Son of God' in Norman L. Geisler and Paul K. Hoffman (eds), *Why I Am A Christian: Leading Thinkers Explain Why They Believe* (Grand Rapids, Michigan: Baker, 2001). Kreeft's opening and closing contributions to: *Does God Exist? The Debate Between Theists & Atheists* (Amherst, New York: Prometheus, 1993) is one of the best things about the volume. Visit Kreeft's home page @ < http://ic.net/~erasmus/RAZ29 .HTM >.

Lewis, C.S.
Clive Staples Lewis (1898–1963), 'Jack' to his friends and probably best known for his *Chronicles Of Narnia*, is widely regarded as the finest Christian apologist of the twentieth century. Second son of Albert and Flora Lewis of Belfast, Jack (a name he picked for himself almost as soon as he could speak) inherited the oratory skills of his Welsh father, who was a solicitor. Lewis was educated at Malvern College, Worcestershire, for a year, and then privately, before gaining a triple first at Oxford University.

After a spell in the army during World War I, during which Lewis was wounded, he studied and briefly taught philosophy at Oxford (where he was president of the philosophical Socratic Club), before moving on to teach literature. After lecturing in Philosophy and then Literature at Oxford, in 1954 Lewis became Professor of Medieval and Renaissance Literature at Cambridge University. Although he engaged in debates with philosophers such as C.E.M. Joad and G.E.M. Anscombe, Lewis was not a professional philosopher. Nevertheless, the good Christian apologist needs to have something of the philosopher about them, and Lewis was perhaps the consummate Christian apologist. Lewis influenced, and his arguments have been defended by, many professional philosophers, including C. Stephen Evans, Norman L. Geisler, Peter Kreeft, John Lucas, Basil Mitchell, Ronald H. Nash, Richard Purtill and Jerry L. Walls. Purtill writes: 'Lewis ... had powerful philosophical abilities, but because he was not a professional philosopher he did not use the jargon of the professionals ... He was a fine writer; one of the foremost prose writers of our time, with an almost unequalled combination of clarity and energy. If you were allowed to read only one twentieth-century defender of rational Christianity, Lewis would be the best choice by far' (*A Christian For All Christians* [London, Hodder & Stoughton, 1990], p. 59). Peter Kreeft adds that: 'Lewis has the typically British stylistic excellence which combines the best of Anglo-Saxon (clarity, simplicity, directness, strong, rock-hard nouns and bright, arrow-like verbs) with the best of Latin (logic, balance, elegance, harmonious structure) in a synthesis of economy, precision, and deceptive ease' (*C.S. Lewis: A Critical Essay* [Front Royal, Virginia: Christendom College Press, 1988], p. 16). Lewis argued that 'good philosophy needs to exist, if for no other reason, because bad philosophy needs to be answered'. Lewis combined romanticism and rationalism in a powerful blend; few writers equal his ability to make the truth of Christianity appear at once so reasonable and so attractive: 'Lewis is, of all things, a romantic rationalist; and Christianity, he would insist, is the catalyst which allows these two diverse elements to combine in the compound of a single soul' (ibid., p. 12). These three strings to Lewis's bow – rationalism, romanticism and Christianity – correspond to his three main literary genres – literary criticism, mythological and allegorical fiction, and apologetics (Lewis also wrote poetry and was a prolific letter-writer). Lewis defended the core beliefs common to Christians of all denominations, beliefs he called 'Mere Christianity', because 'Ever since I became a Christian I have thought that the best, perhaps the only, service I could do for my unbelieving neighbours was to explain and defend the belief that has been common to nearly all Christians at all times' (Preface, *Mere Christianity* [London: Fount, 1997]).

Three consistent themes throughout Lewis's corpus are the rejection of 'chronological snobbery', the objectivity of values and rationality, and the desire he called 'Joy'. Chronological snobbery is 'the uncritical assumption that whatever has gone out of date is on that account discredited. You must find out why it went out of date. Was it ever refuted (and if so, by whom, where, and how conclusively) or did it merely die away as fashions do? If the latter, this tells us nothing about its truth or falsehood' (*Surprised By Joy* [London: Fount, 1991]). Lewis staunchly defended the objectivity of a natural moral law, beauty, and truth, rooting all three in the existence and nature of God: 'Unless all that we take to be knowledge is an illusion, we must hold that in thinking we are not reading rationality into an irrational universe but responding to a rationality with which the universe has always been saturated ... For if our minds are totally alien to reality then all our thoughts, including this thought, are worthless. We must, then, grant logic to reality; we must, if we are to have any moral standards, grant it moral standards too. And there is really no reason why we should not do the same about standards of beauty' (*'De Futilitate'* in *Christian Reflections* [London: Fount, 1991], p. 96). Lewis uses 'Joy' to describe an experience 'of intense longing. It is distinguished from other longings by two things. In the first place, though the sense of want is acute and even painful, yet the mere wanting is felt to be somehow a delight ... In the second place, there is a peculiar mystery about the object of their Desire ... every one of those supposed objects for the Desire is inadequate to it' (Preface, *The Pilgrim's Regress* [London: Fount, 1977]). Lewis argues from this desire that there must be a corresponding object of desire which, since absent from this world, must lie beyond it. Thus Lewis turned Augustine's famous declaration that 'our hearts are restless until they rest in [God]' into an argument for the existence of God, and indeed, of heaven. Lewis also popularized the moral argument for God's existence, argued that metaphysical naturalism was self-undermining (because reason needs to proceed by the laws of logic and not merely by the laws of physics), and forcibly pointed out that, given Jesus' claims to divinity, he was either a liar (if he didn't believe his claims), a madman (if he believed his claims but was wrong) or absolutely right (if he believed his claims and wasn't mad).

For many years an atheist, Lewis became first a theist and then a Christian through a combination of factors, including his own philosophical thought, his professional assessment that the New Testament was not mythical, and his friendship with several Christians, including J.R.R. Tolkien, author of *The Hobbit* and *The Lord Of The Rings*: 'I gave in, and admitted that God was God ... perhaps the most dejected and reluctant convert in England' (*Surprised By Joy* [London: Fount, 1991]).

Lewis married Joy Davidson, a Jewish–American poet. Like Lewis's father and mother, Joy died from cancer, an episode in Lewis's life portrayed in his *A Grief Observed* and in the film *Shadowlands*. Lewis died in bed, on the same day as Aldous Huxley and J.F. Kennedy.

His many books, collections of essays and talks include: *Mere Christianity, Miracles, The Problem Of Pain, The Abolition Of Man, Surprised By Joy, The Great Divorce, The Four Loves, Letters To Malcolm: Chiefly On Prayer, Christian Reflections, God In The Dock* (all published by Fount); *The Space Trilogy* (Macmillan); *The Chronicles Of Narnia* (Macmillan); and *The Discarded Image* (Cambridge University Press). cf. C.S. Lewis Mega Links Page @ < http://ic.net/~eras mus/RAZ26.HTM >; Peter Kreeft, 'The Achievement of C.S. Lewis: A Millennial Assessment' @ < http://www.discovery.org/view DB/index.php 3?command=view&id=511&program=CS%20Lewis %20and%20Public%20Life >; Scott R. Burson and Jerry L. Walls, *C.S. Lewis & Francis Schaeffer: Lessons For A New Century From The Most Influential Apologists Of Our Time* (Downers Grove, Illinois: IVP, 1998); Corbin Scott Carnell *Bright Shadow Of Reality: Spiritual Longing In C.S. Lewis* (Grand Rapids, Michigan: Eerdmans, 1999); William Griffin, *C.S. Lewis: The Authentic Voice* (Tring, Hertfordshire: Lion, 1988); Peter Kreeft, *C.S. Lewis: A Critical Essay* (Front Royal, Virginia: Christendom College Press, 1988); Peter Kreeft, *C.S. Lewis For The Third Millennium: Six Essays On The Abolition of Man* (San Francisco: Ignatius, 1994); Andrew Walker and James Patrick (eds), *Rumours Of Angels: Essays In Honour Of C.S. Lewis* (London: Hodder & Stoughton, 1990).

Moreland, J.P.
J.P. Moreland is Distinguished Professor of Philosophy at Biola University in La Mirada, California. He was previously Professor of the Philosophy of Religion at the Talbot School of Theology in America, where he also directed the MA program in philosophy and ethics. Moreland testifies that: 'As a university student in 1968, I met Jesus Christ personally and He changed my life. I have had close to two decades of walking and fellowshipping with Him and falling more and more in love with Him daily. He has given me a power for life that I did not know before, and I have had personal experiences of Him' (*Does God Exist? The Debate Between Theists & Atheists* [Amherst, New York: Prometheus, 1993], p. 74). Fellow Christian philosopher Dallas Willard (under whom Moreland studied) says that: 'No evangelical now

writing on apologetics surpasses Moreland in philosophical ability.' In addition to his PhD in philosophy, Moreland has a MTh from Dallas Theological Seminary, an MA in philosophy from the University of California at Riverside, and a degree in chemistry from the University of Missouri. Moreland is a strong defender of natural theology (like William Lane Craig, he defends the Kalam argument) and mind–body dualism. He is also a prominent figure in the Intelligent Design Movement. Moreland's most noted book is *Scaling The Secular City: A Defense Of Christianity* (Grand Rapids, Michigan: Baker, 1987), which William Lane Craig called 'the most sophisticated apologetics book I have read', and which Norman L. Geisler lauded as 'a fresh, up-to-date defence of the Christian faith by a bright mind'. Moreland is the author, co-author or editor of fourteen books and numerous articles. cf. Moreland, J.P. @ < http://www.afterall.net/citizens/moreland/ >; J.P. Moreland Publications @ < http://people.biola.edu/faculty/moreland/Publications.html >; 'Integration and the Christian Scholar' @ < http://capo.org/premise/96/april/p960406.html >; 'Philosophical Apologetics, the Church and Contemporary Culture' @ < http://leaderu.com/aip/docs/moreland2b.html >; with Kai Nielson, *Does God Exist? The Debate Between Theists & Atheists* (Amherst, New York: Prometheus, 1993); with Gary R. Habermas, *Beyond Death: Exploring The Evidence for Immortality* (Wheaton, Illinois: Crossway, 1998); (ed.), *The Creation Hypothesis* (Downers Grove, Illinois: IVP, 1994); with Michael J. Wilkins (eds), *Jesus Under Fire: Modern Scholarship Reinvents The Historical Jesus* (Carlisle: Paternoster, 1995); *Christianity And The Nature of Science* (Grand Rapids, Michigan: Baker, 1989); 'Science, Miracles, Agency Theory and the God-of-the-Gaps' in R. Douglas Geivett and Gary R. Habermas (eds), *In Defence Of Miracles* (Leicester: Apollos, 1997); 'The Explanatory Relevance of Libertarian Agency as a Model of Theistic Design' in William A. Dembski (ed.), *Mere Creation: Science, Faith & Intelligent Design* (Downers Grove, Illinois: IVP, 1998); 'Why I have Made Jesus Christ Lord of My Life' in Norman L. Geisler and Paul K. Hoffman (eds), *Why I Am A Christian: Leading Thinkers Explain Why They Believe* (Grand Rapids, Michigan: Baker, 2001).

Paley, William
English classical apologist (1743–1805) who studied mathematics at Cambridge, where he taught for nine years after being ordained into the priesthood in 1767. His three major works are: *The Principles Of Moral And Political Philosophy* (1785); *A View Of The Evidences Of Christianity* (1794); and *Natural Theology* (1802). In the latter work,

Paley gave a now classic exposition of the argument for design from the similarities between the design of a watch and of the nature of the universe. See 'William Paley' @ < http://ourworld.compuserve.com/home pages/rossuk/Paley.htm >; or excerpts from the *Natural Theology* @ < http://www-phil.tamu.edu/~gary/intro/paper.paley.html> ; < http://www.utm.edu/research/iep/p/paley.htm >.

Plantinga, Alvin
John O'Brien Professor of the Philosophy of Religion at the University of Notre Dame, Alvin Plantinga is one of America's leading philosophers and ranks among the top few contemporary Christian philosophers of religion. His ideas have determined the direction of philosophical debate in many areas of the discipline. Plantinga has focused on the epistemology of religious belief, defending the thesis that belief in God may be rational despite lacking support from the arguments of natural theology (although he supports such arguments), a position he calls 'Reformed Epistemology' after the Christian thinkers of the Reformation, such as Calvin, from whom he draws inspiration (cf. *God And Other Minds* [Ithaca, New York: Cornell University Press, 1967]; (ed.) with Nicholas Wolterstorff, *Faith & Rationality* [Notre Dame, Indiana: University of Notre Dame Press, 1983]). Plantinga argues that religious belief is 'properly basic', justified not by other beliefs but by immediate experience. More recently (in *Warrant: The Current Debate* [Oxford: Oxford University Press, 1993]; *Warrant And Proper Function* [New York: Oxford University Press, 1993]; and *Warranted Christian Belief* [New York: Oxford University Press, 2000]) Plantinga has advanced a subtle externalist account of epistemic justification or 'warrant'. Plantinga defines warranted beliefs as (roughly speaking) beliefs produced by a properly functioning cognitive system aimed at truth. With the introduction of the notion of a properly functioning cognitive system Plantinga argues that the very concept of proper function implies the existence of an intelligent designer, and that naturalistic evolution is an inadequate account of the existence of reliable cognitive systems. Plantinga is also a leading theorist in the metaphysics of modality. *The Nature Of Necessity* (Oxford: Clarendon Press, 1978) developed a now standard semantics of 'possible worlds' (maximally consistent states of affairs), and presented what many consider to be the definitive version of the free will defence against the argument from evil, as well as a highly influential modal version of the ontological argument. cf. < http://www.faithquest.com/home.cfm?main=docs/philosophers/plantinga/index.cfm >;
< http://www.homestead.com/philofreligion/Plantingapage.html >;

< http://id-www.ucsb.edu/fscf/library/plantinga/ >; 'Philosophy of Religion' @ < http://www.philosophynow.demon.co.uk/overviewrel.htm >.

Swinburne, Richard
As the Nolloth Professor of the Philosophy of the Christian Religion at the University of Oxford, Richard Swinburne ranks amongst today's top philosophers of religion. Swinburne is best known for his case for the existence of God developed in *The Existence Of God* (Oxford: Clarendon Press, 1991), which proceeds according to scientific patterns of reasoning and employs probability calculus (which is missing from his shorter and more accessible *Is There A God?* [Oxford: Oxford University Press, 1996]). He is also a noted defender of substance dualism. Swinburne often proceeds by spending the first half of a book carefully defining the terms crucial to the argument of the second half. cf. < http://www.faithquest.com/home.cfm?main=docs/philosophers/s winburne/index.cfm >; 'The Justification of Theism' @ < http://www. lead eru.com/truth/3truth09.html >; his tetralogy on the philosophy of Christian doctrine: *Responsibility And Atonement* (Oxford: Clarendon Press, 1989); *Revelation* (Oxford: Clarendon Press, 1991); *The Christian God* (Oxford: Clarendon Press, 1994) and *Providence And The Problem Of Evil* (Oxford: Oxford University Press, 1998); his trilogy on philosophical theology: *The Coherence of Theism* (Oxford: Clarendon Press, 1977, revised 1993); *Faith And Reason* (Oxford: Oxford University Press, 1984); and *The Existence Of God* (Oxford: Clarendon Press, 1991). See also *Is There A God?* (Oxford: Oxford University Press, 1996); and *The Evolution Of The Soul* (Oxford: Clarendon Press 1986).

Ward, Keith
Regius Professor of Divinity at the University of Oxford, and formerly Professor of History and Philosophy of Religion at King's College, London, Ward is the author of several acclaimed books on such topics as the soul, comparative religion, faith and science, and Christian doctrine. cf. *Holding Fast To God* (London: SPCK, 1983); *God, Chance And Necessity* (Oxford: OneWorld, 1996); *Defending The Soul* (Oxford: OneWorld, 1992); *Religion And Creation* (Oxford: Clarendon Press, 1996); *Religion And Human Nature* (Oxford: Clarendon Press, 1998).

Willard, Dallas
Professor Willard teaches at the University of Southern California's School of Philosophy, and is the author of numerous books and papers, including *Hearing God* (London: HarperCollins, 1999); *The Spirit Of The Disciplines* (San Francisco: HarperCollins, 1991); and *The Divine*

Conspiracy: Rediscovering Our Hidden Life In God (London: Fount, 1998). cf. Dallas Willard @ < http://www.dwillard.org/ >; especially his contribution to J.P. Moreland and Kai Nielson, *Does God Exist? The Debate Between Theists & Atheists* (Amherst, New York: Prometheus, 1993): 'Language, Being, God, and the Three Stages of Theistic Evidence' @ < http://www.dwillard.org/Philosophy/Pubs/language_being.htm >.

The following sources may be of interest:

- Theistic Philosophers @ < http://theism.actualism.com/theistic.php3 >
- Kelly James Clark (ed.), *Philosophers Who Believe* (Downers Grove, Illinois: IVP, 1993), with contributions from Mortimer J. Adler, Kelly James Clark, Stephen T. Davis, Basil Mitchell, Terence Penelhum, Alvin Plantinga, Nicholas Rescher, John Rist, Richard Swinburne, Frederick Suppe, Nicholas Wolterstorff and Linda Zagzebski.
- Thomas V. Morris, *God And The Philosophers* (New York: Oxford University Press, 1994), with contributions from Thomas V. Morris, William P. Alston, Peter van Inwagen, Michael J. Murray, William J. Wainwright, C. Stephen Layman, Jerry L. Walls, Robert C. Roberts, Jeff Jordan, Marylin McCord Adams, William J. Abraham, Laura J. Garcia, Arthur F. Holmes, Brian Leftow, George Maverodes, Merold Westphal, Spencer Carr, Eleonore Stump, George N. Schlesinger and David Shatz.

Select Bibliography

These resources are grouped by topic and listed (roughly speaking) in the order that those topics arise in reading this book. They are also graded (where appropriate) by accessibility (*not* cogency): (1) for introductory material, (2) for material of intermediate difficulty and (3) for advanced material. As a guide for comparison I would grade this book as (2).

Visit my web site @ < http://www.peter-s-williams.co.uk/ >. I also maintain an 'about me' patch at that American on-line book shop amazon.com that includes biographical information, book reviews and recommended book lists @ < http://www.amazon.com/exec/obidos/tg/cm/member-fil/-/A1VQXYIQBW3EIZ/103-4894811-5379804 > (alternatively, simply go to amazon.com and do a people search).

Angels and Demons

Web sites

I debated with British atheist Steven Carr on the existence of angels @ < http://www.bowness.demon.co.uk/deb.htm > (2)

Angel.com @ < http://applecity.com/Angels/angels.htm > (1)

Aquinas, Thomas, *Summa Theologica* @ < http://www.newadvent.org/summa/1.htm > (3)

Bohlin, Sue, 'Angels, The Good, The Bad and The Ugly' @ < http://www.leaderu. com/orgs/probe/docs/angels.html > (1)

Catholic Encyclopedia, 'Angels' @ < http://www.newadvent.org/cathen/01476d. htm >

'In Search of Angels' @ < http://members.tripod.com/~StevensD/ >

Kreeft, Peter, 'Satan and the Millennium' @ < http://catholiceducation.org/articles/religion/re0018.html > (1)

Rhodes, Ron, 'Close Encounters of the Celestial Kind: Evaluating Today's Angel Craze' @ < http://home.earthlink.net/~ronrhodes/AngelsArticle.html > (1)

Tunnicliffe, Patty, 'What in Heaven's Name? An Analysis of the Messages and World Views Coming from Aliens and Modern Day Angels' @ < http:// ses.edu/journal/issue2_1/2_1tunnicliffe.htm > (1)

Williams, Peter S., 'Angelology and Biblical Skepticism' @ < http://www. leaderu.com/theology/williams_angel.html > (2)

—, 'New Testament Criticism and Jesus the Exorcist' @ < http://www.quod libet.net/williams-criticism.shtml > (1)

Books

Adler, Mortimer J., *The Angels And Us* (New York: Collier, 1982). (2)

Boyd, Gregory A., *God At War: The Bible And Spiritual Conflict* (Downers Grove, Illinois: IVP, 1997). (2)

—, *Satan & The Problem Of Evil* (Downers Grove, Illinois: IVP, 2001). (2)

Graham, Billy, *Angels* (London: Hodder & Stoughton, 1976). (1)

Green, Michael, *I Believe In Satan's Downfall* (London: Hodder & Stoughton, 1981). (1)

Heathcote-James, Emma, *Seeing Angels: True Contemporary Accounts Of Hundreds Of Angelic Experiences* (London: John Blake, 2001). (1)

Kreeft, Peter, *Angels (And Demons)* (San Francisco: Ignatius, 1995). (1)

—, *The Snakebite Letters* (San Francisco: Ignatius, 1993). (1)

— and Tacelli, Ronald, *Handbook Of Christian Apologetics* (Downers Grove, Illinois: IVP, 1994).

Lane, Anthony N.S. (ed.), *The Unseen World: Christian Reflections On Angels, Demons And The Heavenly Realm* (Carlisle: Paternoster, 1996). (2)

Lewis, C.S., *The Screwtape Letters* (New York: Collier, 1982). (1)

Oropeza, B.J., *99 Answers To Questions About Angels, Demons & Spiritual Warfare* (Eastbourne, East Sussex: Kingsway, 1997). (1)

Peck, M. Scott, *People Of The Lie* (London: Arrow, 1990). (1)

Perry, Michael (ed.), *Deliverance: Psychic Disturbance And Occult Involvement* (London: SPCK, 1996²). (1)

Price, Hope, *Angels: True Stories Of How They Touch Our Lives* (London: Pan, 1995). (1)

Woolmer, John, *Thinking Clearly About Angels* (Crowborough, East Sussex: Monarch, 2002). (1)

Spiritual Warfare

Web sites

Spiritual Warfare @ < http://www.spirithome.com/spirwarf.html >

The Battle Behind @ < http://ourworld.compuserve.com/homepages/CW_Arn hem/battle.html >

Books

Calver, Clive, *The Holy Spirit: Transforming Us And Our World* (Milton Keynes: Scripture Union, 2001). (1)

Colson, Charles and Pearcey, Nancy, *How Now Shall We Live?* (London: Marshall Pickering, 1999). (2)

Kreeft, Peter, *Ecumenical Jihad* (San Francisco: Ignatius, 1996). (1)

Rabey, Steve and Rabey, Lois (eds), *Side By Side: A Handbook – Disciple Making For A New Century* (Colorado Springs: Navpress, 2000). (1)

Willard, Dallas, *The Divine Conspiracy: Rediscovering Our Hidden Life In God* (London: Fount, 1998). (2)

Introducing Christian Philosophy, Apologetics and Integration

Web sites

The Academy of Christian Apologetics @ < http://hisdefense.org/ > (2)

Craig, William Lane, 'The Resurrection of Theism' @ < http://www.leaderu. com/truth/3truth01.html > (2)

Groothuis, Douglas, 'Apologetics for Postmoderns' @ < http://www.gospelcom . net/ivpress/groothuis/TDChapter.html >

—, 'Six Enemies of Apologetic Engagement' @ < http://www.leaderu.com/ comm on/sixenemies.html > (1)

Hazen, Craig J., 'Ideas and Consequences: The Need for Christian Apologetics in the Modern World' @ < http://hisdefense.org/articles/ch001.html > (1)

Williams, Jimmy, 'Apologetics and Evangelism', @ < http://www.leaderu.com/ orgs/probe/docs/apol-eva.html > (1)

Koukl, Gregory, 'The Value of Philosophy' @ < http://www.str.org/free/comm entaries/philosophy/philos.htm > (1)

Moreland, J.P., 'Integration and the Christian Scholar' @ < http://capo.org/ premise/96/april/p960406.html > (2)

—, 'Philosophical Apologetics, the Church and Contemporary Culture' @ < http://leaderu.com/aip/docs/moreland2b.html > (2)

Plantinga, Alvin, 'Advice to Christian Philosophers' @ < http://www.leaderu. com/truth/1truth10.html > (2)

—, 'Augustinian Christian Philosophy' @ < http://www.faithquest.com/home. cfm?main=docs/philosophers/plantinga/augustine.cfm > (2)

—, 'Christian Philosophy at the End of the 20th Century' @ < http://www.faith quest.com/home.cfm?main=docs/philosophers/plantinga/20th.cfm > (2)

—, 'On Christian Scholarship' @ < http://id-www.ucsb.edu/fscf/library/plantin ga/OCS.html > (2)

Books

Burson, Scott R. and Walls, Jerry L., *C.S. Lewis & Francis Schaeffer: Lessons For A New Century From The Most Influential Apologists Of Our Time* (Downers Grove, Illinois: IVP, 1998). (2)

Cowan, Steven B. (ed.), *Five Views On Apologetics* (Grand Rapids, Michigan: Zondervan, 2000). (3)

Geisler, Norman L. and Feinberg, Paul D., *Introduction To Philosophy: A Christian Perspective* (Grand Rapids, Michigan: Baker, 1997). (1)

McGrath, Alister, *Bridge-Building: Communicating Christianity Effectively* (Leicester, IVP, 1992). (2)

— and Green, Michael, *How Shall We Reach Them? Defending And Communicating The Christian Faith To Nonbelievers* (Milton Keynes: Word, 1995). (2)

Morris, Tom, *Philosophy For Dummies* (Foster City, California: IDG, 1999). (1)

Varghese, Roy Abraham, *Great Thinkers On Great Questions* (Oxford: OneWorld, 1998). (2)

World Views

Books

Holmes, Arthur F., *Contours Of A World View* (Grand Rapids, Michigan: Eerdmans, 1983). (2)

Jones, Merve, *The Universe Upstairs* (Leicester: IVP, 1991). (1)

McDowell, Josh and Don Stewart, *Concise Guide To Today's Religions* (Amersham-on-the-Hill, Buckinghamshire: Scripture Press, 1992). (1)

Nash, Ronald H., *Life's Ultimate Questions* (Grand Rapids, Michigan: Zondervan, 1999). (2)

—, *World-Views In Conflict: Choosing Christianity In A World Of Ideas,* (Grand Rapids, Michigan: Zondervan, 1992). (2)

Sire, James W., *The Universe Next Door* (Leicester: IVP, 1997³). (1)

Naturalistic Atheism and Scientism

Expositions

Web sites
Steven Carr, 'The UK's Leading Atheist Page' @ < http://www.bowness.demon.co.uk/ >

Internet Infidels @ < http://www.infidels.org/infidels/ >

Books
Dawkins, Richard, *The Blind Watchmaker* (London: Penguin, 1990). (2)

Dennett, Daniel C., *Darwin's Dangerous Idea* (London: Penguin, 1995). (2)

Le Poidevin, Robin, *Arguing For Atheism: An Introduction To The Philosophy Of Religion* (London: Routledge, 1996). (2)

Martin, Michael, *Atheism: A Philosophical Justification* (Philadelphia: Temple University Press, 1990). (2)
Mackie, J.L., *The Miracle Of Theism* (Oxford: Clarendon Press, 1982). (3)
Russell, Bertrand, *Why I Am Not A Christian* (London: Routledge, 1996). (1)

Critiques

Web sites
Barr, Steven M., review of Dawkins' *Unweaving The Rainbow* @ < http:// catholiceducation.org/articles/science/sc0009.html > (1)
Johnson, Phillip E., review of Dawkins' *Climbing Mount Improbable* @ < http://catholiceducation.org/articles/science/sc0014.html > (1)
—, review of Daniel Dennett's *Darwin's Dangerous Idea* @ < http://www.arn. org/docs/johnson/dennett.htm > (1)
Koons, Robert C., 'The Incompatibility of Naturalism and Scientific Realism' @ < http://www.leaderu.com/offices/koons/docs/natreal.html > (3)
Plantinga, Alvin, review of Daniel Dennett's *Darwin's Dangerous Idea* @ < http://id-www.ucsb.edu/fscf/library/plantinga/dennett.html > (2)
Willard, Dallas, 'Knowledge and Naturalism' @ < http://www.dwillard.org/ Phil osophy/Pubs/knowledge_and_naturalism.htm > (3)
—, 'Reflections on Dawkins' *The Blind Watchmaker*' @ < http://www.dwillard. org/Philosophy/Pubs/dawkins.htm > (2)

Books
Balfour, Arthur J., *Theism And Humanism* (Seattle: Inklings, 2000). (3)
Broom, Neil, *How Blind Is The Watchmaker?* (Leicester: IVP, 2001). (2)
Cook, David, *Blind Alley Beliefs* (Leicester: IVP, 1996). (1)
Craig, William Lane and Moreland, J.P. (eds), *Naturalism: A Critical Analysis* (London: Routledge, 2001). (3)
Denton, Michael J., *Evolution: A Theory In Crisis* (Bethesda, Maryland: Adler & Adler, 1986). (3)
Johnson, Phillip E., *The Wedge Of Truth: Splitting The Foundations Of Naturalism*, (Downers Grove, Illinois: IVP, 2000). (1)
Lewis, C. S, *Miracles* (London: Fount, 1998²). (2)
Nash, Ronald H., *World-Views In Conflict: Choosing Christianity In A World Of Ideas* (Grand Rapids, Michigan: Zondervan, 1992). (2)
—, *Life's Ultimate Questions* (Grand Rapids, Michigan: Zondervan, 1999). (2)
Sire, James W., *The Universe Next Door* (Leicester: IVP, 1997³). (1)
Ward, Keith, *God, Chance and Necessity* (Oxford: OneWorld, 1996). (3)

Christianity and Science

Web sites
Access Research Network @: < http://www.arn.org >
Christians in Science @ < http://www.cis.org.uk/ >
Forster, Roger and Paul Marston, *Reason, Science and Faith* @ < http://www.
    reason-science-and-faith.com/ > (2)
Koons, Robert C., 'The Incompatibility of Naturalism and Scientific Realism'
    @ < http://www.leaderu.com/offices/koons/docs/natreal.html > (3)
Kreeft, Peter, 'Science and Religion' @ < http://catholiceducation.org/articles/
    apologetics/ap0063.html > (1)
Moreland, J.P., 'Is Science a Threat or Help to Faith?' @ < http://www.afterall.
    net/citizens/moreland/papers/jp-threatscience.html > (1)
Plantinga, Alvin, 'When Faith and Reason Clash: Evolution and the Bible' @
    < http://www.asa3.org/ASA/dialogues/Faith-reason/CRS9-91Plantinga1. html >
    (2)

Books
Colson, Charles and Pearcey, Nancy, *Developing A Christian Worldview Of
    Science And Evolution* (Wheaton, Illinois: Tyndale House, 2001). (1)
Moreland, J.P., *Christianity And The Nature Of Science* (Grand Rapids,
    Michigan: Baker, 1989). (3)
— and Reynolds, John Mark (eds), *Three Views On Creation And Evolution*
    (Grand Rapids, Michigan: Zondervan, 1999). (2)
Polkinghorne, John, *Serious Talk: Science And Religion In Dialogue* (London:
    SCM, 1995). (2)
Ratzsch, Del, *Science & Its Limits: The Natural Sciences In Christian Perspec-
    tive* (Leicester: Apollos, 2000). (2)

Mind–Body Dualism

Web sites
Damaris Centre for Soul and Consciousness Studies @ < http://www.damaris.
    org/dcscs/index2.htm >
Descartes, René, *Meditations On First Philosophy* @ < http://www.cola.
    wright. edu/DesCartes/Meditations.html >
Koukl, Gregory, 'All Brain, No Mind' @ < http://www.str.org/free/commenta
    ries/philosophy/nomind.htm > (1)
—, 'Dominoes, Determinism, and Naturalism' @ < http://www.str.org/free/
    commentaries/evolution/dominosd.htm > (1)
Willard, Dallas, 'Knowledge and Naturalism' @ < http://www.dwillard.org/
    Philosophy/Pubs/knowledge_and_naturalism.htm > (3)
—, 'A Non-Reductive and Non-Eliminative Physicalism?' @ < http://www.dwi
    llard.org/Philosophy/Pubs/non-reductive.htm > (3)

Williams, Peter S., 'Why Naturalists Should Mind About Physicalism, and Vice Versa' @ < http://www.damaris.org/dcscs/readingroom/2000/willia ms1.htm > (2)

Books

Cooper, John W., *Body, Soul & Life Everlasting* (Leicester: Apollos, 2000). (2)

Craig, William Lane (ed.), *Philosophy Of Religion: A Reader And Guide* (Edinburgh: Edinburgh University Press, 2002). (3)

—, and Moreland, J.P. (eds), *Naturalism: A Critical Analysis* (London: Routledge, 2001). (3)

Habermas, Gary R. and Moreland, J.P., *Beyond Death: Exploring The Evidence For Immortality* (Wheaton, Illinois: Crossway, 1998.) (2)

Hasker, William, *The Emergent Self* (Ithaca, New York: Cornell University Press, 1999). (3)

Lewis, C.S., *Miracles* (London: Fount, 1998^2). (2)

Moreland, J.P., *Scaling The Secular City* (Grand Rapids, Michigan: Baker, 1987). (2)

— and Rae, Scott B., *Body & Soul: Human Nature & The Crisis In Ethics* (Downers Grove, Illinois: IVP, 2000). (3)

Swinburne, Richard, *The Evolution Of The Soul* (Oxford: Clarendon Press, 1986). (3)

The Existence of God

General

Web sites

Aquinas, Thomas, 'Does God Exist?' from *Summa Theologica* @ < http:// newadvent.org/summa/100203.htm > (2)

Chesterton, G. K, 'The Ethics of Elfland' (from *Orthodoxy*) @ < http://www. leaderu.com/cyber/books/orthodoxy/ch4.html > (2)

Craig, William Lane @ < http://www.leaderu.com/offices/billcraig/menus/ index.html > (2–3)

Descartes, René, *Meditations On First Philosophy* @ < http://www.cola. wright. edu/DesCartes/Meditations.html > (2)

Evans, C. Stephen, 'The Mystery of Persons and Belief in God' @ < http:// www.leaderu.com/truth/3truth07.html > (1)

Kreeft, Peter, @ < http://catholiceducation.org/articles/apologetics/ap0002. html > (1)

—, 'Can You Prove That God Exists?' @ < http://catholiceducation.org/articles/ apologetics/ap0060.html > (1)

—, 'The Reasons to Believe' @ < http://catholiceducation.org/articles/apologe tics/ap0002.html > (1)

Plantinga, Alvin, 'Two Dozen (or so) Theistic Arguments' @ < http://www. homes tead.com/philofreligion/files/Theisticarguments.html > (3)

Swinburne, Richard, 'The Justification of Theism' @ < http://www.leaderu. com/truth/3truth09.html > (2)

Vitz, Paul, 'The Psychology of Atheism' @ < http://catholiceducation.org/art icles/religion/re0384.html > (1)

Willard, Dallas, 'Language, Being, God, and the Three Stages of Theistic Evidence' @ < http://www.dwillard.org/Philosophy/Pubs/language_being. htm > (2)

Books

Clark, Kelly James (ed.), *Readings In The Philosophy Of Religion* (Peterborough, Ontario: Broadview Press, 2000). (2)

Craig, William Lane (ed.), *Philosophy Of Religion: A Reader And Guide* (Edinburgh: Edinburgh University Press, 2002). (3)

Davies, Brian (ed.), *Philosophy Of Religion: A Guide And Anthology* (Oxford: Oxford University Press, 2000). (3)

Davis, Stephen T., *God, Reason And Theistic Proofs* (Edinburgh: Edinburgh University Press, 1997). (3)

Evans, C. Stephen, *Why Believe? Reason And Mystery As Pointers To God* (Leicester: IVP, 1996). (1)

Geisler, Norman L. and Corduan, Winfried, *Philosophy Of Religion* (Grand Rapids, Michigan: Baker, 1988²). (2)

— and Bucchino, Peter, *Unshakable Foundations* (Minneapolis, Minnesota: Bethany House, 2001). (1)

— and Hoffman, Paul K. (eds), *Why I Am A Christian* (Grand Rapids, Michigan: Baker, 2001). (2)

Geivett, R. Douglas and Sweetman, Brendan (eds), *Contemporary Perspectives On Religious Epistemology* (New York: Oxford University Press, 1992). (2)

Hick, John (ed.), *The Existence Of God* (New York: Macmillan, 1964). (2)

Miethe, Terry L. and Habermas, Gary R., *Why Believe? God Exists!* (Joplin, Missouri: College Press, 1998). (2)

Moreland, J.P., *Scaling The Secular City* (Grand Rapids, Michigan: Baker, 1987). (2)

Peterson, Michael, Hasker, William, Reichenbach, Bruce and Basinger, David (eds), *Philosophy Of Religion: Selected Readings* (New York: Oxford University Press, 1996). (2)

Plantinga, Alvin, *Warranted Christian Belief* (New York: Oxford University Press, 2000). (3)

Stump, Eleonore and Murray, Michael J. (eds), *Philosophy Of Religion: The Big Questions* (Oxford: Blackwell, 1999). (2)

Swinburne, Richard, *The Existence Of God* (Oxford: Clarendon Press, 1991). (3)

—, *Is There A God?* (Oxford: Oxford University Press, 1996). (2)

Vitz, Paul C., *Faith Of The Fatherless: The Psychology Of Atheism* (Dallas, Texas: Spence, 2000). (1)

Ward, Keith, *God, Chance and Necessity* (Oxford: OneWorld, 1996). (3)

Williams, Peter S., *The Case For God* (Crowborough, East Sussex: Monarch, 1999). (2)

Debates on God's Existence

Web sites

Craig, William Lane @ < http://www.leaderu.com/offices/billcraig/menus/index.html >

Books

Miethe, Terry L. and Flew, Antony, *Does God Exist? A Believer And An Atheist Debate* (San Francisco: HarperCollins, 1991). (2)

Moreland, J.P. and Nielson, Kai, *Does God Exist?* (Amherst, New York: Prometheus, 1993). (2)

Russell, Bertrand and Copleston, F.C., 'A Debate on the Existence of God' in Hick, John (ed.), *The Existence Of God* (New York: Macmillan, 1964). (1)

Smart, J.J.C. and Haldane, J.J., *Atheism and Theism* (Oxford: Blackwell, 1996). (3)

God and Evil (cf. Arguments from Value)

Web sites

Clark, Kelly James, 'I Believe in God, the Father, Almighty' @ < http://www.calvin.edu/academic/philosophy/writings/ibig.htm > (2)

Kreeft, Peter, 'The Problem of Evil' @ < http://catholiceducation.org/articles/religion/re0019.html > (1)

Williams, Peter S., 'Terror from the Skies and the Existence of God' @ < http://www.damaris.org/writing/articles/other_articles/worldtradecentre3.htm >

Books

Boyd, Gregory A., *Satan & The Problem Of Evil* (Downers Grove, Illinois: IVP, 2001). (2)

— and Boyd, Edward, *Letters From A Skeptic* (Eastbourne, East Sussex: Kingsway, 2000). (1)

Clark, Kelly James, *Return To Reason* (Grand Rapids, Michigan: Eerdmans, 1998). (2)

Geisler, Norman L. and Bucchino, Peter, *Unshakeable Foundations* (Minneapolis, Minnesota: Bethany House, 2001). (1)

Howard-Snyder, Daniel (ed.), *The Evidential Argument From Evil* (Bloomington, Indiana: Indiana University Press, 1996). (3)

Lewis, C.S., *The Problem Of Pain* (London: Fount, 1977). (1)

McGrath, Alister, *Suffering* (London: Hodder & Stoughton, 1992). (1)

Miethe, Terry L. and Habermas, Gary R., *Why Believe? God Exists!* (Joplin, Missouri: College Press, 1998). (2)

Perry, John, *Dialogue On Good, Evil, And The Existence Of God* (Indianapolis, Indiana: Hackett, 1999). (1)

Peterson, Michael, Hasker, William, Reichenbach, Bruce and Basinger, David (eds), *Philosophy Of Religion: Selected Readings* (New York: Oxford University Press, 1996). (2)

Plantinga, Alvin, *God, Freedom, And Evil* (Grand Rapids, Michigan: Eerdmans, 2001). (2)

Strobel, Lee, *The Case For Faith: A Journalist Investigates The Toughest Objections To Christianity* (Grand Rapids, Michigan: Zondervan, 2000). (1)

Swinburne, Richard, *Providence And The Problem Of Evil* (Oxford: Oxford University Press, 1998). (3)

Williams, Peter S., *The Case For God* (Crowborough, East Sussex: Monarch, 1999). (2)

Films to watch: *The Fifth Element*, dir. Luc Besson; *From Dusk Till Dawn*, dir. Robert Rodriguez.

The Argument from Mind

Web sites

Swinburne, Richard, 'The Justification of Theism' @ < http://www.leaderu.com/truth/3truth09.html > (2)

Books

Adams, Robert M., 'Flavors, Colors, and God' in Geivett, R. Douglas and Sweetman, Brendan (eds), *Contemporary Perspectives On Religious Epistemology* (New York: Oxford University Press, 1992). (3)

Craig, William Lane (ed.), *Philosophy Of Religion: A Reader And Guide* (Edinburgh: Edinburgh University Press, 2002). (3)

Swinburne, Richard, *The Evolution Of The Soul* (Oxford: Clarendon Press, 1986). (3)

—, Richard, *The Existence Of God* (Oxford: Clarendon Press, 1991). (3)

Ontological Argument

Web sites

Anselm's *Proslogium* @ < http://www.ccel.org/a/anselm/basic_works/htm/i.htm >

Books

Evans, C. Stephen, *Philosophy Of Religion* (Leicester: IVP, 1985). (1)

Peterson, Michael, Hasker, William, Reichenbach, Bruce and Basinger, David (eds), *Philosophy Of Religion: Selected Readings* (New York: Oxford University Press, 1996). (2)

Plantinga, Alvin, *God, Freedom, And Evil* (Grand Rapids, Michigan: Eerdmans, 2001). (2)

Stump, Eleonore and Murray, Michael J. (eds), *Philosophy Of Religion: The Big Questions* (Oxford: Blackwell, 1999). (3)

Arguments from Value

Web sites

Craig, William Lane, 'The Indispensability of Theological Meta-Ethical Foundations for Morality' @ < http://www.leaderu.com/offices/billcraig/docs/meta-eth.html > (2)

Moreland, J.P., 'The Ethical Inadequacy of Naturalism' @ < http://www.afterall. net/citizens/moreland/papers/jp-naturalism2.html > (2)

Williams, Peter S., 'Terror From the Skies and the Existence of God' @ < http://www.damaris.org/writing/articles/other_articles/worldtradecentre3.htm > (2)

—, 'Aesthetic Arguments for the Existence of God' @ < http://www.quodlibet. net/williams-aesthetic.shtml > (2)

Books

Balfour, Arthur J., *Theism And Humanism* (Seattle: Inklings, 2000). (3)

Beckwith, Francis J. and Koukl, Gregory, *Relativism: Feet Planted Firmly In Mid-Air* (Grand Rapids, Michigan: Baker, 2001). (1)

Chamberlain, Paul, *Can We Be Good Without God?* (Downers Grove, Illinois: IVP, 1996). (1)

Copan, Paul, *'True For You, But Not For Me': Defeating The Slogans That Leave Christians Speechless* (Minneapolis, Minnesota: Bethany House, 1998). (1)

Craig, William Lane (ed.), *Philosophy Of Religion: A Reader And Guide* (Edinburgh: Edinburgh University Press, 2002). (3)

Davies, Brian, *Philosophy Of Religion: A Guide And Anthology* (Oxford: Oxford University Press, 2000). (3)

Hick, John (ed.), *The Existence Of God* (New York: Macmillan, 1964). (2)

Lewis, C. S, *Mere Christianity* (London: Fount, 1997). (1)

Sorley, William R., *Moral Values And The Idea Of God* (New York: Macmillan, 1930). (2)

Williams, Peter S., *The Case For God* (Crowborough, East Sussex: Monarch, 1999). (2)

Cosmological Arguments

Web sites

Aquinas, Thomas, 'Does God Exist?' from *Summa Theologica* @ < http:// newadvent.org/summa/100203.htm > (2)

Clark, Samuel L., 'A Discourse Concerning the Being and Attributes of God' @ < http://www.hti.umich.edu/cgi/p/pd-modeng/pd-modeng-idx?type=HTM L&rgn=DIV0&byte=8985960 > (3)

Groothuis, Douglas, 'Leo and the Mechanic: A Cosmological Narrative' @ < http://www.gospelcom.net/ivpress/groothuis/leocosmo.htm > (1)

Willard, Dallas, 'Language, Being, God, and the Three Stages of Theistic Evidence' @ < http://www.dwillard.org/Philosophy/Pubs/language_being. htm > (2)

Books

Beck, David W., 'God's Existence' in Geivett, R. Douglas and Habermas, Gary R. (eds), *In Defence Of Miracles* (Leicester: Apollos, 1997). (2)

Craig, William Lane (ed.), *Philosophy Of Religion: A Reader And Guide* (Edinburgh: Edinburgh University Press, 2002). (3)

Davies, Brian, *Philosophy Of Religion: A Guide And Anthology* (Oxford: Oxford University Press, 2000). (3)

Peterson, Michael, Hasker, William, Reichenbach, Bruce and Basinger, David (eds), *Philosophy Of Religion: Selected Readings* (New York: Oxford University Press, 1996). (2)

Reichenbach, Bruce R., *The Cosmological Argument: A Reassessment* (Springfield, Illinois: Charles C. Thomas, 1972). (3)

Willard, Dallas, 'The Three Stage Argument for the Existence of God' in Geivett, R. Douglas and Sweetman, Brendan (eds), *Contemporary Perspectives In Religious Epistemology* (New York: Oxford University Press, 1992).

Williams, Peter S., *The Case For God* (Crowborough, East Sussex: Monarch, 1999). (2)

Design

Web sites

Access Research Network @: < http://www.arn.org > (1–3)

Behe, Michael J., 'Darwin Under the Microscope' @ < http://catholiceducation. org/articles/science/sc0017.html > (1)

International Society for Complexity, Information, and Design @ < http:// www. iscid.org/ > (3)

Collins, Robin, 'The Fine-Tuning Design Argument: A Scientific Argument for the Existence of God' @ < http://www.discovery.org/viewDB/index.php3? program=CRSC&command=view&id=91 > (3)

Craig, William Lane @ < http://www.leaderu.com/offices/billcraig/menus/ind ex.html > (2–3)

Dembski, William A. @ < http://www.leaderu.com/offices/dembski/index.html > (2–3)

Genetic Music @ < http://www.whozoo.org/mac/Music/ > (1)

Paley, William, *Natural Theology* @ < http://www.hti.umich.edu/cgi/p/pd-mod eng/pd-modeng-idx?type=HTML&rgn=DIV1&byte=53054870 > (2)

Swinburne, Richard, 'The Argument for Design' @ < http://www.faithquest. com/philosophers/swinburne/design.html > (2)

Willard, Dallas, 'Language, Being, God, and the Three Stages of Theistic Evidence' @ < http://www.dwillard.org/Philosophy/Pubs/language_being.htm > (2)

Williams, Peter S., 'Intelligent Design, Aesthetics and Design Arguments' @ < http://iscid.org/papers/Williams_Aesthetics_012302.pdf > (2)

Books

Behe, Michael J., Dembski, William A. and Meyer, Stephen C., *Science And Evidence For Design In The Universe* (San Francisco: Ignatius, 2000). (2)

Broom, Neil, *How Blind Is The Watchmaker?* (Leicester: IVP, 2001). (2)

Colson, Charles and Pearcey, Nancy, *Developing A Christian Worldview Of Science And Evolution* (Wheaton, Illinois: Tyndale House, 2001). (1)

Davies, Paul, *The Mind Of God* (London: Penguin, 1992). (2)

Dembski, William A., *No Free Lunch: Why Specified Complexity Cannot Be Purchased Without Intelligence* (Lanham, Maryland: Rowman & Littlefield, 2001). (2).

—, *The Design Inference* (Cambridge: Cambridge University Press, 1999). (3)

—, *Intelligent Design: The Bridge Between Science & Theology*, (Downers Grove, Illinois: IVP, 1999). (2)

— (ed.), *Mere Creation* (Downers Grove, Illinois: IVP, 1998). (3)

—, and Kushner, James M. (eds), *Signs Of Intelligence* (Grand Rapids, Michigan: Baker, 2001). (2)

Denton, Michael J, *Evolution: A Theory In Crisis* (Bethesda, Maryland: Adler & Adler, 1986). (3)

—, *Nature's Destiny: How The Laws Of Biology Reveal Purpose In The Universe* (New York: Free Press, 1998). (2)

Hick, John (ed.), *The Existence Of God* (New York: Macmillan, 1964). (2)

Moreland, J. P, *Scaling The Secular City* (Grand Rapids, Michigan: Baker, 1987). (2)

— (ed.), *The Creation Hypothesis* (Downers Grove, Illinois: IVP, 1994). (2)

Newman, Robert C. and Wiester, John L., *What's Darwin Got To Do With It?* (Downers Grove, Illinois: IVP, 2000). (1)

Swinburne, Richard, *The Existence Of God* (Oxford: Clarendon Press, 1991). (3)

—, *Is There A God?* (Oxford: Oxford University Press, 1996). (2)

Ward, Keith, *God, Chance and Necessity* (Oxford: OneWorld, 1996). (3)

Williams, Peter S., *The Case For God* (Crowborough, East Sussex: Monarch, 1999). (2)

Epistemological Arguments

Web sites

Plantinga, Alvin, 'An Evolutionary Argument against Naturalism' @ < http://hisdefense.org/articles/ap001.html > (2)

—, 'Naturalism Defeated' @ < http://www.homestead.com/philofreligion/files/alspaper.htm > (3)

Reppert, Victor, 'The Argument from Reason' @ < http://www.infidels.org/library/modern/victor_reppert/reason.htm >

Books

Balfour, Arthur J., *Theism And Humanism* (Seattle: Inklings, 2000). (3)

Markham, Ian, *Truth And The Reality Of God* (Edinburgh: T & T Clark, 1998). (3)

Plantinga, Alvin, *Warrant and Proper Function* (New York: Oxford University Press, 1993). (3)

Taylor, Richard, *Metaphysics* (Englewood Cliffs, New Jersey: Prentice Hall, 1974²). (2)

Williams, Peter S., *The Case For God* (Crowborough, East Sussex: Monarch, 1999). (2)

Miracles (cf. Jesus' Resurrection)

Web sites

Prophecy Proves the Bible @ < http://www.geocities.com/Athens/Aegean/8830/prophecy.html > (1)

Craig, William Lane, 'The Problem of Miracles: A Historical and Philosophical Perspective' @ < http://www.leaderu.com/offices/billcraig/docs/miracles.html > (2)

Geisler, Norman L., 'Miracles and Modern Science' @ < http://www.origins.org/truth/1truth19.html > (1)

Kreeft, Peter, 'Miracles' @ < http://catholiceducation.org/articles/religion/re0021.html > (1)

Books

Chamberlain, Theodore J. and Hall, Christopher A., *Realized Religion* (London: Templeton Foundation Press, 2000). (2)

Geisler, Norman L. and Hoffman, Paul K. (eds), *Why I Am A Christian* (Grand Rapids, Michigan: Baker, 2001). (2)

Habermas, Gary R. and Gievett, R. Douglas (eds), *In Defence Of Miracles* (Leicester: Apollos, 1997). (2)

Poole, Michael, *Miracles: Science, The Bible and Experience* (London, Scripture Union, 1992). (1)

Wilkins, Michael J. and Moreland, J.P. (eds), *Jesus Under Fire: Modern Scholarship Reinvents The Historical Jesus* (Carlisle: Paternoster, 1996). (2)

Desire

Web sites
Evans, C. Stephen, 'The Mystery of Persons and Belief in God' @ < http://www.leaderu.com/truth/3truth07.html > (1)

Books
Kreeft, Peter, *Heaven: The Heart's Deepest Longing* (San Francisco: Ignatius, 1989). (1)

Williams, Peter S., *The Case For God* (Crowborough, East Sussex: Monarch, 1999). (2)

Experience

Web sites
Alston, William P., 'The Experiential Basis of Theism' @ < http://www.leaderu.com/truth/3truth04.html > (2)

—, 'Why I am a Christian' @ < http://www.leaderu.com/truth/1truth23.html > (1)

Books
Alston, William P., 'Perceiving God' in Clark, Kelly James (ed.), *Readings In The Philosophy Of Religion* (Peterborough, Ontario: Broadview Press, 2000). (3)

Moreland, J.P., *Scaling The Secular City* (Grand Rapids, Michigan: Baker, 1987). (2)

Swinburne, Richard, *Is There A God?* (Oxford: Oxford University Press, 1996). (2)

Williams, Peter S., *The Case For God* (Crowborough, East Sussex: Monarch, 1999). (2)

Meaning

Books
Geisler, Norman L. and Bocchino, Peter, *Unshakeable Foundations* (Minneapolis, Minnesota: Bethany House, 2001). (2)

Geisler, Norman L. and Hoffman, Paul K. (eds), *Why I Am A Christian* (Grand Rapids, Michigan: Baker, 2001). (2)

Kreeft, Peter, *Three Philosophies Of Life* (San Francisco: Ignatius, 1989). (1)

Morris, Thomas V., *Making Sense Of It All* (Grand Rapids, Michigan: Eerdmans, 1998). (1)

Moreland, J.P., *Scaling The Secular City* (Grand Rapids, Michigan: Baker, 1987). (3)

Williams, Peter S., *The Case For God* (Crowborough, East Sussex: Monarch, 1999). (2)

Zacharias, Ravi, *Can Man Live Without God?* (Dallas, Texas: Word, 1994). (1)

The Bible

Web sites

The Bible Gateway @ < http://bible.gospelcom.net/ >

Kreeft, Peter, 'The Bible: Myth or History?' @ < http://catholiceducation.org/articles/apologetics/ap0065.html >

Stump, Eleonore, 'Modern Biblical Scholarship, Philosophy of Religion and Traditional Christianity' @ < http://www.leaderu.com/truth/1truth20.html >

Williams, Jimmy, 'Are the Biblical Documents Reliable?' @ < http://www.leaderu.com/orgs/probe/docs/bib-docu.html >

Prophecy Proves the Bible @ < http://www.geocities.com/Athens/Aegean/8830/prophecy.html >

Archaeology Confirms the History Recorded in the Bible @ < http://www.geocities.com/Athens/Aegean/8830/history.html >

Bible Believers Archaeology @ < http://www.biblehistory.net/ >

Books

Barnet, Paul, *Is The New Testament Reliable? A Look At The Historical Evidence*, (Downers Grove, Illinois: IVP, 1986). (1)

Blomberg, Craig L., *The Historical Reliability Of The Gospels* (Downers Grove, Illinois: IVP, 1987). (2)

—, *Jesus And The Gospels* (Leicester, Apollos, 1997). (2)

Bruce, F.F., *The New Testament Documents: Are They Reliable?* (Leicester: IVP 1960). (1)

Elwell, Walter A. and Yarbrough, Robert W., *Encountering The New Testament* (Grand Rapids, Michigan: Baker, 1998). (1)

Geisler, Norman L. and Hoffman, Paul K. (eds), *Why I Am A Christian* (Grand Rapids, Michigan: Baker, 2001). (2)

Jauchen, John Stephen (ed.), *NIV Thompson Student Bible* (Indianapolis, Indiana: Kirkbride Bible Company, 1999) – includes study aids, archaeological notes and other helpful features.

Kreeft, Peter and Tacelli, Ronald, *Handbook Of Christian Apologetics* (Downers Grove, Illinois: IVP, 1994). (1)

Sheler, Jeffery L., *Is The Bible True?* (London: HarperCollins, 2000). (1)

Strange, William, *The Authority Of The Bible* (London: Darton, Longman & Todd, 2000). (2)

Wilson, Ian, *The Bible Is History* (London: Weidenfeld & Nicolson, 1999). (2)

Winter, David, *But This I Can Believe* (London: Hodder & Stoughton, 1980). (1)

Jesus

General

Web sites

'Who is Jesus?' @ < http://www.ccci.org/whoisjesus/interactive-journey/ > (1)

France, R.T., 'The Gospels As Historical Sources for Jesus, the Founder of Christianity' @ < http://www.leaderu.com/truth/1truth21.html > (1)

Kreeft, Peter, 'The Divinity of Christ' @ < http://catholiceducation.org/articles/religion/re0020.html > (1)

Books

Craig, William Lane (ed.), *Philosophy Of Religion: A Reader And Guide* (Edinburgh: Edinburgh University Press, 2002). (3)

Evans, C. Stephen, *Why Believe? Reason And Mystery As Pointers To God* (Leicester: IVP, 1996). (1)

France, R.T., *The Evidence For Jesus* (London: Hodder & Stoughton, 1986). (1)

Geisler, Norman L. *Christian Apologetics* (Grand Rapids, Michigan: Baker, 1976). (2)

—, and Hoffman, Paul K. (eds), *Why I Am A Christian* (Grand Rapids, Michigan: Baker, 2001). (2)

Kreeft, Peter, *Socrates Meets Jesus* (Downers Grove, Illinois: IVP, 2002). (1)

—, *Between Heaven & Hell: A Dialog Somewhere Beyond Death With John F. Kennedy, C.S. Lewis & Aldous Huxley* (Leicester: IVP, 1982). (1)

McDowell, Josh, *The New Evidence That Demands A Verdict* (Nashville, Tennessee: Thomas Nelson, 1999). (2)

—, and Wilson, Bill, *He Walked Among Us: Evidence For The Historical Jesus* (Carlisle: Paternoster, 2001). (2)

McGrath, Alister, *Jesus: Who He Is And Why He Matters* (Leicester: IVP, 1994). (1)

Miethe, Terry L. and Habermas, Gary R., *Why Believe? God Exists!* (Joplin, Missouri: College Press, 1998). (2)

Moreland, J.P., *Scaling The Secular City* (Grand Rapids, Michigan: Baker, 1987). (2)

Strobel, Lee, *The Case For Christ: A Journalist's Personal Investigation Of The Evidence For Jesus* (Grand Rapids, Michigan: Zondervan, 1998). (1)

Wilkins, Michael J. and Moreland, J.P. (eds), *Jesus Under Fire: Modern Scholarship Reinvents The Historical Jesus* (Carlisle: Paternoster, 1996). (2)

Jesus' Resurrection

Web sites

Links to resources on the resurrection @ < http://members.tripod.com/~vant illian/resurrection.html >

Craig, William Lane vs Brian Edwards, 'Did the Resurrection Really Happen?' @ < http://www.gospelcom.net/rzim/radio/easter.shtml > (mp3 File) (1)

Guthrie, Shandon L., 'Evidence For The Resurrection Of Jesus' @ < http:// sguthrie.net/resurrection.htm > (2)

Kreeft, Peter and Tacelli, Ronald, 'Evidence for the Resurrection of Christ' @ < http://hometown.aol.com/philvaz/articles/num9.htm > (1)

McDowell, Josh, 'Evidence for the Resurrection' @ < http://www.leaderu.com/ everystudent/easter/articles/josh2.html > (1)

Books

Beasley-Murray, Paul, *The Message Of The Resurrection* (Leicester: IVP, 2000). (1)

Clifford, Ross, *The Case For The Empty Tomb: Leading Lawyers Look At The Resurrection* (Claremont, California: Albatross, 1991). (1)

Copan, Paul (ed.), *Will The Real Jesus Please Stand Up? A Debate Between William Lane Craig And John Dominic Crossan* (Grand Rapids, Michigan: Baker, 1998). (2)

—, and Tacelli, Ronald (ed.), *Jesus' Resurrection: Fact Or Figment? A Debate Between William Lane Craig and Gerd Ludemann* (Downers Grove, Illinois: IVP, 2000). (2)

Craig, William Lane, *The Son Rises: The Historical Evidence For The Resurrection Of Jesus* (Chicago, Illinois: Moody Press, 1981). (2)

Davis, Stephen T., *Risen Indeed: Making Sense Of The Resurrection* (London: SPCK, 1993). (3)

Habermas, Gary R. and Moreland, J.P., *Beyond Death: Exploring The Evidence For Immortality* (Wheaton, Illinois: Crossway, 1998.) (2)

— and Flew, Anthony, *Did Jesus Rise From The Dead? The Resurrection Debate*, Miethe, Terry L. (ed.), (San Francisco: Harper & Rowe, 1987). (2)

Miethe, Terry L. and Habermas, Gary R., *Why Believe? God Exists!* (Joplin, Missouri: College Press, 1998). (2)

Moreland, J.P., *Scaling The Secular City* (Grand Rapids, Michigan: Baker, 1987). (2)

Strobel, Lee, *The Case For Christ: A Journalist's Personal Investigation Of The Evidence For Jesus* (Grand Rapids, Michigan: Zondervan, 1998). (1)

Wilkins, Michael J. and Moreland, J.P. (eds), *Jesus Under Fire: Modern Scholarship Reinvents The Historical Jesus* (Carlisle: Paternoster, 1996). (2)

Christian Philosophers and Apologists On Line

Access Research Network @: < http://www.arn.org >
Alston, William P. @ < http://www.homestead.com/philofreligion/Alston.html >
Craig, William Lane @ < http://www.leaderu.com/offices/billcraig/ >
Davis, Stephen T. @ < http://www.faithquest.com/philosophers/StephenT.Davis >
Dembski, William A. @ < http://www.leaderu.com/offices/dembski/menus/ articles.html >
Guthrie, Shandon L. @ < http://sguthrie.net/index.php >
Hackett, Stewart C. @ < http://www.mindspring.com/~cole-t/p-r/hackett/ >
Koons, Robert C. @ < http://www.leaderu.com/offices/koons/ >
Kreeft, Peter @ < http://ic.net/~erasmus/RAZ29.HTM >
Lewis, C.S., Mega Links @ < http://ic.net/~erasmus/RAZ26.HTM >
McDowell, Josh @ < http://www.josh.org >
Moreland, J.P. @ < http://www.afterall.net/citizens/moreland/ >
Plantinga, Alvin @ < http://www.homestead.com/philofreligion/Plantingapa ge.html > & < http://id-www.ucsb.edu/fscf/library/plantinga/ >
Sudduth, Michael @ < http://www.homestead.com/philofreligion/main.html >
Swinburne, Richard @ <http://www.faithquest.com/philosophers/swinburne/ >
Theistic Philosophers @ < http://theism.actualism.com/theistic.php3 >
Willard, Dallas @ < http://www.dwillard.org/ >
Zacharias, Ravi @ < http://www.gospelcom.net/rzim/ >

Finally, I highly recommend a subscription to *Philosophia Christi*, the excellent peer-reviewed journal of the Evangelical Philosophical Society. Requests regarding subscriptions (currently an annual fee of $25 or $15 for students) should be sent to: EPS Secretary–Treasurer, Biola University, McNally 66, 13800 Biola Avenue, La Mirada CA 90639-0001. E-mail: < philchristi@biola.edu >; web site: < www.ep society.org >.

Scripture Index

Subject Index

Names Index